STRATEGIES
for
CURRICULUM
DEVELOPMENT

Edited by

Jon Schaffarzick
and
David H. Hampson

National Institute of Education
Department of Health, Education, and Welfare

McCutchan Publishing Corporation
2526 Grove Street
Berkeley, California 94704

ISBN 0-8211-0756-9

Library of Congress Catalog Card Number: 75-24652

This work was produced with financial support from the National Institute of Education, Department of Health, Education, and Welfare. However, the content does not necessarily reflect the position or policy of that Agency, and no official U.S. Government endorsement should be inferred.

The editors received no compensation whatsoever for the work done in writing their chapters or in editing the collection.

Preface

The essays in this book should interest beginning students of curriculum development, more advanced curriculum developers who are interested in learning about a range of approaches to development, and researchers who are interested in designing studies to compare alternative approaches to development. Included in the book are an introductory overview of the history of curriculum development during the past two decades, chapters in which nine developers describe and analyze the developmental procedures they use and recommend, and a concluding analysis of the similarities and differences among these diversified procedures and a discussion of the prospects for carrying out comparative research studies that might assess their relative strengths and weaknesses.

When we asked the nine developers to write these essays, both of us were affiliated with NIE's Career Education Program, which is now called the Education and Work Program. In addition to working with some large curriculum development projects that had been initiated in the Office of Education, we were beginning to plan for future development endeavors. Realizing that the initiation of two or more new curriculum development projects might provide a unique opportunity to use, study, and compare alternative developmental procedures, we decided to begin learning more about some of the main alternatives that might be used and compared and some of the variable elements of developmental approaches that might serve as focuses for comparative research. The preparation of these essays was the first step in this process.

We were very pleased with the quality of the papers and agreed with other early readers that the collection could be useful to an audience much wider than the NIE staff. Therefore, we began editing, preparing introductory and concluding chapters, and securing a publisher through a competitive selection process (which was required by government regulations because the papers had been written under an NIE contract). We are required to also point out that all of our work in preparing this book for publication has been accomplished on our own time, as students of curriculum development rather than as employees of the Institute.

Because these essays provide relatively succinct explanations, we hope that they will benefit beginning students and developers who desire an initial familiarization with a variety of procedural options rather than a comprehensive understanding of one or two approaches. We hope, moreover, that they will assist researchers to design comparative studies that will yield more reliable indications of the assets and liabilities of different developmental approaches. Such indications should, in turn, assist active developers to make appropriate choices from the array of procedural possibilities available to them.

We have enjoyed working on this book, both because we have learned much from our interactions with the writers of the chapters and because all of the authors have been so pleasant to work with. We would like to express special thanks to Pat Fox, who has strengthened all of the chapters through her fine editing, and John McCutchan, who has ensured expeditious publication.

Jon Schaffarzick
David H. Hampson

Contributors

Leo Anglin, Teaching Assistant, Department of Curriculum and Instruction, School of Education, University of Wisconsin-Madison

Larry J. Bailey, Professor of Education, College of Education, Southern Illinois University

M. Vere DeVault, Professor, Department of Curriculum and Instruction, School of Education, University of Wisconsin-Madison

Elliot W. Eisner, Professor of Education and Art, Stanford University

David H. Hampson, Senior Associate and Chief of the Career Exploration Division, National Institute of Education, Department of Health, Education, and Welfare

Robert Karplus, Associate Director, Lawrence Hall of Science; Director, Science Curriculum Improvement Study; Professor of Physics, University of California, Berkeley

Howard D. Mehlinger, Professor of Education and History; Director, Social Studies Development Center, Indiana University

W. James Popham, Professor, Department of Education, University of California, Los Angeles

Alan C. Purves, Professor of English Education, College of Education, University of Illinois at Urbana-Champaign

Lauren B. Resnick, Associate Professor, Departments of Psychology
and Educational Psychology; Associate Director, Learning Research and Development Center, University of Pittsburgh

Jon Schaffarzick, Research Associate with the Program on School
Capacity for Problem Solving, National Institute of Education,
Department of Health, Education, and Welfare

Ralph W. Tyler, Director Emeritus, Center for Advanced Study in
the Behavioral Sciences; Senior Consultant, Science Research
Associates

Contents

1 Perspectives on Curriculum Development

David H. Hampson

Conceptions of Curriculum

There are many different, often conflicting, conceptions of what is meant by the term "curriculum." For some it is a loose term encompassing the range of content of a course of study, while for others, it is the singular textbook to which the class is assigned. Curriculum developers and users have begun more recently to think in terms of curriculum as that planned set of identified educational goals and learning experiences that are organized in a manner to facilitate evaluation of learner outcomes.

Confusion has been fueled, in addition, by the debate among curriculum developers as to how what is to be taught should be organized and delivered to students. One major school of thought focuses on the upgrading and refinement of the subject matter as the best method of improving curriculum. This group has been successful primarily on the secondary level where subject-matter specialists still prevail. There is, on the other hand, the school of thought that begins with the subject matter, but is primarily concerned with the problems of delivery, as exhibited in individually prescribed materials, computer-aided instruction, and process-oriented approaches.

Proponents of this school have had their greatest successes in the elementary school, where subject-matter boundaries are more easily crossed.

Until recently two major dilemmas predominated. The first concerned the substantive nature of curriculum, and the second involved the more subtle question of the emphases in curriculum development. During the last ten years another dilemma has emerged which underpins the others: how should one decide what should be taught?

In its eagerness to become scientific and to appear to be technically and logically sound, the field of curriculum development (perhaps merely as a reflection of the total field of education) has too infrequently questioned the dominant theme in curriculum, Tyler's syllabus,[1] which first appeared in 1949. This is not to say that Tyler's work has not played and will not continue to play a major role in the future conceptualization of ideas concerning curriculum. The point is, merely, that until recently much of what occurred in the field tended to reflect in gray tones the influence of Tyler's seminal thinking. While many people have added specifics and details, a good number, including Taba,[2] Goodlad,[3] Popham,[4] and Mager,[5] follow Tyler's directional compass.

Underpinning this directional compass has been the acceptance of curriculum as a process of ends and means. The apparent logic of this technical conception of curriculum is exemplified by Tyler's four questions: What educational purposes should the school seek to attain? What educational experiences can be provided that are likely to attain these purposes? How can these educational experiences be effectively organized? How can we determine whether these purposes are being attained?[6] It is only relatively recently that the acceptance of this technical conception has been openly called into question.

Symptomatic of this emerging questioning has been the "great objectives debate." Though not a frontal attack on this school, the work of Eisner in 1967[7] and Kliebard in 1968[8] pointed out the serious limitations of the doctrine of behavioral objectives. It is noteworthy that both traced the involvement of curriculum developers with the notion of behavioral objectives back well beyond the contemporary influence of Tyler to the work of Franklin Bobbitt in the 1920s.

Macdonald in 1965 argued even more directly that the technical conception emerging from Tyler's syllabus, with its apparent rationality, could not stand close scrutiny. He suggested that curriculum developers following such a syllabus, far from being scientific, prescribed instructional practices on the basis of possibility, but with unknown probability of validity; that the leap from description to prescription is based upon factors not necessarily relevant to instruction; and that objectives are only known, in any final sense, after the completion of an act of instruction.[9]

Schwab has criticized most directly the technical notion of curriculum.[10] Taking a position similar to that of Macdonald, Schwab argues that the field of curriculum is moribund and in need of new principles and methods if it is to contribute to the advancement of education. He feels that existing theories are inadequate to tell us what to do with human beings. He suggests that the "stuff" of theories is an abstract or idealized representation of real things and, therefore, questions their utility as the basis for the framing of curriculum which, in action, treats real things, real acts, real teachers, and real children. He argues further that, even if appropriate, theory is inadequate to the tasks of curriculum; we should, consequently, divert our energies to the practical, the quasi-practical, and the eclectic.

It is evident from the debate that the field of curriculum is entering a most interesting period. The work of such people as Macdonald, Schwab, and, more recently, Walker[11] demonstrates that for the first time in over twenty years a major alternative conception of curriculum is emerging. The recent work of Eisner, Schwab, and Walker in a report to the National Institute of Education further supports this view.[12] As this alternate conception takes shape, it will stimulate both new research and new ways of organizing the thinking in the field of curriculum. Whether the technical conception of curriculum as an ends-means process will be displaced is doubtful, at least in the short term. Its proponents should benefit, however, from being forced to rethink many of the basic assumptions they have so readily accepted. The expected opportunity for debate bodes well for the future of curriculum as a field of examination, study, and professional endeavor.

The Curriculum Reform Movement Since 1950: An Overview

In restricting my discussion of curriculum reform to post-1950 I may appear to be denying the historical antecedents. This is not the case; time, space, and the existing work of others limit the opportunity and need for such a discussion. (For further reading in this area, however, one should consult the work of Cremin,[13] Eisner,[14] and Bellack.[15])

The beginning of the curriculum reform movement is usually thought to be 1957. The launching of Sputnik is typically considered the moving force behind the "new" mathematics, the "new" physics, the "new" biology, and, subsequently, the "new" forays into the social sciences. While Sputnik was undoubtedly influential in bringing about needed educational change, it is too simplistic to view that event as "the (space)ship that launched a thousand curricula." There is much evidence to support the fact that the concern for curriculum reform went back several years before 1957. Both Goodlad[16] and Grobman,[17] make extensive references to the earlier work of the University of Illinois Committee on School Mathematics, and Grobman draws specific attention to the long-standing interest in educational problems exhibited by the American Institute of Biological Sciences. It is fair to say, however, that without Sputnik the curriculum reform movement would have progressed more slowly.

Prompted by the criticism leveled against the educational system subsequent to the launching of Sputnik, a number of large-scale efforts in the field of curriculum were begun in the late 1950s and early 1960s. As Goodlad noted, by the mid-1960s "a new alphabet soup of curriculum projects—BSCS, CBA, ESS, PSSC, SMSG—[had become] part of the diet of American children and youth in school."[18] Support for these efforts came largely from the National Science Foundation (NSF), joined later by the U. S. Office of Education, and from an assortment of private foundations, one of the most important of which was the Ford Foundation. Millions of dollars were provided to support the new efforts. For example, the NSF granted the Biological Sciences Curriculum Study (BSCS) over $10,000,000,[19] and the Chemical Education Material Study (CHEM) almost $3,000,000.[20]

When these projects first began in the late 1960s few developers had a sense of either the probable costs or the time necessary to complete such efforts. By the early 1970s, however, developers were beginning to come to grips with these issues. James J. Gallagher was able to state in hearings before the Select Subcommittee on Education of the Committee on Education and Labor of the House of

Representatives, that "a major national curriculum project . . . such as a new mathematics program or a new social studies curriculum . . . would cost about 10-15 million dollars." He further suggested that such a project would take between five and seven years to complete.[21]

Two major characteristics emerge from the curriculum efforts of the 1950s and 1960s. Perhaps because they are so obvious, they need reexamination, rethinking, and possibly revision.

First, the curriculum reform movement was discipline oriented. Developmental activities concentrated on the upgrading of content traditionally taught in schools. The stress was on the academic, with the ends and means of the curriculum to be derived from organized bodies of knowledge known as disciplines. Though the emphasis on subject matter dominated the secondary level, it was partially mitigated at the elementary level. Whether this stemmed from the fact that subject-matter specialists were not entrenched at the elementary level or from a genuine desire on the part of developers to concentrate on the delivery aspects of curriculum to the student is still open to question. Ample evidence is available to show that curriculum developed for the elementary school was aimed at a more inclusive school population for that age group, as opposed to the exclusivity exhibited by many of the curricula developed for secondary school students.

A second major characteristic of the reform movement concerns the types of individuals and groups selected (or self-selected) to undertake the developmental activities: most were not professional educators. They were mathematicians, physicists, biologists, and others drawn from the academic disciplines and based in university departments of the arts and sciences or in professional learned societies such as the American Chemical Society, the American Institute of Biological Sciences, and the American Mathematical Society. Thus, while the efforts were national in scope, both in the desired impact across a wide range of students and in federal support, the direction of the effort was in the hands of relatively few scholars with little, if any, input from local school systems, state agencies, or even the federal agencies providing the funding.

The emphasis on upgrading subject matter and the involvement of discipline-based scholars to guide the efforts have produced many positive results. Reflected in the new curricula are the subject-matter advances of the twentieth century, the underlying structure of the disciplines, and the primary principles and methods of inquiry. It is also possible, however, to detect some unintended consequences. For example, the curricula developed did much to perpetuate subject-matter compartmentalism, particularly at the high school level, and the "college preparatory" nature of many of the curricula has led to the exclusion of a good number of students from the offerings.

The preceding comments were largely directed at the curriculum reform efforts that were concluding by the late 1960s and were directed mainly at the high school level. These efforts are being followed by a second wave of curriculum development that is focus-ing on the elementary level and is attempting to circumvent many of the problems generated by the earlier reform activities. A new breed of curriculum developer, based on regional educational laboratories and centers, has emerged concurrent with this second wave. These developers are primarily educational product developers rather than subject-matter experts. They bring to curriculum development activ-ities an increasingly sophisticated technology with regard to the crea-tion and testing of their products. Though it is too early to pass final judgment on their performance, preliminary observation of the prod-ucts developed by such institutions as the Southwest Regional Labo-ratory and the Learning Research and Development Center in Pitts-burgh suggests they are producing high quality curricula that avoid many of the problems created by the earlier subject-matter-based approaches.

In the following chapters, particularly those by Resnick and Pop-ham, the reader will have an opportunity to critique and question some of these emerging developmental efforts.

Persistent Dilemmas Facing Curriculum Developers

There is more to the process of curriculum development than organizing or arranging a predetermined set of information and ex-periences. Curriculum development has made great progress, both as an art and as a science, particularly when one considers that the principal responsibility of the curriculum developer in the fairly recent past was to order a series of textbook chapters.

In the following section four dilemmas facing the curriculum de-veloper are examined. I suggest that the developer pay particular and persistent attention to them, for they influence both the substance and the setting of new curriculum development. Without attention to these dilemmas, the best curriculum conceptions may come to naught; with attention, the future potential of curriculum development efforts may have greater impact in terms of speed of adoption and size of audience than have those efforts in the past.

Evaluation

The major role of evaluation in curriculum development is to assist the developmental process at every step by examining the procedures and materials developed. This type of evaluation is, therefore, formative in nature. The distinction between "formative" and "summative" evaluation is not one of substance or method; it is, rather, a distinction in use. Those evaluative procedures which are meant to provide publishers and funding sources with data on the impact on learners, the extent of use by teachers, and so forth, in an attempt to "sell" a finished product, are summative, and they are essentially useless to the product itself. If, however, the developer is interested in using the evaluation data to improve and shape the end product, then the evaluation is formative. Formative evaluation is, therefore, a major part of the ongoing developmental effort. The guiding question in formative evaluation should be: how might every element of the program be examined in order to improve its outcome? In order to answer this question, formative evaluation must be built into the developmental effort from the outset.[22]

Though it is possible, in theory, to comprehend the differences in roles of formative and summative evaluation, as distinguished by such writers as Scriven,[23] in the practice of curriculum development this delineation becomes extremely fuzzy, with the role and form of the latter, as a conceptual distinction, being called into serious question by the iterative nature of a good formative evaluation design and activity. This distinction, or lack of it, is an issue to be addressed at the outset of a developmental effort if the developer is to avoid both the semantic and methodological questioning that emerges during the life of the program.

An additional concern in the area of evaluation has arisen recently and with due cause: postrelease or postpublication evaluation. Though systematically neglected to date, this problem must now be faced squarely by the curriculum developer. California has passed Bill

AB 531, Section 9426, which brings to the forefront the concept of "learner verification" and attempts to provide feedback on the usage of the curriculum to the publisher-developer for use in subsequent updating and modification of the material. It is apparent, then, that developers are going to have to build serious postpublication evaluation into their future curriculum development plans.

Dissemination

Curriculum developers have traditionally been naive about the ultimate dissemination of their products. They have usually postponed the necessary thinking and planning for dissemination until the developmental effort has been almost completed. In some cases they have taken no responsibility in this area, delegating the task to some other group, mainly publishers.

As federal funds for curriculum development become tighter and as the practitioner and those allocating funds (Congress) increasingly question the impact of the funding of research and development on practice, dissemination will probably become the cause célèbre in education of the late 1970s and early 1980s, rivaling the attention paid to evaluation in the previous decade. This assumption is demonstrated by the increasing demand and support by Congress for an adequate system of disseminating educational products that have been developed with federal funding. Thus, the National Institute of Education is allocating a large portion of its budget to the support of activities related to dissemination.

Curriculum developers can no longer perpetuate the syndrome of "leaving it on the stump." They must, rather, make dissemination a part of their developmental effort from the outset.

Experimentation

The term "experimentation" immediately conjures up confusion in the minds of many educators, schooled in the behaviorist tradition, with "experimental"—as in "experimental design." This confusion must be cleared up.

The field of education should not be despaired of as an environment for experimentation, as many who wish to view experimentation as synonymous with pre- and posttesting and control-experimental groups would claim. True experimental design is not, however, suitable for dealing with the notion of experimentation within the setting of practice. Schools must be responsible to their students and to those who pay taxes. To supply different groups with different curricula raises a serious political question concerning the provision of optimum experiences for all students. Rather than being discouraged, the curriculum developer should consider alternate ways of designing experiments and collecting data than those advocated by the proponents of "true experimental design." Systematic observations over time, as employed by the astronomer or by in-depth clinical studies, iteratively confirming or not confirming hunches or hypotheses, may well be starting points for thinking about this issue. Only as the profession of education builds up a body of such experimental work will the curriculum developer become confident "that the tail of experimental design does not wag the dog of educational experimentation."

Staff Development

The importance of materials to aid the teacher, to accompany the curriculum for the student, is accepted as a major component to be built into all curriculum development efforts. The teacher is, in the vast majority of cases, the "curriculum gatekeeper." Without adequate attention to the teacher's day-to-day role, the entire curriculum may founder.

Staff development has usually taken place in summer institutes, in-service conferences during a school term, and even yearlong programs. Two major characteristics have marked the conduct of most previous staff development activities: their predominantly in-service nature, and their cost as an addition to the price of implementation and dissemination. It is to be expected, given the propensity of new curriculum programs to change existing practice in the classroom, that the in-service characteristic will remain, though alternate approaches may well be beneficial. An area that curriculum developers have persistently neglected, however, is the preservice preparation of teachers in order that they might benefit from new or emerging curricular trends. The preparatory institutions must assume partial responsibility for this problem. Many teach methods courses that fail to include the body of good practice that presently exists. Many schools and teachers were further isolated by being bypassed by the curriculum reform movement of the 1950s and 1960s, which had its roots, as previously mentioned, outside of professional education. These problems must be solved.

One approach may be to take advantage of state university and college systems; working with state education agencies may well provide the method for doing this. Many state authorities are increasingly using their university and college systems to conduct in-service programs. Georgia, for example, has an outstanding record in this area. If the capacity to handle the in-service aspect of teaching can be transferred to those institutions traditionally concerned with the preservice aspect, the possibility exists that there can be developed a powerful device for infusing preservice programs with a constant updating of emerging curricular concepts and programs. Whatever the solution, it is an issue to be addressed by curriculum developers.

The second major characteristic of programs of staff development has been their cost. In most cases staff development has meant reimbursement of teachers during summer months or release time during the school year with the concomitant payment of substitute teachers. Staff development, therefore, has traditionally been costly. Its delivery has also remained fairly uniform, with the institute or workshop predominating.

Curriculum developers should address themselves to two needs: to make staff development a component of the curriculum development effort and thereby include its cost initially; and to examine alternate forms of delivery, with the intention of cutting costs. If one works through state institutions, can costs be lowered by using an existing group of professionals? Can staff-development programs for new curriculum be included in the initial requirements for awarding or updating of certification? Can the curriculum developer make greater use of individualized packages or the mass media to deliver staff development programs? These are important questions that the curriculum developer should consider, for the ultimate success of the curriculum may well depend on the effectiveness of staff development.

Considerations for Curriculum Developers to Ponder

The first consideration concerns the origins and leadership of recent efforts at curriculum development and what this means for future activities. The major efforts of the 1950s, 1960s, and early 1970s originated outside of the school system they were designed to serve. This was reflected at first in the preponderance of subject-matter experts who became overnight directors of curriculum efforts aimed at serving the nation's schools, teachers, and students, largely without input from those quarters. In later efforts the responsibility for curriculum development has largely passed to a new breed of leaders, again situated outside the school system and located in educational centers and laboratories especially created to undertake research and development. There are potential problems in this situation because the United States has long venerated the tradition of local control of education. It also runs counter to the reemergence of the individual states as the important unit of analysis in attempting to bring about or account for educational change. The situation is further strained by the current political mood, which appears to distrust "bigness," whether it be in government, business, or even curriculum.

In education, as in many other areas of social policy, the American people are reacting negatively to being told that something is good for them. For curriculum developers this means that they must look more to the existing state of practice as the source for their ideas and problems; they should consider taking smaller, more incremental bites at the "curricular apple"; and they must involve the professional educator, the student, and the community, both in framing the goals of curriculum and in participating in its development. It will no longer be possible for curriculum developers to see schools merely as test sites.

From this involvement will come two valuable results. First, at the substantive level, the curriculum developer will gain an accurate sense of the scope of the problem to be addressed by the intended curriculum, and of the potential solutions available. By working with educators, students, and the community and by taking advantage of their inputs, the developmental effort will benefit qualitatively. Second, at the level of improving relations with the constituency, commitment from the potential users will aid in the political acceptance of the development effort; it will also be a positive step in the future dissemination of the curriculum product.

The second consideration concerns the ability of curriculum alone to bring about significant changes in the form of education. The curriculum projects of the last twenty years had as an intended outcome the upgrading of the quality of education the student received. They were intended to increase the effectiveness of the nation's schools by correcting the inadequacies, particularly in science and mathematics, that were brought to light by Sputnik. Curriculum was seen as the way to solve these problems.

Today, as we witness the continuing decline of standardized test scores, increasing unemployment among youth, and high dropout rates, it is becoming more and more obvious that changes in curriculum in isolation from changes in other areas, such as educational organization and delivery, will only have a limited success. Curriculum developers must, therefore, seek ways to align their efforts with efforts at change in other areas of education, and, where possible, to become part of broader changes in society.

This could be achieved by forming large multidisciplinary teams that would completely revamp the educational process. The curriculum developer would be part of the team, providing direction and leadership on the type and process of what should be taught. The relationship of curriculum to other parts of the intended educational program could be weighed constantly. This would result in large-scale educational change with the components integrated, balanced, and supporting one another. Even at the other end of the continuum, where the curriculum developer continues to work alone, it is imperative that much greater attention be given to the place of curriculum among the parts of the educational process. Without this sensitivity to the other parts, significant educational change cannot occur.

The third consideration concerns the underpinning rationales that prompt curriculum change.[24] As mentioned previously, much recent curriculum reform was related to subject matter. Pressures for change from the political-social arena were not absent from these reforms; indeed Sputnik provoked an amount of bellicosity concerning education without parallel in recent times. Nevertheless, modernization of the subject matter was of prime importance. The developers were able to improve segments of the curriculum without having to seek the approval of the politician, the evangelist, or the prophet.

Developers must now increasingly cope with social and economic forces external to the educational system, which may result in a modification of the system. Developmental efforts will, therefore, stem from broad political and social considerations, rather than from narrow educational considerations. The best contemporary example in the United States is career education. While the career education movement has borrowed much of its curriculum development technology from its subject-based predecessors, it represents a major departure in curriculum development in that it cuts across subjects and focuses on a vital current problem: the role and relationship of education in conducting the remainder of one's life.

In meeting the pressures generated by these forces, the curriculum developer must constantly balance them with the pressures of local involvement. Thus the developer may emerge as a mediator bringing together national priorities and local needs, providing a point of contact and a touchstone of reality.

The fourth consideration returns to the point raised at the outset of this chapter: the conceptions of curriculum. As previously mentioned, the technical conception of curriculum epitomized by Tyler's framework is being questioned; the intention here is not to reiterate that discussion. The point is raised again because the debate will continue to engage all of us and have implications for our work. We must, therefore, analyze the arguments of both sides carefully.

Summary

This chapter has offered a series of perspectives on curriculum development. The four sections have examined conceptions of curriculum, the curriculum reform movement since 1950, some persistent dilemmas facing the curriculum developer, and considerations for curriculum developers to ponder. It is hoped that the chapter will provide a series of common beginning questions for the reader to consider as he examines the remaining chapters.

Each of these chapters stands alone and offers insight into the variety of ways in which curriculum development is, and has been, conducted. The essays were specifically chosen to offer a range of such insights. The final chapter by Schaffarzick analyzes the varied essays and draws conclusions about the common characteristics that are beginning to emerge.

Notes

1. Ralph W. Tyler, *Basic Principles of Curriculum and Instruction* (Chicago: University of Chicago Press, 1949).

2. Hilda Taba, *Curriculum Development: Theory and Practice* (New York: Harcourt, Brace and World, 1962).

3. John I. Goodlad and Maurice N. Richter, Jr., *The Development of a*

Conceptual System for Dealing with Problems of Curriculum and Instruction, USOE Contract No. S.A.E. 8024, University of California at Los Angeles, 1966.

4. W. J. Popham *et al., Instructional Objectives,* American Educational Research Association Monograph Series on Curriculum Evaluation, No. 3 (Washington, D. C.: American Educational Research Association, 1969).

5. Robert F. Mager, *Preparing Instructional Objectives* (Palo Alto, Calif.: Fearon, 1962).

6. Tyler, *Basic Principles of Curriculum and Instruction.*

7. Elliot W. Eisner, "Educational Objectives: Help or Hindrance?" *School Review* 75 (No. 3, 1967): 250-260.

8. Herbert Kliebard, "Curricular Objectives and Evaluation: A Reassessment," *High School Journal* 51 (No. 6, 1968): 241-247.

9. James B. Macdonald, "Myths about Instruction," *Educational Leadership* 22 (May 1965): 571-576, 609-617.

10. Joseph J. Schwab, *The Practical: A Language for Curriculum* (Washington, D. C.: National Education Association, 1970).

11. Decker Walker, "A Naturalistic Model for Curriculum Development," *School Review* 80 (No. 1, 1971): 51-65.

12. Elliot W. Eisner, Joseph Schwab, and Decker Walker, "Starting Points and Procedures in Curriculum Development," in *Career Education: The State of the Idea and Its Prospects for the Future,* NIE Contract No. NIE-C-74-0048, Stanford University, October 1974, prepared for the Career Education Division, NIE, Washington, D. C.

13. Lawrence A. Cremin, *The Wonderful World of Ellwood Patterson Cubberley* (New York: Bureau of Publications, Teachers College, Columbia University, 1965); *id., The Genius of American Education* (New York: Random House, 1966).

14. Elliot W. Eisner, "Franklin Bobbitt and the Science of Curriculum Making," *School Review* 75 (No. 1, 1967): 29-47.

15. Arno A. Bellack, "History of Curriculum Thought and Practice," *Review of Educational Research* 39 (No. 3, 1969): 283-292.

16. John I. Goodlad *et al., The Changing School Curriculum* (New York: Fund for the Advancement of Education, 1966).

17. Arnold B. Grobman, *The Changing Classroom: The Role of the Biological Sciences* (Garden City, N. Y.: Doubleday, 1969).

18. Goodlad *et al., The Changing School Curriculum.*

19. Grobman, *The Changing Classroom.*

20. Richard J. Merrill and David Ridgway, *The Chem Study Story* (San Francisco: W. H. Freeman, 1969).

21. Statement of Dr. James J. Gallagher, Director, Frank Porter Graham Child Development Center, University of North Carolina, in hearings to establish a National Institute of Education before the Select Subcommittee on Education of the Committee on Education and Labor of the House of Representatives, Washington, D. C., February 18, 1971.

22. David H. Hampson, *Educational Product Development and Evaluation*

(Raleigh: Center for Occupational Education, North Carolina State University, 1973).

23. Michael Scriven, "The Methodology of Evaluation," in *Perspectives of Curriculum Evaluation*, ed. Ralph W. Tyler *et al.*, American Education Research Association Monograph Series on Curriculum Evaluation, No. 1 (Chicago: Rand McNally, 1967).

24. Much of the material for this discussion was drawn from Hampson, *Educational Product Development and Evaluation*.

2 Specific Approaches to Curriculum Development

Ralph W. Tyler

The term "curriculum" is used in several different ways in current educational literature. In its most limited sense, it is an outline of a course of study. At the other extreme, the curriculum is considered to be everything that transpires in the planning, teaching, and learning in an educational institution. In this chapter the term will be used to include the plans for an educational program. The term "curriculum development," then, will refer to developing the plans for an educational program, including the identification and selection of educational objectives, the selection of learning experiences, the organization of the learning experiences, and the evaluation of the educational program.

Approaches to curriculum development are likely to vary with different kinds of educational institutions: those used in professional schools are not usually like those used in liberal arts colleges, and those appropriate for colleges may not be feasible in elementary schools. The focus of this chapter is on approaches to curriculum development in American public elementary and secondary schools.

The term "approach" also has a variety of meanings in contemporary educational discourse. Here it will be used to include the various aspects of the development process, including the assumptions, the purposes, the criteria, the procedures, and the participants in curriculum development projects.

The content of this chapter is derived from my experience in curriculum development beginning in Nebraska in 1925. Although many of the projects in which I have been involved have been in colleges or professional schools, a considerable part of my activities has been with elementary and secondary schools, for example, the Eight Year Study with high schools and the Neighborhood Education Center involving four elementary schools in an inner-city, "disadvantaged" area.

The Nature of Curriculum Development

Curriculum development is a practical enterprise, not a theoretical study. It endeavors to design a system to achieve an educational end and is not primarily attempting to explain an existential phenomenon. The system must be designed to operate effectively in a society where a number of constraints are present, and with human beings who have purposes, preferences, and dynamic mechanisms in operation. Hence, an essential early step in curriculum development is to examine and analyze significant conditions that influence the construction and operation of the curriculum.

Preliminary Analysis

One important factor for early analysis is the need or problem that has led to the decision to construct or reconstruct a curriculum. For example, the many recent attempts to develop new curricula for disadvantaged children have been largely stimulated both by the recognition that children from low-income families, especially minorities, are making little progress in their academic work and by the pressure on the schools exerted by active minority groups. The several national curriculum development projects in science and mathematics were mainly promoted by scientists and mathematicians who pointed to the out-of-date content that they found in high school textbooks and who were concerned by the small percent of high school students taking advanced courses in science and mathematics.

The current interest in building new curricula for "career education" appears to derive from several needs or problems that are now recognized. One problem is the large-scale lack of understanding on the part of children and youth of the modern world of work. Another is the increasing alienation of youth from the adult society, including lack of plans or planning for their occupations. A third is the current high level of unemployment of youth between the ages of sixteen and twenty-one, and a fourth is the lack of vocational courses in the high school for job areas that are experiencing increasing demand.

Most curriculum approaches do not involve a systematic analysis of the needs or problems that have stimulated the interest in a given curriculum project. As a result, it is likely that some of the curriculum development efforts will not adequately provide for the needs or solve the problems, or the local schools will not adopt the new curricula because they do not appear to be responsive to the problems that are recognized locally. For example, the most expensive curriculum development project undertaken to that time was the high school physics course produced by the Physical Science Study Committee.[1] In spite of the large expenditures both in development and in teacher institutes to help physics teachers understand and utilize the materials, schools using them today as the committee intended them to be used are in a distinct minority. Part of this ineffectiveness can be attributed to other factors, but one obvious error made by PSSC was its failure to work with local schools sufficiently to know what problems and difficulties they were having in physics courses and to see that the new physics curriculum would furnish a way of solving some of these problems or overcoming some of their difficulties.

Far too often the following questions are asked: "How can we get the schools to change?" or "Why aren't the schools innovative?" The school ought not change for the sake of change nor innovate for the sake of innovation. The school has a mission which it performs more or less well. Where it believes it is succeeding in its mission, it sees no reason to change. Where it encounters problems or discovers it is failing in its mission, the school is usually interested in doing something likely to solve the problem. The schools accepted the diagnosis of physicists that the content of high school physics textbooks was out of date, and they welcomed the efforts of PSSC to produce authentic, up-to-date material. They did not, however, recognize the necessity for a new kind of learning experience and a new kind of teaching strategy. Hence, as Goodlad and his colleagues found in their observations of a sample of PSSC classrooms,[2] the PSSC materials were being utilized in the same way that previous textbooks had been used. It is doubtful, furthermore, whether many high schools considered the relatively small enrollment in advanced physics classes as a serious problem. Had they done so, they might have helped the Physical Science Study Committee analyze possible causes for this enrollment situation and develop more effective plans than were represented by the PSSC course. It is interesting that neither the PSSC nor Project Physics has stopped the downward trend in enrollment in high school physics classes.

Another important facet of analyzing the problem is to identify the particular category of students who are having difficulties with the present curriculum or for whom no satisfactory learning system is available. In the field of primary reading, for example, 75 to 80 percent of American children achieve the skills required to comprehend typical newspaper items and children's stories by age thirteen. However, 20 to 25 percent do not learn to read adequately. These children are usually found in the inner cities and in very rural areas. They commonly come from low-income families where the parents have had little education. Designing a more effective reading curriculum for these categories of children is a different task than the effort to develop a curriculum to be used for all primary children.

Similarly, an analysis of the problem of the individualization of learning reveals certain categories of children who devise their own individual sequence of learning and proceed at their own rate while others require a curriculum specifically designed to enable them to learn and to progress sequentially. It is an inefficient use of resources to design an individualized curriculum for those who develop one for themselves.

It is still early enough for major curriculum development projects in career education to analyze the problems more fully before designing curricula to deal with them. The proponents of some of these are, nevertheless, telling the community, and especially low-income parents, that the new curriculum when in operation will largely guarantee the employment of graduates who do not go on to postsecondary schools. An analysis of the problem would have shown that it is not primarily the lack of occupational skills that prevents the large-scale employment of seventeen-year-olds. Most employing institutions will not hire youth under age twenty-one no matter how skilled they may be. If this be true, the implication for the design of curricula for occupational skill training would connect it directly with employment, possibly through cooperative education or through postsecondary technical training. The main point I wish to make is that curriculum development projects must begin with an analysis of the needs or problems that have stimulated the decision to develop a new or revised curriculum.

Related to the analysis of the relevant problems, the approach should examine the contemporary educational environments, including the home, the peer group, the larger community, and the school, in order to identify dynamic factors that influence the problem and the constraints that must be considered in designing an effective curriculum. For example, an analysis of the large environment of young children in a slum neighborhood might reveal a pervasive negative attitude toward the school and schooling that strongly influences the children's work in school; thus many of them consider their time in school not only as irrelevant but boring, unhappy, and often painful. A curriculum that assumes that the students want to learn what the school has to teach will be ineffective. Some way of influencing the out-of-school environment is necessary, or a curriculum must be designed with highly potent internal rewards.

Particular attention should be given to teachers when one is considering the positive and negative dynamic factors that must be taken into account in the curriculum development project. A curriculum designed as a complete, almost teacher-proof, learning system will not usually be acceptable to teachers in any field in which they feel confident that they can teach and do not dislike the teaching role. The curriculum preferred and more likely to be used by teachers is one with components from which the teacher can make selections and/or adaptations in terms of what he perceives to be necessary for the conditions under which he works and what he believes best utilizes his skill, ingenuity, and personal style. A rigid learning system that permits or requires very little artistry on the part of the teacher is likely to be accepted only when the teacher dislikes the teaching task—as in routine drill in spelling, handwriting, or computation—or feels that he does not have the competence to teach it well. The curriculum development plan will, in most cases, need to include means for working with teachers to assure that the curriculum meets their needs and that they can handle their roles effectively.

One of the limiting factors requiring attention in many curriculum projects is the conscious or unconscious assumption on the part of the school that it is fully as much a sorting institution as it is an educational one. In the past these two functions largely went together. Many children from families with educated parents went to school with some notion of what they were expected to learn and how to go about learning it. This made it possible for them to be guided by the existing curriculum, including textbooks and other learning materials, and to use them successfully. A number of students, on the other hand, did not understand the purposes or the learning tasks they were assigned and saw no connection between the curriculum and those things that were important to them. The class activities and the learning materials neither caught their attention nor stimulated their efforts. Normal school practice was to assign high marks to those who found meaning and satisfaction in the curriculum and low marks to those who did not carry on the learning tasks successfully. Thus "good students" were encouraged to continue their education while "poor students" were discouraged and dropped out or were pushed out.

It has been common in the past to place responsibility for failure on the quality of students rather than on the adequacy of the curriculum, and, since the society did not appear to suffer when "poor students" did not learn, the school was not attacked for sorting them out. Now, however, an uneducated person is a costly liability to American society, and the schools are expected to educate all children. It is also widely recognized that every child who has no serious physical handicap is capable of learning the kinds of behavior emphasized by the schools.

This change in expectation necessitates not only new orientation on the part of many teachers but also new understanding and skills. In curriculum development it requires the formulation of learning objectives that are understood both by teachers and students and believed by both to be desirable and attainable. An approach that seeks to develop a curriculum that will be meaningful and helpful to students who have not learned much heretofore involves working with such children and their teachers to clarify meaningful educational goals and to find learning experiences that stimulate the children's attention and interest and that they can carry through successfully.

Some constraints arise from the traditional role of the public schools in America. In the past children and youth learned outside of school most of what was required to be a constructive adult. They gradually were inducted into adult life because the barriers separating them from adults were neither many nor rigid. By the time they were fifteen or sixteen they had participated with adults in most of life's arenas: home, work, church, playing field, and social and civic activities. But the school was expected to expand the horizon of children by opening up the resources of scholarship, which went far beyond the firsthand experience in the community. The school was not to be a substitute for direct experience but a means of enlarging it. Reading, writing, history, geography, literature, mathematics, science— these were subjects that could open up a vast world of experiences, ideas, and knowledge that could free young people from the limitation of their parochial environment. Hence, teachers were sought who had had scholarly preparation. Now, a bachelor's degree is a minimum requirement for teacher certification in all states. Scholarly interests and background are assets for much teaching, but they are a constraint when teachers are expected to provide vocational guidance relating to occupations that are foreign to academic college programs. Ginzberg's study of career guidance[3] shows its inadequacy in the typical American high school. A scholarly teacher is unlikely to know much about blue-collar jobs and to be a role model for them; he is also likely to have low esteem for such jobs and to communicate this to his students. Such a constraint needs to be considered in planning career education curricula in order to determine what is possible in a school and what will have to be learned elsewhere.

Although I have used career education as an extreme example of a constraint that must be recognized in the typical teaching staff, most curriculum development projects will find that teachers or other school personnel have not yet acquired the attitudes, understanding, or skills necessary to guide some of the desirable learning experiences. Where such constraints are identified, they need to be dealt with by providing for necessary teacher education, by allocating the learning activities to other institutions or individuals, or by eliminating them from the curriculum.

When the education or preparation of teachers, administrators, parents, or others is an essential part of the curriculum plan, the feasibility in terms of the efficient allocation of resources for this task is frequently overlooked. In Israel, for example, the Science Teaching Center developed a new science curriculum that required extensive further education of teachers in order for them to guide the learning of their students. After the materials were developed, the expenditures for the teacher education program were estimated. Much to the consternation of the project staff, it was found that the cost of educating Israel's high school science teachers to use the new course would require all of the in-service education funds of the Ministry of Education for ten years. And there was, in the meantime, great demand for curriculum development in the field of social studies. The total requirements, including personnel, equipment and supplies, consultations, and the further education of teachers, should be carefully estimated when a major curriculum project is undertaken. In the past many, if not most, such projects have failed to come to full fruition because the practical requirements could not be met.

Rationale for Curriculum Building

After identifying the needs or problems to which the curriculum development project should be responsive and the constraints under which the curriculum must operate, the curriculum builders have a clearer picture of the requirements the curriculum will have to satisfy, and it is then possible to work on the several components of the total project. To guide these activities a rationale is helpful, if not essential. Various rationales are described in the current educational literature, and several of them have been used successfully. However, I prefer the one outlined in my syllabus, *Basic Principles of Curriculum and Instruction,*[4] because it is comprehensive and has been employed effectively in a number of curriculum projects.

In this rationale, four major tasks serve as the focuses of curriculum construction: the selection and definition of the learning objectives; the selection and creation of appropriate learning experiences; the organization of the learning experiences to achieve a maximum cumulative effect; and the evaluation of the curriculum to furnish a continuing basis for necessary revisions and desirable improvements.

In the case of projects that seek to construct the total school curriculum, the selection and definition of the learning objectives will commonly be attacked first, but a project that deals with only one subject or curriculum area may begin with the evaluation of an earlier curriculum, and then move to objectives, learning experiences, and organization. In some cases, as in building a curriculum in the field of literature, the first step may be the selection of literary works that appear to offer a variety of new experiences for students and then to consider what can be learned from the reading of these materials that is important for the students. Whichever of the four major tasks is undertaken first, the complete development project will involve them all, often moving to and fro among them several times as ideas emerge that are checked and rechecked among the several components of the curriculum.

Selecting and Defining Objectives

Curriculum building is not a process based on precise rules, but involves artistic design as well as critical analysis, human judgments, and empirical testing. In selecting objectives, for example, curriculum makers need current data and future estimates about opportunities and problems in various sectors of society—occupational, sociocivic, home and family, recreational. These data should be accurate and reliable, but the interpretations drawn from them as to what students can learn that enables them to respond to the opportunities or help solve the problems are judgments that are not precise and become more dependable only as they are tested in actual curriculum practice. Similarly, information about the interests of particular students, their abilities, and their problems should be accurate and reliable, but the interpretations drawn from them as to what these students can learn that will broaden their interests as well as satisfy them, that will furnish a more comprehensive set of abilities as well as build on those already acquired, and that will enable them to deal successfully with their problems are judgments that become more dependable as they are tested in the operation of the curriculum. Even more matters of human judgment are the decisions concerning what students can learn of significance from a given subject-matter field—its concepts, generalizations, questions for inquiry, methods of inquiry, skills, attitudes, and facts. When it comes to the enhanced emotional responses that can be learned from the study of literature and other arts, human judgments and the results of actual curriculum practices are the major bases for selecting objectives.

Recognizing the importance in selecting objectives of human judgments based on experience as well as relevant data systematically collected and analyzed, I recommend the procedure of group deliberation as described by Joseph J. Schwab in his "The Arts of the Practical" and illustrated in some detail by Seymour Fox at the AERA Convention in 1971.[5] Suggestions and judgments of teachers, subject-matter specialists, curriculum specialists, psychologists, sociologists, and specialists in human development can be considered and their probable consequences deliberated in ways that lead to constructive decisions that form the basis of initial objectives to be tested for their attainability and their effects in real curriculum projects.

This procedure of deliberation is also helpful in defining the level of generalization on which to focus an objective. Since 1910 American curriculum practice has alternated between two extremes: learning objectives stated so generally that they failed to clarify the kind of behavior the student was to be helped to learn; and objectives that are so specific that they fail to provide for the level of generalization of behavior of which human beings are capable. To state that an objective of arithmetic is to teach students to "think" is obviously too general to guide the selection of learning experiences, the activities of the student or of the teacher, but to formulate more than 3,000 objectives of arithmetic as E. L. Thorndike[6] did more than fifty years ago is to caricature human learning. Children can, for example, acquire the "idea" of addition and learn to add with a score of illustrative examples without practicing on each of the one hundred combinations of one-digit numbers taken two at a time. When I wrote in 1931[7] of the need for stating objectives in terms of behavior, I made definite reference to the fact that an objective could be clearly defined in terms of generalized behavior if the students involved were able to generalize at that level. An objective can be clear without being specific.

During the Second World War, when large numbers of workers had to be trained quickly to carry on specific tasks like soldering electronic circuitry, the training directors emphasized specific objectives. After the war this was carried over into education without scrutinizing the difference between objectives appropriate for very short training programs for specific jobs and long-term educational programs in schools. In making judgments about the level of generality to be the focus of a given educational objective, one should use the process of deliberation carried on by the types of groups suggested above.

The syllabus mentioned earlier comments on the use of the school's educational philosophy as a screen or set of criteria for selecting objectives, particularly for distinguishing the more important from the less important ones. The syllabus also points out the way in which knowledge of the psychology of learning can be used to estimate the probability of attaining a given objective under the conditions found in a particular school. It is obvious that the effort to develop learning experiences for an objective that has small likelihood of being attained will be wasted.

The selection and definition of objectives for a curriculum are a complex but necessary—and continuing—task. It is continuing both as the rest of the curriculum tasks are carried on and after the curriculum is operating because new external conditions and experiences with the curriculum in the school will be providing new information and the bases for new judgments about objectives. A curriculum must be ever relevant in the best sense of that word.

Selecting and Creating Learning Experiences

Creating learning experiences is an even more artistic enterprise than the selection of objectives. It is true that certain conditions must be met for an experience to aid the student in reaching the objective. The student must, for example, carry on the behavior that is the learning objective in order to learn it. The learner must, furthermore, obtain satisfaction (reinforcement) from the desired behavior in order for it to become part of his repertoire of behavior. Opportunities for practicing the behavior and for feedback to inform the learner when his performance is not satisfactory so that he can try again are also conditions to be met by a set of learning experiences. But these are criteria largely used in appraising possible learning experiences, not means of creating them. Not all teachers or curriculum builders are able to create new and effective learning experiences. A procedure I have found useful is to ask each of those involved in the curriculum development project to suggest a few learning experiences that seem to him appropriate and then to use the deliberative process to review, criticize, and identify those offering promise enough for further development. The persons who, in this preliminary exercise, created some experiences that held up under deliberative review are then encouraged to produce more.

In creating learning experiences, it is important to use the perspective of the different kinds of students for whom they are designed. The initial activities should attract the attention of each student and seem worth doing because they can help him learn something he wants to learn, because they are interesting to do, or because persons he respects are doing them. These activities should also be well within his present ability to carry on successfully so that he can gain confidence in going on with further activities. Although practice is essential in learning, repetitive drill soon becomes boring, and the student does not give adequate attention to it. This effort to use the student's perspective is often overlooked in creating learning experiences. It is necessary to keep firmly in mind that human learners rarely, if ever, want to be "shaped" by others. Each one has purposes and interests of his own and utilizes much energy and effort to further his purposes and satisfy his interests. If a school activity is perceived as interesting and/or useful for his purposes, he enters into it energetically, whereas if it seems irrelevant or boring or painful, he avoids it, or limits his involvement as much as he can. I have found that observing and interviewing students when they are actively engaged in learning things they think important help me to develop initial outlines for experiences that will help these students learn things the school seeks to teach.

Another important principle to keep in mind is to make use of peer-group influences as far as they can be appropriately employed in the development of the desired objectives. Solitary activities are hard for children to carry on for long periods of time. Group projects and games, group discussions, group attacks on problems, and group planning of emotionally charged experiences are illustrations of activities that provide powerful learning experiences. A two-student group is a special case in which learning can be enhanced. The two may be of different ages in a tutoring relationship, of the same age in a cooperative endeavor, or of the same age in a competitive contest. When participants in a curriculum development project are encouraged to explore the many types of social learning, they usually are able to create a wider range of effective learning experiences than they produced before.

Learning experiences that facilitate transfer usually require explicit attention. Every educational program seeks to aid students in developing new ways of thinking, feeling, and acting that will be employed by them in the various appropriate situations they encounter in their lives. Education has been unsuccessful if the student does not transfer what he learns in school to his life outside. Because many things to be learned in school are new ways of viewing situations, new ways of attacking problems, new ways of understanding and explaining phenomena, new ways of responding emotionally to aesthetic experiences, new kinds of interests, and new social, intellectual, and communication skills, they are often in sharp contrast to the habits, ideas, and practices of many students. Without learning experiences that furnish help to apply these new things to life situations the student is encountering, he may not transfer school learning to his life outside the classroom. Hence, for every objective, the participants in curriculum development will find it helpful to consider the ways in which, and the conditions under which, the behavior being learned can appropriately be employed by the student outside the classroom. Thus, an important criterion for a set of learning experiences is the inclusion of a number that stimulate the student to use outside the school what he is learning in school. Too frequently the curriculum omits this important component.

Organizing Learning Experiences

The syllabus referred to earlier discusses the relatively minor changes in student behavior that result from single, isolated learning experiences. However, when they are organized so that each subsequent experience builds on what has been learned in earlier ones and so that the student can perceive the connection between what he is learning in one field and what he is learning in another, the cumulative effect in changes in the learner's behavior is greatly enhanced. The purpose guiding the task of organizing learning experiences in the curriculum is to seek to maximize their combined impact. In obtaining a larger cumulative effect, attention should be given both to the sequence of experiences within each field of learning, such as mathematics, social studies, and occupational planning, and the extent of integration among the fields. By integration is meant the learner's perception of meaningful connectives from one field to another so that what he learns day by day in the several fields will be part of his repertoire of behavior, and he can draw upon the learning in all the fields as he encounters situations or problems where they are appropriate.

To plan for sequence and integration, organizing elements such as concepts, skills, and values are helpful. This means, for example, that the curriculum makers identify major concepts that are useful in explaining and controlling phenomena and that are sufficiently complex and pervasive to enable the student to gain increasing depth of understanding and increasing breadth of application of them as he progresses from week to week and year to year in the curriculum. Some concepts may also be related to phenomena in other fields or problems that cut across several fields so that they are useful elements for aiding integration of learning.

Curriculum makers can also identify significant skills that are sufficiently complex and pervasive to serve as organizing elements to achieve sequence and integration. And, for objectives involving attitudes, appreciations, interests, and personal commitments, curriculum makers can identify important values that can serve as organizing elements.

The syllabus comments on the variety of organizing principles that are found in current curriculums. I doubt if there is a single organizing principle that is to be preferred because it clearly contributes to a greater cumulative effect of the learning experiences. The principles can generally be selected on the ground that they furnish a sequence or an integration that is meaningful and effective with the students and teachers who are expected to use them.

In addition to criteria, elements, and principles of organization, the curriculum makers must deal with the problem of the organizing structures, such as courses, units, topics, lessons, and their relative rigidity or flexibility. The recent debate on individualization of instruction furnishes an initial list of issues and criteria with regard to the size and definition of useful structures, while the debates on the open classroom fairly well outline the issues and criteria to guide in developing an appropriate balance between flexibility and rigidity.

Curriculum Evaluation

The term "evaluation" is used in several different ways in current educational publications, ranging from the inclusion of all information needed by decision makers in education to the other extreme in which it is restricted to the use of an objective testing program. I shall employ the term to include the process of comparing the ideas and assumptions involved in curriculum development with the realities to which they refer. Most of the planning, the monitoring, and the reporting of curriculum activities is guided by the conceptions the participants have about the persons, processes, and objects involved. Unless there is continuous checking to ascertain the probable validity of these notions, the curriculum development project will have little relation to the actual situations that are being encountered. Evaluation is this checking process.

The checking process should be applied at four different stages in curriculum development. When one or more ideas are proposed for developing a program, a set of materials, or an instructional device, evaluation should be undertaken to find out whether there is any evidence from earlier experiments or experience that indicates the probable effectiveness of the idea. In reviewing recent curriculum development projects, I am disappointed to see how frequently ideas are accepted that have been tried or tested in the past and found fallacious. It is unfortunate that so many of the project directors are newcomers to curriculum development and are unfamiliar with its detailed history because much wasted effort is likely to be avoided by evaluation at the idea stage.

Evaluation is also essential in the implementation stage. When a plan is presumably in operation an actual check of the school situations usually reveals a number of places reporting the plan is in operation when, in fact, it is not. In some cases this is due to a lack of understanding of the essential features of the plan, so that the implementation lacks salient conditions essential to the idea. In other cases those implementing the plan feel that it will not work, and so they establish a program that they think is better. There are even cases where an old procedure is continued while it is professed that the new idea is in operation. I found in the study of activity schools in New York City in 1942 that less than half the classrooms in these schools were actually carrying on activity programs.

Various techniques have been developed for sampling the actual implementation of educational programs. John Goodlad and his colleagues have devised a rather comprehensive schedule for his current *Study of Schooling in the United States.*[8] Seymour Fox and his colleagues in the Hebrew University of Jerusalem have developed an analysis procedure that relates the actual operations to the purposes and guiding principles of the plan.[9] In our study of activity schools we used a checklist of sixty-one items based on an analysis of the plan for these schools.

A third stage in which evaluation contributes to the effectiveness of the curriculum is during its actual operation, both in guiding its development during early trials and also in monitoring its continuing use. Placement tests, mastery tests, and diagnostic tests can keep students and teachers in touch with the actual learning process and can furnish information to guide them. An assessment program conducted once or twice a year can provide data that serve to alert the principal or the central administration regarding problems needing special attention. The yearbook of the National Society for the Study of Education entitled *Evaluation: New Roles; New Means* describes some of these procedures.[10]

Finally, evaluation needs to be conducted to find out the extent to which students are actually developing the patterns of behavior that the curriculum was designed to help them learn. Before curriculum makers had developed sophisticated achievement tests, this kind of evaluation was conducted with norm-referenced achievement tests that were not based on a sample of behavior that the students were expected to learn but only on those exercises which differentiated among pupils. This often meant that the exercises did not reflect what the curriculum was designed to help students learn, but involved behavior not in the curriculum, which sharply differentiated students who came from backgrounds where they experienced these things from students who did not. Because schools attempt to help all children learn, the exercises that sample what the children are really learning in school often do not differentiate sharply among them.

Curriculum makers have recently become more interested in using criterion-referenced tests rather than norm-referenced ones. They have also become aware of various other devices that indicate what students have learned. It seems likely that evaluation of the outcomes of new curricula will be increasingly valid.

Conclusion

The approach outlined in this chapter is pragmatic. It assumes limited resources for curriculum development and effective implementation. It seeks, therefore, to utilize available knowledge and experience at each step. A grand, comprehensive, total school curriculum is assumed to be impracticable to develop and implement with the resources available. Hence the first step is to identify serious difficulties or problems with the present curriculum that should be given primary attention. The second step is to outline explicitly the constraints under which a new curriculum must operate. To maximize the constructive participation in curriculum development a group procedure, including group deliberation, is suggested. The construction process itself is outlined in terms of four major tasks: selecting objectives, developing learning experiences, organizing learning experiences, and evaluation. This approach has been successful in my own experience, and I believe it has value for others.

Notes

1. The Physical Science Study Committee, chaired by Jerold Zacharias of the Massachusetts Institute of Technology, obtained in 1959 the first grant from the National Science Foundation to produce a new high school physics course.

2. John I. Goodlad, Frances M. Klein, *et al.*, *Looking Behind the Classroom Door*, revised edition (Worthington, Ohio: Charles A. Jones, 1974).

3. Eli Ginzberg, *Career Guidance: Who Needs It, Who Provides It, Who Can Improve It* (New York: McGraw-Hill, 1971).

4. Ralph W. Tyler, *Basic Principles of Curriculum and Instruction* (Chicago: University of Chicago Press, 1969).

5. Joseph J. Schwab, "The Practical: Arts of Eclectic," *School Review* 79 (August 1971): 493-542; Seymour Fox, "A Practical Image of the Practical," paper presented at the symposium on Joseph J. Schwab's *The Practical: A Language for Curriculum* (Washington, D. C.: National Education Association, 1970), at the American Educational Research Association Annual Meeting, February 4, 1971.

6. E. L. Thorndike, *Psychology of Arithmetic* (New York: Macmillan, 1922).

7. Ralph W. Tyler, "A Generalized Procedure for Constructing Achievement Tests," Ohio State University, *Educational Research Bulletin*, 1931.

8. John I. Goodlad *et al.*, "Study of Schooling in the United States" (in progress).

9. This work by Seymour Fox *et al.* is now in progress.

10. *Evaluation: New Roles; New Means*, Sixty-eighth Yearbook of the National Society for the Study of Education, Part II, ed. Ralph W. Tyler (Chicago: University of Chicago Press, 1969).

3 The Science and Art of Curriculum Design

Lauren B. Resnick

Education, broadly viewed, is any process that results in expanded knowledge and competence for those who engage in it. We normally think of education as going on in certain institutions—schools, colleges, training centers—but, in fact, the educational process is not limited to such institutions. It can, and does, occur in virtually all life encounters, in unplanned as well as planned ways.

Curriculum, by contrast, constitutes a planned intervention for the purpose of education. A curriculum can be thought of as a series of activities explicitly designed to change the knowledge and competence of those who engage in it. Whenever an educational experience is planned, whenever explicit efforts are made to optimize learning and development, a curriculum is being designed. The curriculum may be tight or fluid in style; it may specify activities in great detail or only in general outline; the instructor may control most moves, or

The author would like to thank her many colleagues at the Learning Research and Development Center who have helped, over several years of association, to give shape and substance to her ideas on curriculum design. She would also like to express special appreciation to Wendy Ford for assistance in the substantive editing of this paper. Errors of statement or interpretation, however, are her own.

much may be left to learners. Whatever the particular strategy or ideology of education employed, it is appropriate to speak of a curriculum whenever education is not simply left to chance.

In some societies, the largest part of the individual's education is "informal" in the sense that it takes place in the context of normal work or social activity.[1] While some verbal instruction or demonstration may be offered, this is always done in a concrete context; thus relatively little linguistic and symbolic activity is required, and direct application to culturally relevant tasks is assumed. In a society such as ours, however, which demands complex symbolic abilities and flexibility in applying them across a range of contexts, learning would be too inefficient without some planned educational intervention. Completely "informal" learning would be too tied to the context in which it was taking place to permit the flexible applications demanded in an industrialized environment. Environments explicitly designed for learning are therefore necessary in our society. Such environments are designed to convey both general cultural skills— such as literacy, mathematics, or reasoning—and specific knowledge or technical competence. They are also, in principle, designed to convey such skills and knowledge reliably, that is, in a manner that assures individuals the possibility of learning. The design of environments for learning, and of components of these environments, is the task of curriculum design.

Curriculum Design as Applied Science

Curriculum design can be viewed as a special case of engineering or applied science. So viewed, it becomes pertinent to ask what the scientific basis for design in the curriculum domain is, and how that scientific base interacts with the practice of design. The dominant view of the relationship between science and social applications holds that science produces general principles or laws, and these are studied by individuals—engineers—who apply the laws to practical problems. According to this model, which is schematized in Figure 3-1, the flow of information is unidirectional. Scientists provide information to technologists, but technologists do not provide information to scientists. Furthermore, technologists do not even participate actively in providing questions for scientists to work on. Rather, scientific activity responds primarily to questions generated by previous

Science

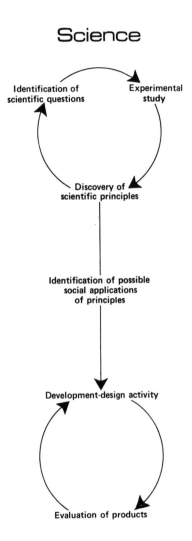

Technology

Figure 3-1. A unidirectional flow of information between science and technology

theoretical research. Thus, if the scientist ever leaves the laboratory, it is to give "advice" to engineers or to translate his findings into forms understandable to a wider audience. The scientist is not, according to this view, directly responsible for what is done with his principles. He is not expected to study directly the social outcomes of his work; he is responsible only for producing knowledge.

Probably no one actually engaged in scientific or technological work has ever really believed in the unidirectional model of information flow. When wartime exigencies demanded technological applications, physical scientists organized themselves into special working groups, focusing on technological outputs yet yielding major new scientific knowledge. The hot and cold war conditions of the 1940s and 1950s probably only highlighted the extent to which science normally feeds upon technological demand.

In education the question of the relationship of science to technology has barely begun to be asked. People working at the technological, or design, end of the continuum—that is, in instructional development—have become aware, in a general way, of the failure of the unidirectional model of science and technology. Rarely in their experience have principles from psychology or the social sciences been directly applicable to the problems of instruction. At the least, translation has been needed. Sometimes the principles themselves have seemed so far from practical concerns that developers have felt the need for research deriving from their own questions rather than from the theoretical questions of the laboratory or basic scientist. But mechanisms even for communicating design-oriented questions have been lacking, and scientists in education's "base disciplines" have, until fairly recently, remained quite aloof from questions of application.

Occasionally, experimental psychologists seriously attempting to probe the relevance of their own and their colleagues' work to social affairs have reached conclusions similar to those of the designers. An interesting case in point is William Estes' recent survey[2] of several decades of research on learning. Estes examined this research for what it could offer as guidelines in the design of instructional programs for individuals with learning disabilities. He explicitly sought empirically validated relationships between learning, as studied in the experimental laboratory, and individual differences in mental capacity. Estes concluded that although a few encouraging developments in both theory and application could be noted, "contacts between learning theory and the empirical study of mental development have been sparse and unsystematic."[3] He pointed out, further, that where progress had been made, it was generally with respect to the severely retarded—the most socially conspicuous educational failures. This concentration on a specific population meant that little had been learned about fostering higher cognitive processes.[4]

A few psychologists whose careers have moved relatively freely between basic research and applied concerns have addressed the question of the possibilities for a science of instructional design. Bruner[5] has pointed out that a theory of instruction must be prescriptive in the sense of providing rules for effective ways of bringing about desired learning effects. Atkinson, in several papers,[6] has described procedures for "optimizing" learning outcomes by varying parameters of time, item selection, and other variables in relation to characteristics of students. Suppes and his colleagues[7] have devoted intensive study to the details of cognitive performance on school tasks, using data from ongoing computer-assisted instruction in arithmetic.

Addressing the question of design in general, Simon, in *The Sciences of the Artificial*,[8] has considered what the requirements for a science of design would be and in what ways such a science would differ from the sciences of natural events. Design, Simon argues, is concerned with more than description and explanation; it is concerned with construction of artifices (hence "sciences of the artificial") to meet goals. This is done, in general terms, by adapting the substance and organization of the artifact to the surroundings in which it operates. When one applies Simon's analysis to education, the artifact is the curriculum or instructional environment, including materials and instructions for what to do with them. The "surrounding" for an instructional program, the condition that must be understood in order to design effective artifacts, is the nature of the learner, both as an individual and as a member of a social group and culture. A science of instructional design, following this general conception, would involve the study of instructional materials and educational environments; the study of the learner; and the study of how the learner and the educational artifact interact, with particular emphasis on how modifications of the instructional artifacts change the nature of this interaction.

These considerations suggest that a new conception of the relationship between science and technology, in education as elsewhere, is required. This conception must allow for a more symmetrical relationship between basic research and social application, thus forcing science into active contact with the problems of design. Without such contact, science will continue to take its questions as well as its methods from prior theory, and its findings will probably continue to be so distant from practical concerns as to offer little guidance to the designer. To correct this state of affairs, to bring science and design—in the present case, psychological science and instructional design—into fruitful interaction with one another, it is necessary to abandon the unidirectional model of the flow of information between science and technology and substitute an interactive model.

Figure 3-2 suggests what is meant. The science-to-technology information flow is complemented by a technology-to-science flow; communication is bidirectional. Science continues to use its carefully controlled methodologies and to pursue questions of data or theory that arise in the course of such research, but some of its questions are now drawn from attempts at social application, from attempts to design products or environments to meet social needs. In a similar way design technology still draws its principles from science, and it still depends heavily upon a cycle of observation, test, and revision that is needed for honing and sharpening its products. Now, however, technology takes on a further function. Its products and the accumulating data on their functioning can be searched for patterns and questions that seem general to a number of products rather than specific to any one. These are the observations that provide stimulus for further scientific work; they are the questions that keep scientific research in productive touch with problems of design and application.

The preceding comments on the general nature of curriculum development as design and applied science provide the setting within which the following description and discussion of particular strategies of curriculum development should be interpreted. In subsequent sections I shall describe several curriculum design efforts with which I have been associated that can serve as illustrations of how science and curriculum design can interact. All are projects undertaken over the past ten years by various groups within the Learning Research and Development Center (LRDC) at the University of Pittsburgh. Extensive reports on each of the projects are available and will be

Science

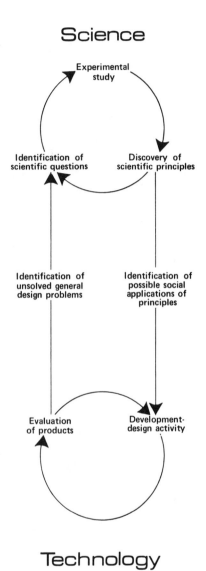

Technology

Figure 3-2. An interactive model of the relation between science and technology

cited throughout the chapter, but only brief discussions will be possible here.

Throughout the chapter, but only occasionally expressed, another set of assumptions will operate. Curriculum design, like design in all other fields, contains elements of both science and art. Instructional design is scientific to the extent that it consciously applies validated principles of the natural and social sciences to problems of educational intervention and to the extent that it develops and uses systematic methods for testing its products and revising them on the basis of performance. It is artistic to the extent that inventiveness and intuition are used in initial instructional development, and, further, to the extent that aesthetic criteria play a role in judging the final products. The relationship between disciplined science and artful design should become clearer as some of LRDC's curriculum design efforts are described; the possibility and desirability of these relationships will receive more explicit treatment in a later section.

Each of the examples of curriculum design discussed here is drawn from the subject matter of the elementary or preschool and is thus closely allied with developmental and child psychology, as well as with learning psychology. Further, all have shared a common commitment to developing programs of education that are adaptive to individual needs and to the abilities of learners. They thus have many specific features in common, such as an emphasis on diagnostic description of children's capabilities and some reliance on self-instructional material. What is equally important for the present discussion is that each curriculum has been developed with a strong degree of conscious attention to deriving general principles from design activity by studying curriculum products and their functioning in schools for clues to general principles of instruction as well as for effectiveness in meeting an immediate goal.

The curriculum design projects will be discussed not in their chronological order of development but rather in the context of a set of considerations that seems to be central both to the development of instructional products and to the development of a theory of instructional design. These considerations, outlined in an earlier paper by Glaser and Resnick, are: analysis of the task properties of the knowledge domain or, more practically, a description of the state of knowledge to be achieved; diagnosis of the characteristics of the learners, that is, a description of the learner's initial state; actions that can be taken or conditions that can be implemented to transform the initial state, that is, design of the curriculum or instructional environment; assessment of specific instructional effects; and evaluation of generalized learning outcomes.[9]

What Is to Be Learned: The Analysis of Tasks

Classically, specification of what is to be learned has been the prime requisite for the design of curriculum. It has often been assumed that experts in any domain make the best developers of curricula. It was this point of view that lay, in part, behind the major curriculum reform movements of the 1950s and early 1960s. Scientists and other scholars, working at the frontiers of their disciplines, began to examine the content of school curricula and found it not to reflect their own understanding of the disciplines. The new curricula of the period (PSSC and SMSG, for example) were designed to present to novices, sometimes even in the elementary school, the concepts considered essential by experts in the disciplines.

Work in instructional design has made it increasingly clear that while expert knowledge of the field to be taught is certainly required for curriculum design, the subject-matter expert alone will rarely be able to provide a description of his competence in a form that can guide development for novices. Bruner[10] pointed this out when he stressed the need to transform the expert's version of concepts into forms comprehensible to younger or less experienced individuals rather than presenting them in their original form. More recently Glaser[11] has emphasized a distinction between knowledge structures as organized for the expert to facilitate use of previously learned bodies of knowledge and those organized for the learner to facilitate acquisition of competence. The expert's inability to describe fully the bases of his own performance has also emerged in recent work in cognitive psychology, work that attempts to simulate the performance of expert performers of complex tasks.[12] Skilled performers of a task cannot always describe well what they know; even more rarely can they describe the psychological processes called upon when they use their knowledge; and they are further still, in most cases, from being able to describe how they acquired their expertise—how they changed from novices to experts.

Task Analysis in Cognitive-Developmental Psychology

A distinction between skilled performance and developing competence has been stressed as a general scientific observation by many developmental psychologists, and study and description of children's competence in various kinds of tasks have been a major focus of cognitive-developmental psychology over at least the past decade. The tasks studied have frequently been drawn from Piaget's pioneering work and sometimes from traditional adult laboratory learning tasks, now reexamined as developmental phenomena. Occasionally, developmental study of phenomena directly related to school tasks such as reading has been undertaken.[13] The results of this large body of research in developmental psychology serve to highlight the task facing curriculum designers: the research makes it evident that adult concepts and skills are not "born" full-grown, that children—and, presumably, learners of all ages—pass through successive stages of understanding and ability on the way to what we view as mature competence, and that each such stage has a kind of logic to it. "Unskilled" performances make sense if understood in their own terms; further, they are the route to competence, a route that must be probed and clarified if instruction is to match optimally the developing capabilities of learners.

Influential as this research has been in demonstrating the general question of how changes in competence occur, the strategies and assumptions of most research in developmental psychology make it difficult to apply the findings directly to instructional problems. Most developmental research is expressly "noninterventionist." The aim is to discover and describe "natural" sequences of development. There operates in this work an often unspoken but nonetheless powerful driving assumption that the sequences thus discovered will be universal and independent of environment. "General experience" rather than any specific set of environmental interactions is thought to produce developmental changes.[14] What is implied but rarely tested explicitly in developmental research is that natural environments are similar in crucial ways and that they will therefore facilitate development of the same kind. Recent cross-cultural work[15] is beginning to substantiate the long-argued suggestion that environments may differ quite radically in their demands and that adult cognitive competence and style vary accordingly. But developmental psychology as a whole still lacks a theory or even a good set of descriptors of the environment. Thus, it is difficult to cull from developmental theory any but the most general guidelines for design of environments specifically intended to bring about changes in competence.

Rational Task Analysis and Learning Hierarchies

What is needed for purposes of instructional design is a description of desired educational outcomes in a form that specifies the psychological processes called upon in skilled performance and also suggests less sophisticated organizations of skill and knowledge that are capable of leading to or producing skilled performance. We need, in other words, analyses of learning goals that specify both the nature of competent task performance and simpler tasks that will facilitate learning. These "facilitative" tasks, organized and sequenced to maximize the match between current abilities and new demands, will constitute a curriculum.[16]

Over several years of work in designing an early learning program for preschool and primary grade children (The Primary Education Project),[17] we have developed a method of task analysis explicitly designed to meet these objectives. The strategy yields hierarchies of tasks similar to those proposed by Gagné,[18] but with more specification of the actual processes involved in performance. A detailed description of the method as applied to an introductory mathematics curriculum appears in Resnick, Wang, and Kaplan.[19] Figure 3-3 illustrates the process. Each box in the figure describes the situation as presented to the child and the child's expected response. Thus the top box (Ia) should be read, "*Given* a set of moveable objects, *the child can* count objects, moving them out of the set as he counts." This provides verbal specification of the task to be analyzed. The first step in performing an analysis is to describe in as much detail as possible the actual steps involved in skilled performance—that is, the "components" of the task. The results of this analysis are shown in level II of the figure. Once the components are identified, each is considered separately, and abilities that are prerequisite to or facilitative of learning the components are identified. For example, the tasks described in IVa and IVb facilitate learning IIIa, which in turn facilitates learning IIa and IIb. Analysis of this kind can result in charts showing several levels of tasks with complex interrelationships

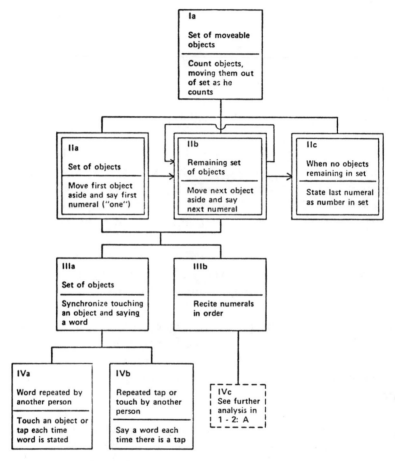

*Figure 3-3. Task analysis of an early mathematics objective (from
L. B. Resnick, M. C. Wang, and J. Kaplan, "Task
Analysis in Curriculum Design: A Hierarchically
Sequenced Introductory Mathematics Curriculum,"*
Journal of Applied Behavior Analysis, *6 [No. 4, 1973]:
Figure 1-2:B)*

among them (shown in the figure by connecting lines). Frequently, when a set of tasks from a single curriculum domain is being analyzed, one task in the set appears as a prerequisite to another in the set. These relationships provide the basis for sequencing the separate tasks of a curriculum in a way that will optimize transfer and maximize the likelihood of success in learning. Frequently, too, the same abilities appear as prerequisites to several different tasks. In this case a generalized ability has been identified, one to which special diagnostic or instructional attention should probably be devoted in order to optimize instructional effectiveness and efficiency for learners of varying characteristics.

Although the example given here is for a very simple task, counting a set of moveable objects, the strategy of analysis is a general one and can be applied to tasks in various domains. The level of specificity—that is, the fineness of detail with which given tasks are analyzed—depends upon the task and the population for whom instruction is being designed. As a general rule, no further prerequisites would be specified when a level of behavior is reached that can be assumed in most of the student population in question. Further, the initial analysis should describe components of the task at a level of detail consonant with what one expects is already a reasonably well-organized behavior pattern in the learner's repertoire. Even in a curriculum for kindergarten children, as in the present example, much is left unspecified. It is assumed (box IIa), for example, that the child will be able to recognize a grouping of separate elements. Similarly, it is assumed that the motor acts of moving an object or saying a word are already organized and need not be further analyzed.

We have used these strategies of task analysis in developing curricula for a variety of preschool and primary grade programs.[20] In each case, careful attention has been devoted to validation of the analyses either through special validation studies[21] or through careful study of the curriculum itself.[22] These studies not only serve to validate proposed curriculum sequences, but also yield basic information on natural sequences of development[23] and on the nature of transfer relationships among hierarchically related tasks.[24] Thus, they exemplify a form of interactive research and development, cases in which efforts to develop optimal curricula have generated research on questions of basic scientific interest.

Information Processing Analyses

The analyses just described can be appropriately characterized as informal "process models" of performance at different stages of expertise. As process models, they specify hypothesized components and temporal organization of performance and attempt to identify the underlying memory, perceptual, linguistic, and other processes that are embedded in the more complex tasks. More formal methods of task analysis, drawn largely from the work of current information processing psychology, also deserve consideration as possible bases for future instructional work. Formalized task analyses require both more completely specified performance models than the ones we have used in curriculum development up to now and more precise empirical validation. The most demanding current criterion for a complete performance model is that it be written as a computer program that is capable of performing the task. A program of this kind encourages precision in modeling (computers take their instructions quite literally), but can be written so as to engage in quite sophisticated "heuristic" behaviors.[25]

Technologies for computer modeling of this kind exist. It would be a tedious but not highly inventive undertaking to turn each of the many informal process models we have written into programs that assured us of the completeness—in this technical sense—of our analysis. With that accomplished, we would still need to test the programs as models of human performance. Our work on validation of learning hierarchies has provided an initial test of these models. The models are accurate enough to predict well transfer between tasks and the general order of task acquisition. A variety of specific performances might, however, produce the same general patterns of sequence and transfer; more rigorous methods of validation are required in order to lend credence to the details of any given process model. Methods for such validation include detailed analysis of individual verbal and behavioral protocols, study of differences in reaction times for slight variants of a task, analysis of frequency and type of errors, and so forth—in short, virtually the entire range of methods now used in the field of cognitive psychology.

It is obvious that the use of formalized models is expensive, and consideration must be given to when the added cost of formal specification and empirical study is likely to add enough instructional power to make the effort worthwhile. In subject-matter fields where much is known, where successful examples of instruction abound and where the subject matter has an inner logic that lends strong face validity to hypothesized analyses, the added effort of formalized analysis may have relatively small direct payoff for instruction. Where little is known, where even strong hypotheses concerning actual process are difficult to find, much may be gained through the discipline of formal analysis. Many unlikely or less than optimal paths for instruction may be eliminated, and strategies likely to be effective may be suggested.

A contrast between analysis of mathematics and reading tasks at different stages may help to make this point. In a general sense, mathematics, especially early mathematics of the kind we have studied and analyzed, presents relatively few ambiguities. The subject matter is a closed logical system, within which informal analyses are likely to reflect actual performance reasonably faithfully and thus to guide instructional design effectively. The same is largely true of early reading, where letter-sound correspondences are relatively easily specified and ordered. By contrast, it is very difficult to develop process descriptions for language comprehension and for advanced mathematical thinking. Many competing analyses are possible. In language, especially, the subject-matter domain is "open" and highly dependent on context, on past experience, and on details of the task as presented. It is by now quite widely agreed[26] that comprehension is not a simple linear process, that it involves use of redundancy in the structure of the language and a search for meaning —in short, it is a very complex cognitive process. For this kind of subject matter, formal process analyses and empirical tests are likely to have especially high payoff. At present, for example, there exists no generally accepted model of how a prose passage is comprehended when read, of the processes involved in taking and interpreting information from a text. In this situation much may be gained through the disciplining effort of formalized task analysis and related empirical research leading to the development of psychological models of comprehension processes.

One example of a case where formal analysis of an academic task has led to an unusual and potentially productive instructional design comes from spelling. An original model for how children spell was written by Simon and Simon.[27] This was a formal model in the sense that it took into account existing data on the structure of the sound-symbol correspondences of the language and the typical errors made by children in spelling; was written as a computer program; and was validated, in part, on the basis of the ability of the program to match actual performance both in terms of correct spellings generated and in terms of the kinds of errors typically produced. Spelling programs that embody some of the processes identified in this analysis have been written under the direction of Karen Block at the Learning Research and Development Center. These spelling lessons, which are computer based and utilize the special responsive characteristics of the computer, include practice in generating alternative spellings for given sounds, in sorting spellings according to patterns used to represent the same sound, and in choosing among alternative spellings. This work virtually embodies the interactive mode of curriculum design. The initial analysis of spelling was motivated by an applied instructional need. The resulting model provided the basis for lesson design, which in turn can provide one of the pieces of converging evidence needed to validate the model itself. If children trained in the processes identified in the model improve in spelling and continue to match the program in terms of quality as well as correctness of output over successive levels of competence, validation of the model will have been provided in the course of instruction.

Formal and empirical process analyses are likely to yield much instructional power when the aim is to identify and find ways of instructing what we call "generative skills," that is, basic abilities that are used in a variety of learning and other performance situations. Current cognitive psychological theory is pointing with increasing consensus to the existence of certain basic processes, such as memory, perception, and inference strategies, that are quite general in human functioning and thus would produce generalized learning abilities were we to find ways of enhancing them. These abilities are embedded in academic tasks and in on-the-job tasks of various kinds. Some of these abilities appear to be tapped indirectly by the kinds of tasks that are found in most widely used intelligence and aptitude tests. But the abilities are deeply embedded; they are not visible in cursory forms of task analysis as, for example, in job analysis techniques, and they require complex study to be detected and understood. It seems likely that formal task analysis procedures will prove to be an effective means of identifying generative skills and suggesting methods for their instruction. The power of such analyses in the domain of instructional design remains only a promise at this time, but it is a promise worth serious investigation.[28]

Diagnosis of Learner Characteristics

Closely allied to the problem of describing what is to be learned is the problem of describing the capabilities of the learner as he enters the learning environment. This step is crucial if curricula are to be adaptive to individual differences. It is necessary to know what the learner is like: what he can do that is directly relevant to the subject matter to be learned, what he can do that constitutes a more generalized learning-to-learn skill, what motivates him, and so on. With this knowledge in hand, it becomes possible to design curricula that adapt to these characteristics. The description of these characteristics must be in terms relevant to educational decision making. For this reason, typological descriptions generally are not useful, as compared with descriptions of specific competencies and behaviors that can be observed under specifiable conditions. Describing individuals as being of high or low intelligence, for example, gives little guidance in the selection of instructional treatments that are most likely to be effective. The weakness of such approaches is documented in much of the literature on aptitude-treatment interactions: years of research have yielded little information on how to adapt instructional treatments to individual differences, as measured by traditional aptitude tests.[29] Thus traditional approaches to testing and differential psychology, developed and validated for purposes of selection and prediction, are, in their present form, of relatively little value for instructional diagnosis. New ways of conceptualizing the nature of individual differences are required and, along with them, new ways of assessing these differences.[30]

Describing the learner is not something that is done at the outset of instruction and then left alone until final assessment of the outcome of instruction. Rather, it must be a more or less continuous process. As the learner proceeds through a curriculum, his or her capabilities change. They change in terms of both specific knowledge acquired and generalized abilities available for further learning. These changes can result either from general experience during the period coterminous with instruction or from engaging in the instruction itself. Thus, to maintain an effective curriculum over an extended period of time, it is necessary to describe changes in the learner's capabilities as instruction progresses and to do this in a form that is useful in making decisions as to the course of succeeding instruction.

The discussion in the previous section on analysis of the subject matter has already alluded to some of the ways in which this problem can be attacked. Hierarchies of learning tasks, generated through formal or informal task analysis, provide a way of describing the learner's capabilities in terms of the tasks and underlying abilities that make up the curriculum itself. Describing the tasks an individual can already perform within a hierarchy and those yet to be learned tells the instructor (or the learner himself) which tasks are likely to be easily learned and which are likely to be too difficult. Thus the learner's capabilities can be described in terms of the curriculum content itself and its underlying processes. Further, they can be described as a changing function of progress, or lack of it, through the curriculum. The hierarchy of tasks thus serves as a map that delineates both present location and possible directions of movement of any individual learner under consideration.

The Role of Criterion-Referenced Testing

Implementing this mapping function of curriculum hierarchies requires a form of testing that is explicitly designed for ongoing instructional decision making, one that will help in placing individual children in the curriculum structure and provide diagnostic information for use in making specific instructional assignments. Considerable effort was devoted to developing such a testing strategy in LRDC's first major curriculum development undertaking, Individually Prescribed Instruction (IPI). A paper by Glaser outlined the major evaluation requirements for a system of education that adapted instruction to individual requirements:

1. Outcomes . . . of learning are specified in terms of observable learner performance and the conditions under which this performance is to be exercised.
2. Detailed diagnosis is made of the initial state of a learner entering a particular instructional situation.
3. Educational alternatives are provided which are adaptive to the classifications resulting from the initial student ability profiles.

4. As the student learns, his performance is monitored and continuously assessed at longer or shorter intervals appropriate to what is being taught.
5. Instruction and learning proceed in interrelated fashion, tracking the performance and selections of the student.
6. The instructional system collects information in order to improve itself, and inherent in the system's design is its capability for doing this.[31]

These requirements were met in IPI by elaboration and application of the notion of criterion-referenced testing.[32] Such tests are equivalent to "work samples" as a means of assessing job performance. Criterion-referenced tests were used to assess entering level in the curriculum sequence (placement tests), immediate mastery of individual skills as they were taught (curriculum-embedded tests), and mastery of a unit of related objectives (pre- and posttests). With younger children in the Primary Education Project (PEP) and subsequent adaptive curricula the tests were administered orally on a one-to-one basis and frequently involved the use of manipulative materials appropriate to the task and age level. Teachers used these tests as part of the regular instructional process. The tests, along with observation of the children's activities as they worked on instructional materials, guided the teachers both in placing children in the curriculum structure and in adapting the instruction to individual needs.

Use of criterion-referenced tests in the manner described for individualized instruction raised a series of questions, which in subsequent years commanded the attention of researchers within LRDC and elsewhere.[33] One set of questions has concerned the strategy for specifying objectives and creating pools of test items that would adequately sample the specified domain. Initial efforts at test development were informal and iterative: an objective was described verbally; test constructors wrote items that appeared to match the statement of the objective; the items were reviewed by the curriculum designer, and either items, stated objectives, or both were revised until a consensus was reached that the test reflected the curriculum developer's intent. There was no formal procedure for specifying the objective to be tested or for sampling among test items for inclusion in the tests. Further, standards for passing and failing, mastery and nonmastery, were informally and largely arbitrarily set in terms of passing or failing some fixed number of items on the test.

Some Examples of New Approaches to Testing
for Instructional Design Making

In the case of test theory, as in the case of task analysis, serious work on theoretical questions has been prompted by the demands and the successes of instructional development. Two cases of interwoven development and research activity in testing illustrate this point. The first concerns the use of the computer as an aid in "tailored" or "adaptive" testing. It is possible, using a computer, to tailor testing to the individual's performance by limiting the number of items given to those actually needed to reach a decision and by branching to new classes of items for further diagnosis. To accomplish this, systematic rules are required both for generating items in a class and for making pass-fail decisions. The first requirement was met by an adaptation of the strategy of "item forms"[34] so that the computer could generate a large number of specific items based on a limited set of stored parameters and generation rules. Two different kinds of decision rules, one based on traditional statistical theory and the other on Bayesian theory, have been investigated. Both permit evaluation of successive "pass" and "fail" cases as they cumulate, and both allow testing to stop as soon as a reasonably certain decision is reached. This is much the way a skilled diagnostician proceeds: if the individual being tested passes several items in sequence, a positive or "mastery" decision can be made; if he fails several in sequence, a negative or "nonmastery" decision can be made; if the individual vacillates between passing and failing items, a longer period of testing is needed to reach a decision. Further detail on these theoretical investigations and their applications to tailored testing can be found in papers by Ferguson and Hsu, Carlson, and Pingel.[35]

The second case of interest here grows out of the successful development of diagnostically oriented tests of visual and auditory skills by Jerome Rosner[36] and by Rosner and Simon.[37] The tests Rosner developed correlate positively and strongly with existing tests (in the case of visual skills) and also predict performance on related academic tasks such as beginning reading (in the case of auditory skills). They are distinguished from past tests of these skills by the fact that they are tied directly to curricula designed to teach the skills tested. Tests used in predicting academic performance normally lose their predictive validity when the tasks appearing in the tests are directly taught. Studies conducted to date suggest that this is not the case with Rosner's tests—that instruction oriented to improving test performance can be successful and that the improved performance will be reflected on other tasks not directly taught. This kind of finding validates the procedure of using criterion-referenced tests as targets for instruction.

Design of Instructional Materials and Environments

A major and important aspect of curriculum design work has been completed when task analysis and diagnostic instruments are available. Task analysis translates general statements about curriculum content into specific concepts and skills to be taught and, in many cases, also provides a sequential structure for the content. Criterion-referenced diagnostic tests, in addition to their use in instructional decision making, serve as working definitions of the specific content.

Yet, despite the structure imposed by task analysis and criterion-referenced tests, there is a large, and largely intuitive, leap to be made from these specifications to an interesting and effective instructional program. Examination of "systems" approaches to curriculum development will reveal that there is no good set of prescriptions available for designing instructional materials. Instead, there is heavy dependence on a cycle of iterative development and testing. This process serves to validate the effectiveness of intuitive translations of curriculum specifications into instructional procedures; it cannot, however, substitute for artful design work at the outset, for tests will only reveal successes and failures, not prescribe alternative strategies. The actual design of instructional materials or instructional environments, then, is a matter of art as well as science and requires a special facility for combining intuitive and scientific knowledge.

Design of Adaptive Learning Environments

The need for an effective combination of art and science becomes especially apparent when one is concerned with designing entire environments for learning rather than the separate components or instructional materials. A "curriculum" is often thought to consist of the "lessons" that students will encounter—the "things" of instruction. Only rarely in discussions of curriculum does one find much explicit consideration of the role of the total environment in promoting (or hindering) learning. Yet the social context within which instructional materials are used can enhance or diminish their effectiveness to an extraordinary degree, and, conversely, instructional materials can encourage or discourage certain kinds of social expectations and behaviors that are essential to learning.

The history of LRDC's work in designing adaptive educational programs illustrates the importance of the general environment as an instructional variable and the ways in which instructional materials and social environments for learning interact with one another. IPI began as an attempt to apply general principles of individualized instruction to an entire elementary school. It was not a lesson-design project, but rather a school-design project, with the necessity for curriculum development following from a conception of how a school adaptive to individual differences ought to run.

The goal of IPI was to develop a form of instruction that would embody principles of individualization in a form that could be disseminated to and was usable in a broad array of public schools. Individualization had a long history in educational theory and in relatively isolated instructional practice; but in the early 1960s it had not been shown to be a principle that could actually work outside of a few specially staffed demonstration schools. To translate individualization into a widely usable concept, it seemed necessary to provide a manageable means for teachers to diagnose children's strengths and needs in any given learning domain and then to provide instruction suitable to these diagnoses.

Adapting Existing Materials to an Individualized Environment

Initial efforts of the IPI project were directed at identifying and organizing existing instructional materials for individualized use rather than designing new lessons or related material. Thus, in keeping with the principles discussed earlier, work proceeded on specification and sequencing of objectives and on design of tests for monitoring the progress of students. The intent was to use the tests diagnostically and then make assignments in a variety of texts and workbooks to match individual needs. These early efforts made clear the extent to which instructional materials and instructional environments were interdependent. The existing textbooks had not been written for an individualized school, and it proved more difficult than expected to key existing materials to IPI sequences of objectives and tests. It was not easy to find in the texts lessons that fully taught new concepts since it was generally expected that these concepts would be presented by the teacher in group instruction and that the exercises engaged in by children would serve largely as practice. Further, close analysis revealed that most textbook lessons confounded the teaching of several concepts or skills. The lessons were often designed simply to expose children to concepts rather than to assure mastery of those concepts. These features of the textbook materials discouraged independent work by children and thus implicitly encouraged the continuation of teacher-oriented instructional practice. In a public school, even one that enjoyed a greater than usual number of paraprofessional aides, this inevitably meant group instruction and expository rather than participatory instructional styles—in short, a less than optimally adaptive environment.

Designing Instructional Materials to Shape the Environment

These observations, based on trials in an entire elementary school, led to increased attention to the development of instructional materials themselves. The IPI and PEP curricula, as they are publicly known and used today, are the results of this "materials development" phase of LRDC's work. These curricula continue to embody a general system for managing structured individualized teaching. Heavy emphasis is placed on the specification of learning objectives in observable form and on testing that allows placement of children in the various curriculum sequences according to their actual level of mastery at a particular time. Emphasis is also placed on keying instructional materials to tests so that assignments can be matched to children's performance on these tests. Finally, tests and instructional materials are arranged in such a way that children have access to them and can use them on their own or with the help of paraprofessional aides, thus permitting them to work independently of the teacher's moment-to-moment direction and with a considerable degree of self-management. The result in practice has been a substantial difference in the rates at which children progress through the curriculum.[38] The program has also resulted in some substantial changes in the patterns of social interaction in the classroom. In various studies teachers have been observed to engage in more instructional (as opposed to management- or discipline-oriented) interactions with children, and more of these have involved individual children rather than groups. There are more student-initiated communications, and there is generally less teacher-oriented behavior on the part of the children. Thus, this instructional design effort has demonstrated that substantial amounts of individualization, at least with respect to rate of learning, are possible in the public school classroom, given appropriate design and organization of the instructional materials. It has also made it clear that such individualization, if seriously pursued, has potentially profound implications for the social organization of the classroom.

Designs for Organizing and Running an Adaptive Classroom

LRDC's curriculum development efforts led to the realization that although individualized instructional materials encouraged adaptation to individual differences, they could not, in and of themselves, ensure it. Indeed, quite new forms of classroom organization and teacher behavior were required if the curricula were to function optimally. With twenty-five or so children working on almost as many different activities, the traditional model of the teacher demonstrating or explaining to groups of children could not work. Some teachers, given the instructional materials and the help of an aide for administering or scoring the various tests that formed part of the program, invented for themselves a way of managing this complex social environment. Others foundered.

Observation of and consultation with teachers who were successful in using the program eventually led to the development of a model for classroom management and organization. The model specified open display of instructional materials and a coding system that would allow even a very young child to interpret instructions on a "ticket" that specified which activities he should engage in. It also specified the various teaching functions that needed to be carried out in the individualized classroom: testing, tutoring individuals, instructing small groups, and "traveling" among the children as they worked to help, to encourage, and to observe. Traveling was the function most foreign to teachers used to traditional classroom organizations, and new teachers needed considerable help in learning the most effective ways of behaving as they circulated in the classroom. Teacher-training strategies had to be developed for this and related forms of behavior.[39] As the program was disseminated, these new modes of interaction became incorporated as a vital part of the definition of the program, thus broadening the "curriculum" to include explicitly the social environment created by the teacher.[40] This broadened definition of curriculum, which includes goals of self-direction and general learning (inquiry) skills and incorporates strategies for managing a classroom in which complex combinations of assigned and child-selected activities occur simultaneously, is also embodied in LRDC's Individualized Science program.[41]

Adapting Curricula to Aptitudes

Observation of the IPI programs in use, and study of the cumulating test data on individual children, made it increasingly evident that for some individuals assumptions the curriculum made concerning abilities upon entering the program were incorrect. In common with other primary-grade programs, IPI assumed a wide range of specific abilities and general "aptitudes" upon entry to school. Ability to focus attention in a directed way, to analyze visual and auditory inputs, to hold material in memory in the face of competing stimulation are all abilities called upon in a large number of different school tasks. They are thus examples of the learning-to-learn abilities discussed earlier in this chapter. They are aptitudes that must be explicitly taken into account in a fully adaptive curriculum that aims to assure mastery for all children.[42]

Two kinds of adaptation to individual aptitudes must be given careful consideration in instructional design. The first is the possibility of teaching aptitudes directly so as to ensure that all individuals entering a given instructional program have at their command the basic process abilities assumed by that program. The second is to design alternative instructional treatments to match or cater to the differences in entering aptitudes within any given population. We have explored both of these approaches.

The notion that aptitudes may be teachable is relatively new both in psychological theory and in educational thought.[43] One of the few domains of aptitude that has been studied in this way in the past is that of perceptual-motor abilities. The relationship of visual and auditory abilities to early school performance has long been recognized, and over the years considerable effort has been devoted to training children recognized as having perceptual-motor dysfunctions. Rosner's work in this area, mentioned earlier, extended this concern to preschool and kindergarten children and was aimed at preparing them for the academic demands of reading and mathematics instruction rather than at offering remedial help once a cycle of failure had manifested itself. In addition, Rosner engaged in both systematic analysis and detailed, iterative testing of instructional materials in order to devise a set of activities that would train the underlying processes of visual and auditory analysis. The result, developed over a period of about five years, is a set of teaching programs for visual and auditory analysis skills[44] that are capable of raising scores on standardized "aptitude tests" and also show transfer to learning early reading and mathematics.[45]

While programs that teach basic aptitudes are extremely powerful because of their generative relationship to other learning, they are not always available or usable. When aptitudes cannot be taught, adaptive education requires that instruction in other programs be matched to the learner's abilities. Our work on modification of the initial IPI reading program illustrates this form of adaptation. The initial program was based on a commercial programmed reading series to which we had added instructional tapes for teaching new sounds and for a variety of additional story reading activities. The program was phonetically oriented, and it assumed, after the introductory unit, that children taught a new letter-sound relationship would be able to apply it to the "sounding out" of new words. Yet a crucial part of the sounding-out process—"blending"—was never really taught. The program we used, like most available beginning reading programs, *told* children to blend ("slide the sounds together"; "say it faster"), but never taught them *how*. Some children, presumably those with better developed auditory skills, invented a procedure; others did not and, as a result, continued to have difficulty with later units in the reading program.

To meet the needs of these children for more explicit instruction, an introductory component was added to the reading program on a trial basis. This component taught children explicit strategies for blending sounds. The results were excellent: there was close to a 100 percent rate of success in learning the blending process, and performance on standardized as well as curriculum-specific reading tests improved. This blending strategy is now being incorporated into a beginning reading system that combines a variety of types of instruction into a highly adaptive program.[46] This form of adaptation to aptitudes offers special support to the learner in an area in which he is weak in the context of a regular subject-matter program. It is a strategy that needs substantial further investigation. One potential effect, suggested by occasional studies in the past,[47] but never seriously investigated in the context of curriculum development, is that the aptitude itself may be increased by subject-matter instruction of certain kinds.

The examples discussed here are representative of design strategies that incorporate long-term study of curriculum effects as well as short-term trials of lessons. New approaches to instruction rather than "patching" of existing programs are often suggested by such study. These long-term studies are superficially costly, but may be inexpensive when considered in terms of ultimate effectiveness. The general strategy is to design and implement a curriculum relatively quickly, building on the best available knowledge combined with a good measure of artistry and invention. Once a curriculum is operating, the needs of the current population of students are being met while at the same time a natural laboratory is formed in which research can proceed. In this way the cost of successive program development is spread over several years of actual use. Meanwhile, research and observation focused on actual instructional effects can proceed, furnishing another example of an interactive research and development mode.

Assessment and Evaluation

Earlier sections of this chapter have alluded to the kinds of strategies we have found most useful in assessing specific instructional effects. The use of criterion-referenced tests as a part of the curriculum has made it easy to follow the progress of children and thus to test the effectiveness of our program in teaching its defined content. Papers by Glaser and Resnick, Wang, and Kaplan[48] describe the way in which this monitoring process can be used in study and revision of curricula and give examples of the kind of data collected. Other studies[49] have shown a substantial relationship between position within the curriculum hierarchy and performance on standardized tests, thus offering an additional validation of criterion-referenced tests and the general program strategy.

Not all objectives of instruction lend themselves easily to frequent criterion-referenced testing. This seems to be the case for domains such as reading comprehension, scientific inquiry, problem solving, and other abilities that are complex and heuristic in character. It is likely that such abilities develop over relatively long periods of time and that the cumulative effect of the total environment—instructional materials, questions raised by peers and teachers, the opportunity to risk new tries—rather than any specific set of lessons produces the effect. If all assessment is left for the long term, however, there is no way of determining which aspects of an instructional program produced the effects observed nor any way of adapting instructional strategies as work proceeds. This raises a new set of tasks for those concerned with assessment of instructional effects. New methods of assessment, probably involving observation of the educational process rather than tests, will need to be developed. Again, though costly, such developmental work is likely to yield rich dividends in educational practice and theory by providing more systematic and usable knowledge about how generative learning skills develop and how environments for teaching them can be designed.

Evaluation in the Field

The value of any curriculum depends, ultimately, upon how it works in the field, away from the watchful and sympathetic ministrations of its developers. The traditional pattern for field evaluations has been to contrast settings using some program with settings not using it. Such evaluations have rarely yielded clear results; nor have they ever been very useful in helping to determine which elements of a program were crucial to maintain and which could be dropped or modified. One reason for the lack of clearly contrasting effects has been suggested earlier: no two teachers implement a program in quite the same way. In order to interpret field test data, it is important to know how the program has been implemented in each site studied and to include implementation data in interpreting outcome data.

Cooley[50] has outlined general strategies for using implementation data in field evaluation of curriculum innovations. These methods have been applied both to LRDC's programs[51] and to a portion of the Follow Through national data.[52] An evaluation approach based on these methodologies, and on related strategies that use implementation measures as part of an evaluation study, is of substantial interest for its contribution to interactive research and development in curriculum. Not only does it yield more interpretable information on outcomes in the field, but it also serves to test—or generate— hypotheses concerning the instructional effects that are the most powerful. It serves, in other words, to abstract from specific programs the features that contribute most to learning outcomes. This information in turn offers guidance in new curriculum development that may incorporate common features into programs that are quite different in other respects.

Conclusion

This chapter began with a discussion of curriculum design as an applied science. The succeeding sections focused largely on describing the present and potential character of an interactive mode of instructional research and development that might yield both curriculum products and scientific knowledge concerning learning and instruction. It remains to make more explicit the assumptions noted earlier concerning the relationships between art and science. By way of conclusion, I turn now to a consideration of the place of art in the science of curriculum design.

Various fields of design have differed in the relative emphasis placed on scientific and aesthetic principles and criteria in their work. In some fields of design, such as architecture, the artistic function is explicitly recognized and accorded status. The designer's function is not simply to apply knowledge produced elsewhere in a mechanical and deterministic fashion, but to use this information to create a product that is aesthetically pleasing as well as functional and economical. Architects cannot function, however, without knowledge of a significant amount of basic physical science as well as knowledge of available materials and their properties. Thus, the profession must also qualify as an applied science.

In fields where aesthetic criteria for the finished products are less pronounced, artistry in creation tends to be played down, and systematic procedures for developing and evaluating products are stressed. This is the case in most fields of engineering, which emphasize their technological (systematic) character and the scientific principles underlying their work. Yet engineering frequently involves artistic processes as well. Heuristics and intuition play a role in the design process—later to be checked and validated systematically—and aesthetic criteria are frequently applied in the form of elegance, gracefulness, economy, and related features of the product.

Curriculum, as a newcomer among fields of design, has not yet developed a firm image or stance on the science versus art dimension. This is perhaps fortunate since it allows us, in conceiving of a discipline of curriculum design, to view it as both a science and an art. Curriculum design, like other fields of design, requires a delicate balance between artfulness and scientific rigor. Without art, the curricular and instructional programs produced are likely to be pedestrian, uninteresting to learners or teachers. Without science, they are likely to overlook useful instructional principles or to embody costly superstitions concerning effective methods. If either art or science is weak, a curriculum is less likely to be effective and attractive than if both are well combined in the design process.

This chapter has had more to say in a direct way about the science than about the art of curriculum design. This is partly because we lack even a language of aesthetics for the field of instruction, and indeed for education in general, while we have at least the working beginnings of a science of instructional design based on the activities of the past dozen or more years in applying principles of psychology and related behavioral disciplines to the task of education. Though we speak easily, for example, of effectiveness and efficiency with respect to instructional design products, we have difficulty in dealing with elegance as a criterion in instruction.

Difficult as "elegant instruction" is to define, distinctions between elegant and inelegant instruction seem possible. Instruction that is playful, that represents complex relationships in simple terms, that engages learners' attention as a result of its internal structure contributes to a sense of elegance in curriculum, and all these attributes are probably related in ways yet to be understood to the more pragmatic goals of effectiveness and efficiency. Thus, while focusing in this chapter on an emerging science, I have tried here and there to point out places where artistic processes and artistic criteria seem to play an important role in what I hope will be the coming shape of a science of curriculum design. The discipline of curriculum design can ill afford the parallel development of two cultures—scientific and artistic. Rather, the two must interact, with the instructional environment ultimately serving as both laboratory and studio, a place where learning and teaching processes are observed and where both scientific and artistic standards are brought to bear in the interests of education.

Notes

1. S. Scribner and M. Cole, "Cognitive Consequences of Formal and Informal Education," *Science* 182 (No. 4110, 1973): 553-559.

2. W. K. Estes, *Learning Theory and Mental Development* (New York: Academic Press, 1970).

3. *Ibid.*, 187.

4. See also W. K. Estes, "Intelligence and Cognitive Psychology," in *The Nature of Intelligence*, ed. L. B. Resnick (Hillsdale, N.J.: Lawrence Erlbaum Associates, in press).

5. J. S. Bruner, "Some Theorems on Instruction Illustrated with Reference to Mathematics," in *Theories of Learning and Instruction*, Sixty-third Yearbook of the National Society for the Study of Education, Part I, ed. E. R. Hilgard (Chicago: University of Chicago Press, 1964), 306-335.

6. G. J. Groen and R. C. Atkinson, "Models for Optimizing the Learning Process," *Psychological Bulletin* 66 (No. 4, 1966): 309-320; R. C. Atkinson, J. P. Fletcher, E. J. Lindsay, J. D. Campbell, and A. Barr, "Computer-Assisted Instruction in Initial Reading: Individualized Instruction Based on Optimization Procedures," *Educational Technology* 13 (No. 9, 1973): 27-37.

7. P. Suppes, M. Jerman, and D. Briar, *Computer-Assisted Instruction: Stanford's 1965-66 Arithmetic Program* (New York: Academic Press, 1968); P. Suppes and M. Morningstar, *Computer-Assisted Instruction at Stanford, 1966-68* (New York: Academic Press, 1972).

8. H. A. Simon, *The Sciences of the Artificial* (Cambridge, Mass.: M.I.T. Press, 1969).

9. R. Glaser and L. B. Resnick, "Instructional Psychology," *Annual Review of Psychology* 23 (1972): 207-276.

10. Bruner, "Some Theorems on Instruction"; *id.*, *Toward a Theory of Instruction* (Cambridge, Mass.: Harvard University Press, 1966).

11. R. Glaser, "Educational Psychology and Education," *American Psychologist* 28 (No. 7, 1973): 557-566.

12. For example, A. Newell and S. Simon, *Human Problem Solving* (Englewood Cliffs, N.J.: Prentice-Hall, 1971).

13. See E. J. Gibson, "Learning to Read," *Science* 148 (No. 3673, 1965): 1066-1072.

14. See L. Kohlberg, "Early Education: A Cognitive Developmental View," *Child Development* 39 (No. 4, 1968): 1013-1062; W. D. Rohwer, "Prime Time for Education: Early Childhood or Adolescence," *Harvard Educational Review* 41 (No. 3, 1971): 316-341.

15. See M. Cole, J. Gay, J. Glick, and D. W. Sharp, *The Cultural Context of Learning and Thinking* (New York: Basic Books, 1971); J. Goodnow, "The Nature of Intelligent Behavior: Questions Raised by Cross-Cultural Studies," in

The Nature of Intelligence, ed. Resnick; A. P. Pick, "The Games Experimenters Play: A Review of Methods and Concepts of Cross-Cultural Studies of Cognition and Development," unpublished manuscript, University of Minnesota, 1974.

16. See J. McV. Hunt, *Intelligence and Experience* (New York: Ronald Press, 1961), for a discussion of this matching process from a different theoretical viewpoint.

17. See L. B. Resnick, M. C. Wang, and J. Rosner, "Adaptive Education for Young Children: The Primary Education Project," in *The Preschool in Action*, ed. M. C. Day and R. K. Parker, 2d ed. (Boston: Allyn and Bacon, in press).

18. R. M. Gagné, "The Acquisition of Knowledge," *Psychological Review* 69 (No. 4, 1962): 355-365; *id.*, "Learning Hierarchies," *Educational Psychologist* 6 (No. 1, 1968): 2-9.

19. L. B. Resnick, M. C. Wang, and J. Kaplan, "Task Analysis in Curriculum Design: A Hierarchically Sequenced Introductory Mathematics Curriculum," *Journal of Applied Behavioral Analysis* 6 (No. 4, 1973): 679-710.

20. Resnick, Wang, and Rosner, "Adaptive Education for Young Children"; C. M. Lindvall, "The LRDC Individualized Mathematics (IM) Project: Program Content, Management System, and Procedures in Development and Implementation," unpublished manuscript, University of Pittsburgh, Learning Research and Development Center, 1974; I. Beck and D. Mitroff, *The Primary Grades Reading System* (Pittsburgh: University of Pittsburgh, Learning Research and Development Center, 1972).

21. See "Hierarchies in Children's Learning: A Symposium," ed. L. B. Resnick, *Instructional Science* 2 (No. 3, 1973): 311-362, for a general discussion of validation strategies.

22. See Resnick, Wang, and Kaplan, "Task Analysis in Curriculum Design."

23. For example, M. C. Wang, L. B. Resnick, and R. F. Boozer, "The Sequence of Development of Some Early Mathematics Behaviors," *Child Development* 42 (No. 6, 1972): 1767-1778; M. C. Wang, "Psychometric Studies in the Validation of an Early Learning Curriculum," *ibid.*, 44 (No. 1, 1973): 54-60.

24. For example, L. B. Resnick, A. Siegel, and E. Kresh, "Transfer and Sequence in Learning Double Classification Skills," *Journal of Experimental Child Psychology* 11 (No. 1, 1971): 139-140; J. L. Caruso and L. B. Resnick, "Task Structure and Transfer in Children's Learning of Double Classification Skills," *Child Development* 43 (No. 4, 1972): 1297-1308.

25. See Newell and Simon, *Human Problem Solving*.

26. *Linguistic Communication: Perspectives for Research*, ed. G. Miller (Newark, Del.: International Reading Association, 1973).

27. D. P. Simon and H. A. Simon, "Alternative Uses of Phonemic Information in Spelling," *Review of Educational Research* 43 (No. 1, 1973): 115-137.

28. For an early example of some possibilities along these lines, see L. B. Resnick and R. Glaser, "Problem Solving and Intelligence," in *The Nature of Intelligence*, ed. Resnick. For a more extended discussion of the general role of information processing task analysis in instructional design, see L. B. Resnick, "Task Analysis in Curriculum Design: Some Cases from Mathematics," in *Cognition and Instruction*, ed. D. Klahr (Hillsdale, N.J.: Lawrence Erlbaum Associates, in press).

29. L. J. Cronbach and R. E. Snow, *Individual Differences in Learning Ability as a Function of Instructional Variables*, Final Report, 1969, School of Education, Stanford University, Contract #OEC 4-6-061269-1217 (Washington, D.C.: Office of Education, Department of Health, Education, and Welfare, 1969); G. H. Bracht, "Experimental Factors Related to Aptitude-Treatment Interactions," *Review of Educational Research* 40 (No. 5, 1970): 627-645.

30. R. Glaser and A. Nitko, "Measurement in Learning and Instruction," in *Educational Measurement,* ed. R. L. Thorndike, 2d ed. (Washington, D.C.: American Council on Education, 1971), 625-670; R. Glaser, "Individuals and Learning: The New Aptitudes," *Educational Researcher* 1 (No. 6, 1972): 5-13.

31. R. Glaser, "Adapting the Elementary School Curriculum to Individual Performance," in *Proceedings of the 1967 Invitational Conference on Testing Problems* (Princeton, N.J.: Educational Testing Service, 1968), 29-30.

32. *Id.,* "Instructional Technology and the Measurement of Learning Outcomes: Some Questions," *American Psychologist* 18 (No. 8, 1963): 519-521.

33. See, for example, A. J. Nitko, "Problems in the Development of Criterion-Referenced Tests: The IPI Pittsburgh Experience," in *Problems in Criterion-Referenced Measurement,* ed. C. A. Harris, M. C. Alkins, and W. J. Popham, CSE Monograph Series in Evaluation, No. 3 (Los Angeles: Center for the Study of Evaluation, University of California, 1974), 59-82.

34. See W. Hively, H. L. Patterson, and S. H. Page, "A 'Universe-Defined' System of Arithmetic Achievement Tests," *Journal of Educational Measurement* 5 (No. 4, 1968): 275-290.

35. R. L. Ferguson, *Computer-Assisted Criterion-Referenced Testing,* Working Paper 49 (Pittsburgh: University of Pittsburgh, Learning Research and Development Center, 1969); T. C. Hsu, M. Carlson, and K. Pingel, "Computer-Assisted Testing," in *A Computer-Assisted Instructional System for Elementary Mathematics* (Pittsburgh: University of Pittsburgh, Learning Research and Development Center, 1974).

36. J. Rosner, *The Visual Analysis Test: An Initial Report* (Pittsburgh: University of Pittsburgh, Learning Research and Development Center, 1971).

37. *Id.* and D. Simon, "The Auditory Analysis Test: An Initial Report," *Journal of Learning Disabilities* 4 (No. 7, 1971): 384-392.

38. Glaser, "Adapting the Elementary School Curriculum to Individual Performance"; Resnick, Wang, and Kaplan, "Task Analysis in Curriculum Design."

39. See G. A. Leinhardt, *Training Program for Selected Teacher Functions* (Pittsburgh: University of Pittsburgh, Learning Research and Development Center, 1973).

40. Resnick, Wang, and Rosner, "Adaptive Education for Young Children."

41. L. Klopfer and A. Champagne, "An Individualized Elementary School Science Program," *Theory into Practice* 13 (No. 2, 1974): 136-148.

42. Glaser, "Individuals and Learning."

43. See *id.* and Resnick, "Instructional Psychology," for a review of literature in the field.

44. J. Rosner, *Perceptual Skills Curriculum* (New York: Walker Educational Book Co., 1973).

45. *Id., The Development and Validation of an Individualized Perceptual*

Skills Curriculum (Pittsburgh: University of Pittsburgh, Learning Research and Development Center, 1972).

46. Beck and Mitroff, *The Primary Grades Reading System.*

47. For example, G. Meuris, "The Structure of Primary Mental Abilities of Belgian Secondary School Students," *Journal of Educational Measurement* 7 (No. 3, 1970): 191-197.

48. R. Glaser, "Objectives and Evaluation: An Individualized System," *Science Education News* (June 1967): 1-3; Resnick, Wang, and Kaplan, "Task Analysis in Curriculum Design."

49. For example, L. B. Resnick and M. C. Wang, *Improvement of Academic Performance of Poor-Prognosis Children through the Use of an Individualized Instructional Program* (Pittsburgh: University of Pittsburgh, Learning Research and Development Center, 1974).

50. W. W. Cooley, *Methods of Evaluating School Innovations* (Pittsburgh: University of Pittsburgh, Learning Research and Development Center, 1971); *id.,* "Assessment of Educational Effects," *Educational Psychologist* 11 (No. 1, 1974): 29-35.

51. G. Leinhardt, *Evaluation of the Implementation of a Program of Adaptive Education at the Second Grade (1972-73)* (Pittsburgh: University of Pittsburgh, Learning Research and Development Center, 1974); *id.,* "Observation as a Tool for Evaluation of Implementation," in *The Use of Direct Observation to Study Instructional-Learning Behaviors in School Settings,* ed. M. C. Wang (Pittsburgh: University of Pittsburgh, Learning Research and Development Center, 1974).

52. W. W. Cooley and J. A. Emrick, "A Model of Classroom Differences Which Explains Variation in Classroom Achievement," paper presented at the meeting of the American Educational Research Association, Chicago, April 1974.

4 Strategies in Curriculum Development: The SCIS Project
Robert Karplus

The Science Curriculum Improvement Study has developed ungraded, sequential physical and life science programs for the elementary school—programs, which, in essence, turn the classroom into a laboratory. Each unit of these programs was carefully evaluated by SCIS staff as it progressed from early exploratory stages to the published edition. The units originated as scientists' ideas for investigations that might challenge children and that illustrate key scientific concepts. The ideas were then adapted to fit the elementary school, and the resulting units were used by teachers in regular classrooms. They were tested several times in elementary schools before they were published.

Central to these elementary school programs are current ideas of intellectual development. A child's elementary school years are a period of transition as he continues the exploration of the world he began in infancy, builds the abstractions with which he interprets that world, and develops confidence in his own ideas. Extensive laboratory experiences at this time enable him to relate scientific concepts to the real world in a meaningful way. As he matures, the continuous interplay of interpretations and observations frequently compels him to revise his ideas about his environment.

The teaching strategy is for the children to explore selected science materials. They are encouraged to investigate, to discuss what they observe, and to ask questions. The SCIS teacher has two functions: to be an observer who listens to the children and notices how well they are progressing in their investigations, and to be a guide who leads them to see the relationship of their findings to the key concepts of science.

The SCIS Materials

Organization of Materials

The SCIS program consists of thirteen units, six for a physical science sequence, six for a life science sequence, and one for kindergarten. The unity of the physical science sequence derives from the fundamental concepts of change and interaction. The six basic units —*Material Objects, Interaction and Systems, Subsystems and Variables, Relative Position and Motion, Energy Sources,* and *Models: Electric and Magnetic Interactions*—introduce and develop scientific and process-oriented concepts considered necessary for scientific literacy (see under "Content," below). The units in the life science sequence focus on organism-environment interactions. The six basic units—*Organisms, Life Cycles, Populations, Environments, Communities,* and *Ecosystems*—make use of the scientific and process-oriented concepts, but add the special considerations appropriate to the study of life. The *Ecosystems* unit attempts a synthesis of the children's investigations in physical and life sciences. Each of the six units roughly corresponds to the sequence of first to sixth grade.

Format

The SCIS materials reach the classroom in the form of kits, which have been designed to simplify and make convenient the use, storage, and reuse of the required equipment and supplies. Each kit is packaged for a teacher and thirty-two children and contains all of the materials needed except standard classroom supplies, dry cells, and the living organisms, which are sent separately when requested by the teacher. For each unit there are a teacher's guide and, in most cases, a student manual, but no textbook.

Content

Central to the SCIS program is the view that changes take place because objects interact in reproducible ways under similar conditions. In the SCIS program, "interaction" refers to relations among objects or organisms that do something to one another, thereby bringing about a change. Students can observe change and use it as evidence of interaction. As they advance from a dependence on concrete experiences to the ability to think abstractly, they identify the conditions under which interaction occurs and predict its outcome. The four major scientific concepts the SCIS program uses to elaborate the interaction viewpoint are matter, energy, organism, and ecosystem. Students' experiences and investigations in the physical science sequence are based on matter and energy; organism and ecosystem provide the framework of the life science sequence. In addition to these scientific concepts, four process-oriented concepts— property, reference frame, system, and model—are used.

Cost

Each unit, packaged in a kit for a typical classroom, costs between $150 and $250. The initial cost of teaching a unit is approximately $5 per pupil, but this varies, depending on whether the kits are shared among teachers. In subsequent years the cost per pupil decreases, as the "permanent" equipment in each kit can be reused.

History of the Project, 1958-1977

The chain of events leading to the SCIS project originated in the summer of 1958, when I perceived a relationship among three activities in which I had participated. These were meetings concerned with high school science teaching that had been stimulated by National Science Foundation-supported curriculum development activities at that level, my "show and tell" science sessions with the elementary school classes of my two school-age children, and the oral examinations of many physics graduate students whose performance gave evidence of a highly compartmentalized and not a broadly integrated understanding of undergraduate physics. All of them indicated to me that there were serious educational problems and that a better utilization of the first nine school years for science education might lead to substantial improvement. This conclusion may seem naive. Still, with encouragement from the NSF, I embarked on what I expected to be a brief side activity in my career as professor of physics; it actually turned into a project of almost twenty years' duration that resulted in a complete professional redirection of my life. In recounting the actual project activities supported by the NSF with grants in excess of four million dollars, it is worthwhile to identify six phases, each about three years long.

Exploration, 1959-1963

The staff consisted of me, an assistant, and occasional consultants during some of the time. I taught and observed elementary school classes, met with teachers and science educators, designed science activities and tried them out, and read publications in science education, developmental psychology, history and philosophy of science, and public policy. Most influential were Bruner's *The Process of Education,* the writings of Jean Piaget, and Kuhn's *The Structure of Scientific Revolutions.* At the end of this period, the educational philosophy and conceptual structure of the Science Curriculum Improvement Study program had been outlined in very general terms. There remained the detailed and demanding tasks of refining this outline in the light of classroom experience and producing curriculum materials that would enable many elementary school teachers to implement the curriculum in their classrooms.

Berkeley Area Trials, 1963-1966

The development of curriculum materials for an articulated program lasting several years required a laboratory school situation in which children and teachers used SCIS materials consistently. Herbert D. Thier, who joined the study as assistant director, took responsibility for establishing three laboratory schools in public schools of the Berkeley area; he also contributed essentially to program development. Chester A. Lawson joined the staff to take responsibility for developing a life science teaching sequence. Sister Jacqueline Grennan of Webster College, Arthur W. Foshay of Teachers College, Columbia University, and John I. Goodlad of U.C.L.A. formed an advisory committee that helped guide the project. The project staff gradually expanded, with the addition of elementary and secondary school teachers, science educators, a psychologist, consulting scientists, an editor, technicians, and artist-designers. The staff prepared trial editions of teachers' guides, student manuals, and laboratory kits for use by local teachers. A newsletter was published, and the teachers' guides were offered for sale to interested individuals.

Preliminary Edition, 1966-1969

Growing public interest and the recommendation of the advisory committee led to the establishment of five trial centers associated with universities in five parts of the United States. These included rural, suburban, small-town, and inner-city schools. To supply these centers and other interested schools with the necessary printed and laboratory materials, publication of primary-grade units in the Preliminary Edition was arranged through D. C. Heath and Company. Development of additional units for the upper grades continued in the Berkeley area laboratory schools, with the staff expanded further to about forty persons. Dissemination activities, relying primarily on local leadership, were begun.

Final Edition, 1969-1972

Revision of the Preliminary Editions with feedback from the trial centers took place three years earlier than scheduled because of difficulties with the publisher and limitations of expenditures placed on the funds granted by the NSF. The final edition was published by Rand McNally & Company. A related project under Dr. Thier's direction adapted the materials for use by blind children.

Evaluation and Teacher Education Materials, 1972-1974

After the completion of the basic teaching materials, the project developed a set of evaluation supplements for classroom use by teachers who wish to identify their pupils' progress systematically. A kindergarten unit entitled *Beginnings* and teacher education materials, including films and a *Handbook,* were also completed. The project staff gradually transferred to other activities.

Public Information and Service, 1974-1977

Supervision of the publications and equipment kits will continue, to assure the necessary quality control and possible minor modifications necessitated by changing availability of supplies, identification of defects in design, and other new conditions. Dissemination will also continue.

Development Strategies

The overall approach to curriculum development by the SCIS has been pragmatic. As goals were set and problems were encountered, the staff devised procedures for solving the problems and attaining the goals. When the available time and resources appeared inadequate to reach a goal or the goal itself seemed intrinsically unattainable, it was modified accordingly. In looking back over our work and that of others during the last fifteen years, we find that much practical experience has accumulated. Yet it is my opinion that there has emerged no curriculum theory that promises to yield better results than a pragmatic approach that relies on highly qualified staff and applies available theories without dogmatism. The reason probably lies in the enormous complexity of the problem that arises from the diversity of institutions, personnel, local practices, and students.

Within the overall pragmatic approach, however, certain strategies were developed and used successfully by the SCIS. Nine of these, each relating to an aspect of curriculum development, are given below together with a brief theoretical justification. In a final section of this chapter, I describe the potentially more general value of these strategies and possible improvements.

Strategy Relating to Personnel

From its very early days the Science Curriculum Improvement Study pursued a strategy of bringing together individuals with backgrounds in the many different areas bearing on instruction in elementary science. The principal developers on the SCIS staff included university scientists, high school science teachers, and elementary school teachers. They were assisted by psychologists, science educators, editors, filmmakers, artists, designers, and technicians. Each development team worked together very closely, but certain primary responsibilities were divided. Thus, the scientists were concerned with providing leadership as regards the conceptual development, the secondary science teachers devised laboratory procedures and designed equipment, and the elementary school teachers outlined classroom procedures. Frequent discussions involving the entire staff helped to refine the content of the units and to establish priorities regarding general objectives.

Personnel recruitment was carried out very carefully, principally by the assistant director, through personal recommendations of scientists and science educators who were sympathetic to the SCIS philosophy. Every candidate for a continuing position was interviewed and then observed teaching a group of students; the teaching style was evaluated in light of the SCIS philosophy. Letters and personnel files were not accepted as providing sufficient information regarding prospective contributions.

Theory behind Personnel Strategy

The study depended on a long-term staff working throughout the year, primarily for five reasons: the slow pace at which children can accept truly new ideas makes summers inadequate for experimental teaching; the interaction of staff with pupils, which results in imaginative new teaching approaches, cannot be compressed into a few weeks' time; the pupils at each grade level must have prior SCIS experience to articulate the units, and that cannot be assured during voluntary summer schools; staff members who conceive a unit must be available to follow the classroom trials and interpret the feedback for revision; staff members working on different teaching units are expected to interact significantly. The three levels of personnel were clearly needed to provide gradation in scientific knowledge and sophistication that could ultimately communicate some modern scientific concepts from the university scientists to nonscientific elementary school teachers and pupils.

Strategy Relating to the Invention of Activities

One of the most important products of a curriculum development project is a set of thoroughly tested activities for pupils that contributes to the overall aims of the project. To invent activities that will hold the children's interest, stimulate them intellectually, have significant science content, fit the conceptual scheme of a unit, are safe, do not require costly equipment, have a reliable outcome, and can be readily understood and supervised by the teacher is a very demanding assignment. All project staff members were, therefore, always encouraged to propose ideas for such activities, and very considerable staff time went into considering, reviewing, laboratory testing, and further developing these ideas. Elementary school teachers and sometimes secretaries on the project staff served as the first "guinea pigs," using the new activity after it had been worked out by its inventors, since their lack of scientific training made them the most naive subjects readily available to the project. It was most important to provide a positive but also realistic supportive environment for the development of new activities. Unless a clear objection arose during internal discussions by members of the project, proposed activities were tried out in elementary school classrooms, where the developers could get feedback from the children rather than having to conform to the theoretical concerns of their colleagues.

From the above remarks it is clear that laboratory facilities and a design shop were important resources of the project.

Theory behind Invention Strategy

Open discussion and a supportive social environment, together with frank intellectual criticism, are the standard conditions for encouraging the expression of creativity. High quality of the personnel was, of course, also essential.

Strategy Relating to Classroom Trials

Classroom trials played an extremely important role in the work of the SCIS and were the ultimate way of acquiring the information on which final decisions regarding segments of the teaching program were based. Classroom experience and the reactions of children and teachers were more important than any theoretical considerations in this respect. Development staff participated in these trials as much as possible.

Classroom trials took place in three stages. The first, called "exploratory teaching," occurred very soon after an activity had been invented and again when a unit was revised. It was carried out completely by project staff members functioning as "guest instructors" in elementary school classrooms. At least two, and sometimes four or five, members of the development staff planned and participated in exploratory teaching. They took the necessary equipment, pages of instructions for students, and sometimes video or audio recording equipment to the classroom. One of the staff members actually conducted the class, while the others observed the sessions, sometimes interviewing children who were experimenting individually concerning their ideas, questions, or intentions. After every exploratory session, one or more of the participating staff members prepared a written report in which the activity, the children's reactions, and the operation of the apparatus were described fully. These reports were filed and later served as raw material for the redesign of equipment, revision of the activity, and preparation of teachers' guides and other publications. The activity was also discussed in a postmortem session in which every participant could express his or her views frankly.

The second stage of classroom trials was carried out by regular teachers in the three laboratory schools (one suburban, two middle-class urban) that had been established in the Berkeley area, after teachers' guides, student manuals, and apparatus kits for the teaching unit had been prepared by the project in the Trial Edition. These classes were visited regularly by the unit's developers and also by other staff members who observed the teaching, occasionally spoke to children if this did not interfere with the teacher's work, and conferred with the teacher concerning any questions the teacher might have. Reports of the observations were filed after the visits and ultimately served as source material for revision of the unit. Individual conferences, feedback meetings, and feedback questionnaires enabled teachers to communicate their reactions to the developers.

Regular teachers in the Berkeley area and in the five trial centers that had been established by the project in 1966 carried out the third stage of classroom trials. These teachers used the Preliminary Edition, published by D. C. Heath. Project staff observed the classes in Berkeley, and local coordinators observed classes in the trial centers. Project staff also visited the trial centers, observed classes, and met with teachers two or three times a year. The coordinators submitted quarterly reports of their experiences in teacher education, classroom observations, suggestions from teachers, and specific comments concerning the teaching activities. All of this information was used in the preparation of the final edition of SCIS units, published by Rand McNally beginning in 1970.

Theory behind Classroom Trial Strategy

The design of the classroom trials involved setting up three feedback loops through which the project staff could test curriculum ideas on an ever-larger scale: first with one class of children or possibly two, then with ten classes and ten teachers, and finally with fifty classes and fifty teachers in five different locations in the United States. The exploratory trials were used to test the children's reactions to proposed activities and equipment and to gather children's ideas to enrich the teaching activities. The Berkeley area trials were used to test the revised activities and to get a first response from teachers concerning the demands placed on them. Ghetto classes were purposely not included at this stage. The country-wide trials, finally, sampled reactions from a larger number of teachers of very diverse backgrounds, with activities that were known to function reliably with children.

Strategy Relating to Pedagogy

The pedagogical organization of all SCIS units is similar and employs the learning cycle of exploration, invention, and discovery. Exploration is the first stage of the learning cycle. Children learn through their own spontaneous behavior relative to objects and events, that is, by handling objects and experimenting with them. Children explore materials with minimal guidance in the form of instructions or specific questions. The materials are always carefully chosen to be easily used and to generate certain questions that the children have not asked before. Exploration affords the teacher informal opportunities for evaluation by observing what individual children actually do, listening to them describe their ideas to one another, and occasionally asking them questions about their intentions.

Invention is the second stage of the learning cycle. Children learn as the teacher provides a definition or term for a new concept, while illustrating with concrete examples from the children's prior explorations. The teacher is asked to be clear and explicit while explaining and to repeat if necessary. To give the children prompt opportunities for using the new concept, the teacher encourages them to identify examples in their everyday life or their recent science activities. These examples also give the teacher feedback concerning the children's understanding. The teacher's role during invention is more directive than during exploration or discovery.

Discovery is the third and last stage of the learning cycle. It refers to activities in which the child discerns a new application for the concept previously explained in an invention session. Several different discovery activities are suggested in the teachers' guides following each invention lesson. The child's discovery experiences enlarge and refine the concept's meaning and also enable the teacher to conduct further diagnostic observations concerning each child's understanding.

The learning cycle is applied in the SCIS program on three levels. On the lowest level, a learning cycle may occupy from two to four weeks of instruction, with one or two class periods for exploration, one for invention, and two to six for discovery; but these are not rigidly prescribed. On this level the structure of the learning cycle helps the teacher to define his role appropriately for each stage. It also prevents successive introduction of new ideas too rapidly for the children to digest, since several discovery activities usually occur between invention sessions. One SCIS unit may encompass two to four learning cycles.

On the next level, each SCIS unit represents a single, larger learning cycle revolving around a major concept such as interaction, community, or energy transfer. Finally, on the highest level, the entire SCIS curriculum can be viewed as a learning cycle extending over several years and revolving around the interaction concept. Thus, the learning cycle provides substantial guidance in the organization of the entire curriculum.

Theory behind Pedagogical Strategy

The most important learning theories are those of association learning, discovery learning, and equilibration learning. The learning cycle combines all three theories in an eclectic combination that does violence to none. Thus, exploration allows discovery learning, invention and discovery allow association learning, and the entire cycle leads to equilibration as the student is first forced to reconsider his conceptual approach during exploration of new phenomena, then hears the suggestion of a new conceptual scheme during invention, and finally, through his own actions and tests, consolidates the new scheme during discovery.

Strategy Relating to Content

Central to modern science and therefore also to the SCIS program is the view that changes take place because objects interact in reproducible ways under similar conditions, as described earlier in this chapter. This conceptual organization was developed by the university scientists on the SCIS staff. Because of its generality and power, it did not substantially restrict the choices of activities used for exploration and discovery. The entire staff, therefore, participated in inventing such activities and identifying the secondary concepts that could also be introduced. Classroom testing determined which of the secondary concepts were understood well enough by children so they could be used in discovery activities. The concepts of relative motion, solution, habitat, and predator were among those found acceptable for the program. Certain other concepts, such as equilibrium, state of a system, and periodic motion, were tried out but had to be eliminated because they were not sufficiently useful to children.

In other words, the overall conceptual viewpoint was well defined early in the history of the SCIS, but many details were determined through classroom testing during the development of the teaching units.

Theory behind Content Strategy

Only the university scientists on the project staff had the knowledge and self-confidence to propose the interaction concept as the central organizing theme. The curriculum elaborations contributed by the university scientists and high school science teachers reflect the project's pragmatic approach, according to which classroom trials and the reactions of children and teachers were given the greatest weight in decision making.

Strategy Relating to Intellectual Development

Many psychologists, but especially Piaget, have described the intellectual development of children during the elementary school years. The developmental stages of children in elementary school were taken into account in the program development in three distinct ways. First, the main thrust of activities had a perceptual emphasis in the very early grades, moved to a conceptual orientation with concrete referents in the intermediate grades, and then introduced some abstract referents for the upper grades. Thus, in the first level of the SCIS, the children observe, describe, and sort objects and organisms according to their properties. In the third-level units, the children deal with predators and prey, with solutions, and with systems and subsystems, all referring to real objects. On the fifth level, however, the children deal with communities of organisms and energy transfer, which refer to abstractions that cannot be directly seen, felt, or heard.

Second, the concepts introduced in the teaching program were of some help in advancing students from one developmental stage to the next, since they called attention to generalizable aspects of the children's observations. Examples are the concepts of properties and habitat (level one), interaction and systems (level two), food chain and variable (level three), producers and consumers (level five), scientific model and ecosystems (level six).

Third, the vast majority of activities could lead to student satisfaction regardless of the children's conceptual level, since each student was free to use the materials in the way he wished and could therefore adapt them to his immediate needs. In their work with electric circuits in the sixth-level physical science unit, for instance, some children got a sense of achievement from lighting their bulb as brightly as possible (preoperational), others investigated the materials that did or did not close the circuit (concrete operational), while still others were concerned with the flow of electricity through the circuit (formal operational). In other words, the teacher could identify preoperational students, concrete operational students, and beginning formal operational students together in the same class, and did not need to expect the same responses from all.

Theory behind Intellectual Development Strategy

Piaget's developmental theory was used to formulate the strategy. In my observation, this theory has not been taken seriously in any other curriculum project and therefore constitutes a unique characteristic of the SCIS program.

Strategy Relating to Dissemination

The dissemination strategy of the SCIS is based on internalization. Basic to this approach is the direct involvement in a leadership role of an individual or team from the community or school system that is adopting the program. It should be noted that this strategy emphasizes dissemination to meet local needs under local control. Accordingly, the implementation procedures have been exceedingly varied.

The following outline describes a typical implementation process:

1. Interest in the SCIS materials originates through reading of the literature, recommendation of nearby school systems, presentations at conventions, contact by the publisher's representative, or teacher education courses.

2. Discussions with the publisher's representative and/or SCIS staff lead to an overall implementation plan. Such a plan usually includes these elements: commitment from an administrator to obtain the necessary funds, arrange for teacher training, and provide intellectual as well as administrative leadership; identification of pilot schools and/or pilot teachers who will use the SCIS materials; selection of one or more individuals to inform themselves about the program in depth, carry on teacher education, and oversee the distribution and maintenance of the laboratory materials kits; a tentative schedule for full-scale implementation.

3. Leadership training for those responsible for educating the teachers takes place either through a study-visit to the Berkeley headquarters of the SCIS or in a Resource Personnel Workshop.

4. There is an in-service workshop conducted by the trained leader for teachers who will use the program.

5. SCIS units, including laboratory kits for the participating teachers, are selected and procured.

The participation of the SCIS staff in the dissemination activities is limited to providing information and serving in a consulting role. The initiative for implementation is expected to come from the community itself.

Theory behind Dissemination Strategy

The "internalization" approach is based on the experience in educational innovation that consistent and persistent on-site leadership is necessary to maintain a new approach. The local educational establishment is subject to so many unpredictable forces—economic, political, personnel, parental—that only local informed and pragmatic leadership can maintain the innovation against the pressures that would either restore the status quo or introduce a still newer innovation, after interest is lost in the present one. Dissemination initiated by the developer could never hope to counter all these forces in the many hundreds of communities using the new curriculum.

Strategy Relating to Teacher Education

Teacher education was accomplished through two principal means: teachers' guides for the conduct of ongoing classroom activities; participation in in-service workshops or preservice courses relating to inquiry-oriented science programs, especially SCIS. Four goals had to be achieved: familiarity with the science phenomena in the units under study; adoption of a child-centered, inquiry-oriented classroom environment; understanding of children's intellectual development; acquaintance with the nature of science and its logical and conceptual structure.

The teachers' guides concentrated on the first two of these goals. They were written in simple and direct terms, to encourage the teacher's use of the program even if he were not well prepared to do so and to help the teacher modify his techniques as necessary in the light of feedback from the children. In particular, the eagerness and interest of the children engaging in scientific activities were seen as a significant tool of teacher education. In this way, the use of the SCIS materials would provide an ongoing experience of teacher education.

All four of the goals were built into materials developed for teacher workshops. These materials include documentary films (completely unrehearsed) of classroom activities using the SCIS units, an *SCIS Teacher's Handbook* with background material relating to all four goals, and an *SCIS Omnibus* containing reprints of articles published by SCIS staff and collaborators, expressing their views at various times during the developmental process. Under the "internalization" concept of dissemination, these teacher education materials are resources for the local leadership personnel who plan and conduct in-service and preservice courses.

Theory behind Teacher Education Strategy

The approach was highly pragmatic, based on the results of classroom trials and teacher reaction to various written materials. It became clear that most teachers have little time to prepare for science teaching, that they are concerned primarily with their most immediate teaching needs, and that extensive changes in teaching style occur only as a result of social experiences involving leadership personnel, other teachers, and children.

Strategy Relating to Educational Objectives

The SCIS has not used explicitly stated educational performance objectives as a curriculum development tool. The considerations described in connection with other strategies were sufficient to select the content and form of the activities. Formative evaluation from repeated classroom trials concentrated on the teaching and learning processes and gave only secondary importance to performance outcomes. The SCIS program has the overall objective of helping students improve their scientific literacy, defined as a combination of basic science knowledge, investigative experience, and curiosity. This goal gives some guidance concerning the program activities, but leaves many options as well.

Educational objectives were used by the SCIS to communicate the possible thrust of activities to the teacher. Objectives are therefore included in each teacher's guide. They are, however, associated with parts of a teaching unit—about a month of instructional time—and not with individual chapters or activities that may occupy one or two class periods. They are, in addition, stated in general behavioral terms rather than in highly specific terms. An example from *Interaction and Systems* is "To detect evidence of interaction by using various senses." The conditions of the interaction and the kind of evidence are left unspecified, as are the reliability of the response, latency, and other details.

Educational objectives were also used in the construction of an evaluation program for use by teachers. Evaluation activities were related to some of the major objectives, though not to all.

Theory behind Educational Objective Strategy

Explicit educational objectives are intended to focus behavior on the stated outcomes and to permit rigorous evaluation. This was unnecessary since the public had no preconceived notion of what children should learn in science. Teachers and schools are, in fact, urged to develop their own objectives for using the SCIS program— objectives that might relate to science learnings, social outcomes, and/or other matters of local concern. Under these circumstances, explicit and detailed educational performance objectives tend to pre-empt local decision making and are counterproductive. The more general objectives included in the teachers' guides serve as helpful guidelines in the absence of local preferences.

General Value and Possible Improvements in Strategies

The pragmatic approach I have described, supplemented by certain theories, has been very satisfactory in the development of the SCIS curriculum materials. As the staff accumulated experience, the procedures underwent changes compared to the initially improvised strategies, so that the items above represent a significant refinement and not the zeroth approximation. Looking back at this point, I find it difficult to identify further significant and substantial areas of improvement that can be clearly seen. In other words, there are, certainly, alternative strategies, but it is not at all evident whether they will be as effective, more effective, or less effective than the strategies actually used by the SCIS project. Their relative effectiveness would surely depend on the educational level, subject matter, and target audience of the new curriculum materials to be developed.

Generalizable Strategies

I believe that the SCIS strategies relating to classroom trials, pedagogy, intellectual development, and dissemination can be applied directly and effectively in any curriculum development project. They do not depend on the science content of the SCIS program, and their applicability is not restricted to an audience of elementary school pupils. The classroom trial strategy has, in fact, become widely accepted as basic to successful curriculum development, and the comparative research design strategy involving predetermined objectives, an experimental group, and a control group has been discredited for this purpose.

The learning cycle in the pedagogical strategy has been used successfully at all educational levels, both in curriculum materials and for making "lesson plans" by an individual instructor. It appears to be a very valuable technique. Of course, the exploratory and discovery activities have to be appropriate for the learner and should provide challenges that involve manipulative, puzzle-solving, self-appraisal, or investigative activities. Likewise, the definition or explanation during invention has to be concrete or abstract and involve practical or hypothetical examples, depending on the learners. These details in using the strategy of the learning cycle have to be worked out as part of curriculum development.

In applying the strategy relating to intellectual development, the age of the learners has to be taken into account. Even though the traditional view has been that the elementary school years are the most important period for development, and that at the secondary level most students are capable of dealing with abstractions at the stage of formal thought, recent studies have shown that this is not true. (See the Proceedings of the Third Annual Meeting of the Jean Piaget Society, Temple University, Philadelphia, May 1973, for a summary.) It is likely that nonacademically oriented students suffer in school precisely because of the mistaken expectations in this respect.

The "internalization" strategy for dissemination does not directly involve the students and is therefore valid at the secondary level. Other approaches, such as those used by the Ford Foundation, that involved implantation of a new program with broad external financial support, appear to be less successful in that the innovation tends to become identified with the support and is discarded as the support ceases. Many ESEA Title III projects have encountered the same difficulty. In other words, it appears essential for long-term implementation that the new curriculum be funded through regular, ongoing budget categories of the institution. In higher education, dissemination has to contend with the self-image of many instructors as highly autonomous individuals. They are likely to accept new curricular materials only through a combination of institutional and individual approaches whose success has not yet been demonstrated. I have nothing to contribute there.

Strategies That Need Modification or Improvement

Several of the strategies employed by the Science Curriculum Improvement Study were specific to the area of elementary school science. These include strategies relating to personnel, invention of activities, content, teacher education, and educational objectives. All of these, of course, are generally relevant, but the specific modifications that are necessary depend on the area of curriculum development. I shall describe some considerations that appear important to me.

One important factor is the age of the learners and school level. The elementary school is a nonselective institution that accepts all children within a very broad range above and below average in physical and mental capacity. No prior learning is expected. Curricula for older students have to recognize their successful or deficient prior school experiences. These curricula may be aimed at students who are selected on the basis of criteria that are subject to influence by the developers or are determined by external agencies and require curriculum adaptation.

The overall goal of the educational experience is a second important factor. The SCIS program tried to enhance scientific literacy as part of the general education of the students. No specific science-related performance or skills are expected of the students by the public. Hence, the content and educational objectives could be treated in very general terms. In some courses of study, such as in the area of reading or in swimming instruction, the public has certain expectations of what children will learn. In other areas, such as typewriting, there are well-defined skills of speed and accuracy that can be appraised unambiguously. For all of these, the open and flexible approach to objectives is unsuitable and must be replaced by more detailed planning. At the same time, I would urge that any objectives originally devised be reviewed continuously in conjunction with classroom trials and that these objectives be considered subject to revision just as the curriculum materials themselves are.

The preparation of teaching materials and teacher education are closely related matters. For the SCIS, an important consideration was the nonscience orientation of most elementary school teachers. If the teachers have a closer professional identification with the curriculum area, which is likely to be the case at the secondary or college level, then the development strategies have to take this into account.

Publication and Distribution

I have not written earlier about publication and distribution because conditions external to the project determined the actions of the SCIS in this regard. These conditions included the publication policy of the NSF and current practices in the publishing industry. A complete account is much too long for this report.

As a matter of fact, the difficulties we encountered arose largely because the SCIS product was innovative, and no existing publisher had the capability to produce and market it. It was necessary, therefore, to arrange for cooperation among several firms, while at the same time controlling the overall cost, and this proved to be difficult. Because of many new products reaching the market, the publishing industry is changing. The experience of the SCIS dating back to the 1960s is, therefore, likely to be of limited value.

Summary

I have described the history of the SCIS project and nine strategies that were employed consciously and consistently to guide the curriculum development activities. The overall approach was pragmatic, with classroom trials and field experience playing the key role in decision making. At the same time, however, the original program design and the responses to the classroom trials were shaped by a conceptual framework of science and an inquiry-oriented educational philosophy that determine the character of the SCIS program.

5 Validated Instructional Materials as the Focus of an Effective Curriculum Development Strategy

W. James Popham

Although not particularly reminiscent of an inkblot, the term "curriculum" might well serve as the educational counterpart of a typical Rorschach projective stimulus. There are almost as many perceptions as to what is involved in curriculum development as there are curricula to develop. Thus, when one is considering any strategy for curriculum development, it becomes imperative to define exactly what is meant by the term curriculum, for it is obvious that substantial strategic variations will hinge directly on how the basic nature of curriculum is conceptualized.

Prevalent Conceptions of Curriculum

While there are literally dozens of substantially different definitions of the term available, a consideration of a few of the more prominent contenders will suffice to reflect the range of meanings educators attach to it and, of course, to the associated activity of curriculum development. In the next few paragraphs a brief examination will be offered of several prevalent conceptions of curriculum—along with an identification of how adherents of such views typically engage in curriculum development.

Scope and Sequence

On the basis of highest frequency of utterance by educators, one might assume that curriculum consists of the scope of instructional events occurring in schools and the sequence in which those events are encountered by learners. Perhaps because the phrase "scope and sequence" possesses a catchy alliterative quality, one does hear it bouncing off the walls in teachers' coffee rooms or in district curriculum offices. Most adherents to the scope and sequence (SAS) conception of curriculum have a pretty loose idea of what SAS really involves. They may phrase it something like this: "A school's curriculum includes all the educational experiences provided for the child under the direction of the school." By this they typically refer not only to formal instructional classes, such as social studies and English courses, but to those nonclass activities such as participation in clubs, work on the school newspaper, and athletics. These nonclass activities are often paradoxically referred to as "extracurricular."

The SAS people use scope to indicate that curriculum covers the total range of educative experiences for which the school takes responsibility. They use sequence to reflect the order in which these experiences are encountered by pupils. Thus, to the scope and sequence curricular specialist, the task of curriculum development is chiefly concerned with identifying and arranging the myriad instructional activities that will be presented to learners. Such activities, once isolated and ordered, are described in written documents to be distributed to teachers and other educational personnel.

Syllabi Savants

There is a sizable group of educators to whom the term curriculum refers mainly to the class syllabi or courses of study distributed by school district offices. When these people think of "curriculum," they do not conjure up images of the educational program resulting from such documents. Rather, they equate curriculum with the actual documents themselves. Surely they recognize the anticipated relationship between what is stated in the documents and what happens in schools, but they truly conceptualize curriculum chiefly in terms of program-defining documentation. There is, of course, the added dividend that they can toss around the appropriate Latin plural for syllabus, smiling condescendingly at any teacher who commits the semantic sin of saying "syllabuses."

For such syllabus devotees the job of curriculum development is essentially one of preparing improved documents. Courses of study have to be refined. Syllabi have to be made clearer and more imaginative. Since curriculum documents from other school districts often contain worthwhile ingredients, there is typically much cutting and pasting in the district curriculum office. For one suspects that more than any other blessing, proponents of this view of curriculum building must rejoice in the fact that few district curriculum divisions have copyrighted their materials.

Content Carving

There are some who equate curriculum with the content to be covered by students while they are in school. Many of the federally funded curriculum development projects of the late 1950s and early 1960s were directed by academicians who conceived of curriculum largely in terms of content and whose job, accordingly, was to discover more defensible content. The proponents of new math and new science were clearly registering dissatisfaction with the content of old math and old science.

Teachers were trained to operate these new curricula by being obliged to master new content. A host of governmentally funded institutes were staged all over the country, primarily to acquaint teachers with the new content that was considered to be the core of these new curriculum efforts.

The content-oriented curriculum specialist conceives of curriculum development primarily as an activity for isolating more meaningful content. In the conduct of this activity are employed such criteria as relevance to the learner and potential value for interpreting other aspects of the subject. The task of the curriculum developer involves excising inappropriate content and introducing preferable content. The types of individuals most useful to accomplish curriculum development of this type are those academicians who have truly mastered the content of a given subject and who can, therefore, judge the appropriateness of both new and old content contenders. Goodlad[1] has described major curriculum development efforts modeled after this content-focused conception of curriculum.

New Fun, New Games

Sharing an orientation in some ways similar to that of the content refiners, we can isolate a group of educators who think of curriculum largely in terms of the activities in which learners engage. Whereas content-oriented curriculum specialists fuss over the substance with which the pupil interacts, activity-focused curriculum planners attend to the procedures to be employed during instruction. Because learners do not engage in activities devoid of content, there is obviously a degree of overlap between these two types of curriculum developers. But the emphasis for those who are activity oriented is the instructional process, with content only providing the framework for the instructional activity. For such curriculum developers the job is obviously one of contriving imaginative, exciting, and effective instructional activities. The most appropriate staff to carry out this sort of curriculum development would be those particularly creative educators who could churn out a variety of innovative instructional tactics.

Curriculum as Goals

In recent years we find an increasing number of educators who think of curriculum as the set of intended outcomes an educational system is designed to produce, that is, the goals or objectives of the system. According to this view, the curriculum consists of the description of the aims or *ends* of an educational enterprise, in contrast to the instructional activities or *means* of accomplishing those ends. By preserving this ends-means distinction, proponents of this view of curriculum hope to provide greater clarity regarding alternative goals, thus fostering more judicious selection of goals.

A curriculum development strategy patterned after this conception of curriculum would focus on the generation and/or selection of more defensible educational goals. One illustration of such activity would be a systematic assessment of educational needs in which a school district attempts to employ data-based procedures in deciding what goals should guide the district's educational program. Another example related to this conception of curriculum development would be the creation of depositories of instructional goals from which educators might make selections appropriate to their particular instructional situations. For instance, the Instructional Objectives Exchange[2] has been engaged in this type of development activity since 1968 and now distributes materials that contain over 4,500 measurable instructional objectives for grades K-12. And in 1973 the Westinghouse Learning Corporation[3] announced a similar service involving more than 8,000 objectives for grades K-8. It is clear that the quality of this form of curriculum development is dependent upon the caliber of the objectives produced.

Strategy Potency

As one reviews the foregoing array of curriculum conceptions and their corollary development strategies, it is important to recognize that they do not represent alternatives in a multiple-choice test question replete with a hidden "correct" answer awaiting discovery. And there is not even an option for us to choose "none of the above."

In the curriculum Olympics, one looks over the field and picks his favorite team, recognizing that other contenders may be capable of making a contribution. But, in order to decide whether one has chosen the winning team, he must have a criterion by which to judge the efficacy of the curriculum development scheme he has selected. The criterion I have chosen to employ is improved learner behaviors —behaviors reflecting important affective, cognitive, and psycho-motor dimensions. It seems incontestable that the chief mission of the schools is, borrowing from Aristotle, to help actualize human potential. Thus, the standard by which we should judge the merits of a curriculum development strategy is the degree to which it results in improvements in the learner with respect to intellectual capabilities, attitudinal dispositions, and so forth.

When one considers the likelihood that the curriculum development strategies just described will bring about any far-reaching improvements in the quality of our schools, he probably cannot be overly optimistic. And if we cannot be reasonably optimistic that a given curriculum development strategy will satisfy the criterion of yielding markedly improved learner behaviors, then we had best search out a new strategy. For even the educational schemes in which we invest the most optimism will typically prove less effective than we thought. To start with an admitted long shot seems injudicious.

The striking feature about the curriculum development strategies just treated is that while they are often quite distinctive, when examined from the viewpoint of their potential impact on the nature of education, they are all essentially the same—impotent. It is not that any of these schemes would not result in some changes in the nature of educational practice, possibly even in some improvements. But as far as promoting widespread, dramatic educational improvements, they are not the answer.

As interventionist strategies they suffer from a common defect: they are almost totally dependent on teacher mediation. No matter whether it is scope and sequence determination, syllabus sharpening, content identification, activity invention, or goal generation, the teacher is the major actor in the play. The teacher stands between the developed curriculum and its effects on the child. If the teacher is ineffective, the strategy fails. If the teacher performs well, the strategy works. Yet, in view of the obviously heterogeneous caliber of public school teachers, each strategy is inordinately dependent on a notoriously undependable transmission agent.

An Alternative Strategy

To avoid this heavy dependence on teacher mediation, some educators have been drawn to a newer and, it is to be hoped, more effective curriculum development strategy: the creation of validated instructional materials. Validated instructional materials are those which, if employed as directed, can demonstrably bring about an intended behavior change in the learners for whom the materials were designed. Furthermore, the nature of the validation is such that data must be accumulated, prior to distribution of the materials, that indicate that they work, that is, that they do indeed promote learner mastery of the aims for which the materials were designed. In order for future utilization to parallel the past utilizations on which such effectiveness data were gathered, it is apparent that validated instructional materials must be designed so that they yield an essentially reproducible instructional event.

It is obvious that even such replicable instructional materials could be subverted by an incompetent or negatively disposed teacher. Teachers do make a difference. But in this curriculum development strategy the difference is minimized as much as is reasonable. It is the instructional artifact, not the teacher, which bears the primary responsibility for whether learners succeed. And because such materials can be disseminated widely, their potential for multiplicative impact is obvious. For example, an effective five-hour set of instructional materials dealing with speed reading skills, after national dissemination, could have an enormously beneficial impact on literally thousands of learners.

The validated instructional materials concept of curriculum development probably traces its lineage to the late 1950s when a group of psychologists and educators became entranced with a teaching technique known as programmed instruction. The essential feature of this approach was that it presented to learners a series of replicable and carefully sequenced (that is, programmed) instructional segments in order that the instructional program itself might assume responsibility for accomplishing one or more measurable objectives. Unlike the typical textbook which attempts to serve two functions—that of an information depository as well as a teaching instrument—programmed instruction sequences were fashioned for a single mission— to teach something. And while the early programmed instruction efforts were often quite primitive, for surely among man's most boring teaching creations were the initial linear and branching programs of the early 1960s, there was also present the germ of a powerful educational idea. A growing number of people realized that it was possible to devise instructional sequences which *in themselves* took responsibility for the student's learning. By a trial and revision approach these materials could generally be made to function effectively. Further, since such materials were essentially exportable, they could be widely distributed and, therefore, become more influential than many alternative instructional interventions.

While the above analysis undoubtedly fails to capture the entire range of reasons that many individuals were drawn to the preparation of validated instructional materials as a potentially powerful curriculum development strategy, it may provide some clues as to why in the mid-1960s we witnessed the establishment of heavily funded regional educational laboratories whose prime mission was to develop exportable instructional materials. Indeed, the beginnings of an emerging curricular specialization,[4] instructional development, were clearly evident. Someone in education was finally beginning to worry about the *D* in educational R & D.

It is important to note that the kind of curriculum development that was beginning in earnest during the mid-1960s was *not* the preparation of traditional instructional materials such as texts, workbooks, filmstrips, and so on. Although all of these media were eligible, the distinctive feature of this new type of development was that the instructional materials being developed were validated, that is, they had been field-tested during and after development in order to ensure that they accomplished the goals for which they were designed. Large-scale development of this type is typified by the work of the Southwest Regional Laboratory for Educational Research and Development (SWRL),[5] a federally funded R & D agency. On a smaller scale, the Vimcet[6] filmstrip-tape programs for teacher education illustrate the application of such a curriculum development strategy.

Basic Elements of the Validated Instructional Materials Strategy

Perhaps the best way to describe the validated instructional materials strategy for curriculum development is to detail briefly the major steps involved in developing such instructional materials. Before doing so, however, it may be useful to offer an even more concise summary of the heart of the strategy. In essence, the approach consists of specifying intended outcomes in measurable terms, developing a replicable instructional sequence that, it is hoped, will accomplish those outcomes, and, on the basis of measured postinstruction performance of learners, revise the sequence until it produces the intended results. In other words, it is a heavily data-based scheme involving trial and revision cycles in order to devise materials that promote measured attainments of students.

To the extent that there is any theoretical basis for the strategy of validated instructional materials of curriculum development, it would probably resemble a basic systems analysis model, for in a systems analysis approach there is a parallel effort to explicate one's goals, devise mechanisms of goal achievement, and then measure system outputs according to previously established criteria. If one wished to add more respectable intellectual trappings, it could be argued that a curriculum development strategy such as that described here can be traced back to many of our most venerated philosophers who urged man to plan rationally prior to acting and to appraise the efficacy of those plans in terms of their results. But, frankly, most of the people who are today feverishly engaged in this form of curriculum development spend little time looking for vindicating theories to support their work. They think this approach represents the most sensible way to promote major improvements in our nation's educational endeavors—a view I share.

The following procedures in developing validated instructional products (used here to signify a set of replicable instructional materials comprised of one or more of a variety of presentation media, such as printed text, film, audiotape, and so forth) by no means represent the definitive steps approved by all proponents of this curriculum development strategy. Yet, with minor variations, they are fairly representative of the step-by-step processes employed by most instructional developers to prepare instructional materials that really instruct.

Goal Selection

The initial step in developing a validated instructional product is to decide, at least in general terms, what it is that the instructional materials are supposed to accomplish. This is a particularly important decision, for the preparation of these sorts of instructional materials is often costly, and mistakes made at this starting point can result in large expenditures on products that do not warrant such an investment. It must be remembered that we are not talking about the preparation of a student textbook where the author gets a typing advance of five hundred dollars from the publisher, whomps up a manuscript that receives an additional massage from the publisher's editorial staff, and then finds its way into print (and, it is hoped, profit) for what must be considered a trifling investment. Since the author derives financial returns from postsales royalties, the publisher truly puts up a pittance in advance capital, mainly associated with printing and promotion costs. All the author has to do is satisfy his or her own standards plus those of an editor or two. It is hard to imagine a thriftier development strategy.

But while an error or two in goal selection can be tolerated when developing such low-cost materials, the risk factor greatly increases when one opts for the validated instructional materials approach. Thus, considerable care must be taken in the original decision regarding what sort of instructional materials to tackle. For example, a careful market survey should be conducted to verify that there is, in fact, a need for the new instructional product, that is, that competitive instructional materials of high quality and reasonable cost do not exist. Another factor concerns the probable cost of the product: will its development require that a prohibitively high price be set? Most importantly, is there reason to believe that the instructional materials, when perfected, can actually promote the goal in question, or is the intended mission too ambitious, given the resources and instructional time available? While this is not an exhaustive list of concerns, these types of considerations should figure in the initial phase of the sequence followed in developing a validated instructional product.

Explicating the Product's Mission

The second step in the enterprise requires that the intended mission of the instructional materials be translated into specifics. For some developers this means stating the objectives for a product in behavioral—measurable—terms. For the more rigorous, this step involves devising the actual criterion-referenced measures which will be used to ascertain the efficacy of the product. And for those sufficiently rigorous to warrant religious veneration by future instructional developers, this step requires the explication of the limits defining the domains of learner behavior to be sought, such domain definitions to be employed in generating and validating the required measuring devices.

Developing the Initial Product

The next task of our instructional developer is to devise the initial version of the instructional materials. This is often accomplished in small segments, trying such segments out with a limited number of learners as the segments are produced.[7] It should be noted that the developer is fully aware that this version of the product is, indeed, an initial one, and that in all likelihood it will be basically modified thereafter on the basis of the results of field tests. Even so, however, the astute developer makes his or her best effort to produce an effective product on the first try, incorporating relevant pedagogical tactics drawn from prior experience and instructional research.

Developmental Testing and Revision

At this point the developer subjects the initial version of the instructional materials to a series of field trials in which the post-instruction performance of learners on the already devised criterion tests serves as the index of the degree to which the materials need to be revised. At this phase of the enterprise there are usually a number of cycles of testing and revision. Here is where the developer calls on formative evaluation techniques to improve the still malleable instructional materials.

This is the phase of the development operation where the costs really start racing, for it is expensive to continue a data-based revision cycle for very long. And the developer is not free to intuit changes in the materials without corroborative performance data. Improvements and, sometimes, mistakes must be carefully documented. Alternative amelioration ploys must, as hypotheses, be tested. Unanticipated side effects must be sought and, if encountered, considered in subsequent revision efforts. This trial-revision phase of the development activity, with learner performance on the stipulated criterion measures serving as the indicator of whether changes in the materials are required, is the heart of this curriculum development strategy. The revision cycle is reiterated until the instructional product demonstrably produces the desired level of learner proficiency, affect, and so forth.

Installation Testing

Along the way the developers should have been worrying about how the product, once refined, would be effectively disseminated. There was a time, as recently as a decade ago, when it was assumed that once an effective instructional artifact had been produced it would be gobbled up and efficiently employed by a ravenous educational clientele. Such dreams have been tempered by experience.

The prudent developer now devotes great attention to the matter of installation, carefully considering how best to diffuse the validated materials so that they will be adopted and, once adopted, used in such a way that their effectiveness is not vitiated. Such installation procedures are often tried out in a large-scale form of tryout, sometimes referred to as field-testing. Often for this type of testing hundreds if not thousands of learners are involved. Naturally, defects in the way the materials are employed dictate modifications in the installation scheme, so that once more the developers are caught up in a trial-revision syndrome. Again, the installation procedures are revised until they work.

Diffusion

Finally, the materials are distributed as widely as possible to the appropriate instructional agencies. Sometimes the development agency tackles this dissemination task. More often than not, a commercial publisher takes over at this point with some sort of royalty payments going to the development agency or the group underwriting the development (for example, the federal government).

Once Over, Lightly

It is clear that the foregoing description of the most prominent procedures used in developing validated instructional materials does not do justice to the enterprise. It was provided to offer the flavor of this type of curricular development. A recent analysis by Baker[8] contains a far more sophisticated account of the major dimensions of the instructional development process. Earlier analyses[9] may also be of some value in providing a fuller picture of what is entailed in the validated instructional materials approach to curriculum development.

Nor should it be suggested that there is heartwarming unanimity among instructional developers regarding how to play their game. Some leaders[10] in the movement believe that the personnel carrying on instructional development should be specialists, such as field testers and installation experts. Others[11] believe just as ardently that the instructional developer should be a generalist engaging in all or most of the phases of instructional development.

These differences in opinion not only lead to substantially divergent schemes for conducting development, but in a sense reflect the extremely early state of instructional development as a distinctive specialization. But while instructional development may be in a primitive state, we should not overlook the considerable potency of this vehicle, particularly when it is contrasted with the potential impact of competing schemes of curriculum development.

Needed Nudging

While it is apparent that any strategy of curriculum development is not totally without defect, and the strategy of validated instructional materials described here surely could be improved at a number of points, there are two major defects that currently limit the potential contributions that this approach might make.

Inadequate Technology Refinement

In view of the nascent status of instructional development as a specialization, it is not surprising that its technical procedures are not particularly sophisticated. And it is equally unstartling to note that the principal financial supporter of this strategy to date (the federal government through its regional laboratories and R & D centers) has been more interested in supporting the actual production of instructional materials than in sharpening the technology by which such materials are produced. It is most shortsighted, nevertheless, not to expend a reasonable proportion of funds for materials production, perhaps 2 to 5 percent, in deliberately attempting to improve the technology of instructional materials development. Many regional laboratories, for example, have been so caught up with the exigencies of developing federally sponsored instructional products that they have had little if any time to refine their approaches to instructional development. Some of these laboratories have operated almost literally with no increase in developmental sophistication since the latter 1960s.

The time has come for a more defensible allocation of funds with no other purpose than to study and improve the procedures by which validated instructional materials are devised. Even in its primitive state, the strategy of validated instructional materials currently offers us our best hope for improving the quality of schooling. With substantial technical refinements, its beneficial impact could be enormous.

Finding the Folk

A second serious deficiency stems from the paucity of qualified personnel available to carry on first-rate instructional development enterprises. Few university training programs exist to prepare such specialists. Few helpful instructional materials can be found. To some extent, of course, this latter point is related to the weak technological base of instructional development. But too many agencies engaged in instructional development have been obliged to hire bright staff members, then hope these people could learn about development either through a rudimentary apprenticeship system or trial and error. This is far too chancy.

We need to expand some resources to create mechanisms by which the talent pool of well-trained instructional developers will be markedly expanded. One approach will surely involve the preparation of instructional materials (validated, obviously) to train such developers. Another approach will probably revolve around more traditional training programs, such as university-based masters' and doctoral programs. Other options include short courses and more extended institutes offered for professionals in other fields who wish to acquire expertise in product development. Though the means can be set aside for the moment, the end should be clear: the creation of an increased capability to prepare the specialists who will operate the curriculum development projects in which validated instructional materials are produced.

Thoughts and Afterthoughts

Space limitations have precluded a particularly intensive exposition of the validated instructional materials strategy of curriculum development. As indicated previously, there are other sources for such analyses.[12] The chief purpose of the present treatment was to describe this strategy against a sketchy backdrop of alternative approaches. While there was no deliberate effort to engage in competitive denegration of alternative strategies of curriculum development, I was probably unable to conceal a belief that the validated materials approach offers education more hope.

If for no other reason than that competing curriculum development strategies have already been given a reasonably decent chance to succeed and have not proved stunningly successful, one is inclined to support the validated instructional materials scheme. Beyond that, certain inherent features of the approach, such as its data-based orientation and multiplication possibilities, are compelling.

While the present analysis was intended to be a description based largely on my personal experience in using a given curriculum development strategy, until the last few paragraphs it was largely nonpartisan. It is my hope that the preceding paragraphs will present the reader with a relatively unbiased opportunity to weigh the probable efficacy of the validated instructional materials strategy for curriculum development.

Notes

1. John I. Goodlad, *The Changing School Curriculum* (New York: Fund for the Advancement of Education, 1966).

2. Box 24095, Los Angeles, California 90024.

3. P. O. Box 30, Iowa City, Iowa 52240.

4. W. James Popham, "Product Research: A New Curriculum Specialty," *Educational Leadership* 23 (No. 6, 1966): 507-513.

5. 4665 Lampson Avenue, Los Alamitos, California 90720.

6. P. O. Box 24714, Los Angeles, California 90024.

7. Markle has offered an excellent account of how those developing validated instructional materials can profitably employ learners in field testing versions of their materials at varying points in the development sequence. S. M. Markle, "Empirical Testing of Programs," in *Programed Instruction*, ed. P. C. Lange, Sixty-sixth Yearbook of the National Society for the Study of Education, Part II (Chicago: University of Chicago Press, 1967), 104-138.

8. E. L. Baker, "The Technology of Instructional Development," in *The Second Handbook of Research on Teaching*, ed. R. M. W. Travers (Chicago: Rand McNally, 1973), 245-285.

9. W. J. Popham and E. L. Baker, "Rules for the Development of Instructional Products," in *Instructional Product Development*, ed. R. L. Baker and R. E. Schutz (New York: Van Nostrand Reinhold, 1971), 129-168.

10. E.g., executives of the Southwest Regional Laboratory for Educational Research and Development.

11. E.g., executives of the Far West Regional Laboratory for Educational Research and Development.

12. Baker, "The Technology of Instructional Development"; Popham and Baker, "Rules for the Development of Instructional Products."

6 The Thought Fox and Curriculum Building

Alan C. Purves

The Thought Fox

I imagine this midnight moment's forest:
Something else is alive
Beside the clock's loneliness
And this blank page where my fingers move.

Through the window I see no star:
Something more near
Though deeper within darkness
Is entering the loneliness:
Cold, delicately as the dark snow,
A fox's nose touches twig, leaf;
Two eyes serve a movement, that now
And again now, and now, and now

Sets neat prints into the snow
Between trees, and warily a lame
Shadow lags by stump and in hollow
Of a body that is bold to come

Across clearings, an eye,
A widening deepening greenness,
Brilliantly, concentratedly,
Coming about its own business

Till with a sudden sharp hot stink of fox
It enters the dark hole of the head.
The window is starless still; the clock ticks.
The page is printed.
—"The Thought Fox," from *The Hawk in the Rain* by Ted Hughes.
Copyright © 1957 by Ted Hughes. Reprinted by permission of
Harper and Row, Publishers, Inc.

What has this poem to do with curriculum? Everything. Hughes
writes about how an author comes to write a poem. He is conscious,
but something outside of his consciousness (or is it entirely in it?)
takes over, and, as a result, the fox of the mind becomes a fox living
on a page. The page is printed. How does this happen? From what
deep part of the brain did the fox and the poem come? How do we
happen to compose a poem? An essay on curriculum building? A
curriculum?

I have been asked to address this question for the purpose of being
helpful to those who may build their own curricula. I have been
building curricula for nearly twenty years—ever since I first planned a
course in writing. I did not think of that as curriculum building. My
real concern was with how I was going to fill fifty minutes and make
people think I was halfway intelligent. Since that baptism, I have
devised college courses, workshops, a Ph.D. program for Trainers of
Teacher Trainers, a segment of a program in Aesthetic Education for
Elementary School Children, a secondary school literature curriculum, and an experimental living-learning unit within a state university. I have done fairly well with some; many have failed to live up to
my expectations. But each year I keep trying.

In reflecting on the curriculum-building process and on the various
experiences I have had, I keep looking for a generalization, a thread
on which to hang both this essay and a set of principles that might be
useful to others. I have examined what the scholars have had to say,
and I even started to write this essay following through the exemplary outline set forth by Ralph Tyler in what must be the seminal
book on curriculum.[1] Having followed through two-thirds of the
outline, my thought fox struck me as very dead indeed. This is not
meant as a criticism of Tyler—I shall have occasion to express my
admiration later—but to speak of the failure to use that model to
shape this essay. *Through the window I see no star*

I shall start with definitions. Curricula consist of materials and
actions arranged in sequence so as to effect people's learning. Cur-

ricula reflect the maker's understanding of the nature and goals of society, the nature of the people who are to be affected and their learning processes, the nature of the concepts, attitudes, or skills that are to be learned. Curricula are planned in that they have goals. Curricula have a means whereby the effectiveness of what has been attempted can be assessed. Curricula are, in sum, rational or systematic approaches to the problem of getting people to learn something. The components of the system are a rationale, a set of objectives, a set of materials, a set of activities, a sequence of those activities and materials, and a means to evaluate or provide feedback about the curriculum. *Something more near / Though deeper within darkness / Is entering the loneliness*

One example—the secondary school literature curriculum on which I worked[2]—addressed, in retrospect, nearly all of the components of the definition. There was a conception of society as it might be—a society that was going to spend more leisure time as an audience and that would be faced with increasing opportunities for choice.[3] There was a conception of the student as a person bombarded with literature through the various media but without a means for seeing how the media affected him. There was a conception of literature as being less a fixed canon of classics than a collection of verbal utterances shaped by the writer to fit his characteristic voice; he sought thereby to embody his experiences and create a response in the reader. The response was important because the reader could never find out the author's intended meaning, could never approximate the author's experience—the result of the nature of language, which instead of being a medium for communication tended to hamper communication. That communications model of Sender⟷Message⟷Receiver has come to be challenged by many people concerned with the nature of language and the relation of language to communication.[4] Because of the indefinite nature of language, particularly ambiguity in meaning, and the variety of connotative overlays, the meaning ascribed to a verbal utterance by the sender cannot be realized by the receiver. The receiver constructs *his* message, which may or may not coincide with the sender's message. The author's intention, therefore, could not be the measure of the appositeness of the reader's response; that measure must come from the commonality among readers or from the logic and clarity with which a reader articulated his response.

Given this set of assumptions, and several more about the nature of response, the curriculum set for itself a number of goals relevant to developing the student's ability to respond and articulate his response to a variety of literary works:

1. An individual should learn to feel secure in his response to a literary selection and not be dependent on imitating someone else's response.
2. An individual should learn why he responds as he does to a literary work—both what in the work and what in himself leads to that response.
3. An individual should learn to respect the responses of others as being as appropriate for them as his is for him.
4. An individual should learn to recognize the common elements in his response and in those of others.

One can see in these goals some assumptions about individual differences and individual liberty; some assumptions about the nature of democratic society; some notions about the limits of general education.[5] Those assumptions can be challenged, but, once they are accepted, the curriculum proposed would logically follow from them, although other logical dependencies might well occur to others.

These goals lend themselves to being rendered in behavioral objectives. Although I recognize there are other ways of thinking about behavioral objectives, my training and predilection (which causes which?) led me to conceive of objectives in terms of a grid of content and behaviors. (See Figure 6-1.) Such a grid speaks to the general objectives I have listed and provides a means for evaluating the success of the curriculum: cognitive or affective measures can be set up to determine whether these objectives have been met. Enabling objectives can be written to cover the application of the cells of specific literary works or groups of works. Whether the grid helps one choose materials, activities, and sequences of the two is quite another matter.[6]

The choice of materials, activities, and content came not from a set of objectives but from another, related, consideration. Literature curricula had generally been subject centered, based upon one of a number of rival conceptions about the nature of literature or about the nature of criticism as an academic discipline. We saw problems with both these starting points and sought to think of curriculum in terms of the mature reader who was not necessarily a specialist.

Piece of writing	Creative	Value	Evaluate	Generalize	Interpret	Relate	Discriminate	Describe
Subject matter in a piece of writing (action, character, setting, theme)								
Voice(s) in a piece of writing (point of view, kind of narrator, tone, authorial distance)								
Shape(s) in a piece of writing (plot, outline, structure)								
Language in a piece of writing (diction, connotation, syntactic peculiarities, rhythm, rhyme, mood, imagery)								
Response to a piece of writing								

Figure 6-1. Grid of content and behaviors

What was it that the mature amateurs did? They read, watched, observed, listened, and talked. Some might draw, some might write, and some might consider acting out or reading aloud; most, however, would talk with a friend or an acquaintance who had also read, watched, observed, listened, and talked. Many, of course, would keep the experience to themselves, but conversation is a fairly natural outcome for a sufficiency of people to warrant our making a generalization. The purpose of talk is to share experiences, and by uttering them (outering them) to help define the nature of the experience. (How do I know what I think until I hear myself talk?) What was the nature of the talk? About whether the experience of reading was pleasurable, worth it? About why the experience happened, about what it meant to the talker? About meaning, about characters, about structure, about language? About anyone of a large number of things?

The curriculum, then, should have selections that stimulate talk or the other forms of response. It should have poems, plays, stories, films, essays, graphics, recordings, kinescopes, and other hybrids in which students evince interest. The canon of "classical" literature may be represented, but classicality is not the prime consideration. Materials might come from both the "high" and the popular culture of our past and present. A variety of cultures—not just the Anglo-Saxon or the Western—should appear, in part because of the pressures that various groups exert upon a curriculum maker ("You really have to have one black writer for every two whites, one woman for every man, one Chicano in every section, and a good number of third world writers." "But if you do that they won't use the books in the South." "That's right, and besides, you can't have any selections that refer to God, drugs, normal parturition, sexual intercourse, homosexuality, violence, or in a derogatory fashion to any group or subgroup." If only "Mary Had a Little Lamb" had been written by Nikki Giovanni!), and in part because of an earnest desire on our part to represent the whole spectrum of the literary imagination.

Material was generally selected on the basis of potential or actual interest of students from various sections of the country. At times banal works were included in hopes that students would remark on their banality. The works were selected more frequently because they might elicit a variety of comments and a variety of ways of being responded to.

The suggested activities included talk, writing, talk, filmmaking, talk, graphics, talk, drama and mime, talk, dance, talk, music, talk, other activities, and talk. The importance of these activities was to get the students to express their responses in some congenial medium and to talk about their responses. The students would read, listen, or watch, and then they would articulate their first responses to what they had received. Talk served as the means for sharing the articulations, for comparing them with those of other students, for testing them against the text, for modifying and refining and clarifying the first responses. The curriculum builds itself around receptive, responsive, and reflective activities. *A fox's nose touches twig, leaf; / Two eyes serve a movement, that now / And again now, and now, and now*

The sequence of those activities is as outlined: reception, response, reflection. Figure 6-2 sets forth a model of the relationship among these three activities. The student begins by having the ability and the disposition to read, as well as a generalized set about the world, literature, and the class. After reading, a response is formulated and uttered: "Ugh!" "It's a good book." "I wonder why the hero did what he did." "I think it's not a typical novel, like *Adam Bede*." Yawn, silence.

Through intervention, a teacher induces the student to expand his response, to make it more detailed and more highly communicable. More often than not, the communication is verbal. As the student expands his response, he brings into play more and more specific facts, terms, and generalizations that he might have acquired. The expanded statement might lead to an exploration of the areas outside the circle—that is, outside the text—but more probably the student will apply knowledge in these areas to the text. The process of expansion might be quite complicated and lengthy, involving as much as a week or a month; it might also take on a nonverbal form: film, enactment through mime, or the like. At the end of the process the student will emerge with a modified set of concepts (the work will have changed him) and a modified interest in reading other similar or dissimilar works.[7]

If such is the sequence of activities with respect to reading and response to one work, what is the large sequence? We argued that the larger sequence could easily be random, that any work could follow any other depending on the predilections of the students and the teacher. If a particular class session was devoted to the expansion of

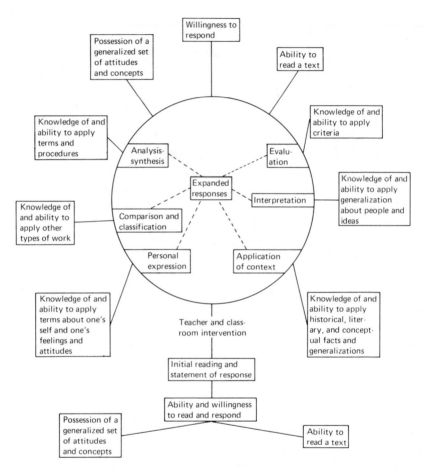

Figure 6-2. Model of instruction and evaluation in literary response and criticism (from A. C. Purves, "Literary Criticism and Educational Measurement," A Guide to Evaluation, RESPONDING [Lexington, Mass.: Ginn & Co., 1973], 73)

response, the teacher could readily suggest a work that seemed to follow from the nature of the talk about the preceding work. If, after reading *Huckleberry Finn*, students seemed concerned with the Mississippi, a teacher might suggest the works of Ben Lucien Berman; if concerned with first person narratives, a teacher might move to similarly structured works; if with growing up, then to other works of adolescence and initiation. No one predetermined sequence seemed more appropriate than any other.[8] There might be a sequence of difficulty of lexicon, syntax, metaphoric structure, theme, and the like, a sequence roughly paralleling what we see as the general growth and development of the individual. Placing works on a continuum of difficulty was, however, not easy. Works could be organized by theme, formal aspect, geography, history, mood, author, and the like, and all connections seemed viable. The selections were therefore ordered in clusters so as to illustrate the variety of possible links between works. The sequence of activities would again be limited only by the expertise of the teacher and by the physical constraints of the classroom or the school. Some teachers are unsure of using improvisation, others of collage. Some schools still have fixed desks. Such factors act to constrain the flexibility of the curriculum, but many can be turned into advantages. Fixed seats can be useful as a foil to informal discussion if the teacher and the class use them as the center of an arena and sit on the floor around them or if they use them as the place for an audience attending a series of dramas in front of the room. . . . *warily a lame / Shadow lags by stump . . .*

From the objectives and the instructional strategy, we set forth a plan of evaluation that focused on three aspects of a student's learning: his ability to read unfamiliar texts with a modicum of perceptiveness, the development of a reasoned pattern of response to what he read, and the development of an interest in literature of any sort. To evaluate these outcomes, we developed multiple-choice tests, essays that allowed for generalization, attitude scales, and inventories of response pattern and interest. All of these, we urged, should be incorporated into an evaluation program both to look at the students' learning and to look at curricular success. The objectives in the grid could be measured, and the diagram of sequence indicated that measurement should be based less on the selections that had been read and on memory and more on selections that had not been read, on developed skills, approaches, and attitudes.

Materials, then, were developed in anthologies, record collections, and book and film lists. Activities were proposed in teachers' guides; measures were developed. Selections were packaged in volumes that were judged attractive and interesting to students. Designers were called in to develop graphics for the volumes, logos for the books, brochures and guides for the teachers. Packaging became important, particularly the physical layout of the pages on which the literature was presented. The works should be attractive; illustrations should be evocative; volumes should appear to be as close to trade books as possible. Teachers' guides should have white space so as to allow room for notations and marginalia.

The decision concerning the teachers' guides came as the result of a long discussion. There is a tradition of fully developed teachers' guides, heavy tomes as big as the text that spell out for the teacher every step in instruction that is to be undertaken. This type of guide was part of a curriculum package that was called "teacher-proof." Many of us argued that the problem with teacher-proof curricula was that teachers resented them. Also, despite the claims, nothing is teacher-proof or student-proof. Would it not be better for the curriculum maker to assume that the teacher was a collaborator rather than an enemy; imaginative rather than cloddish. intelligent rather than stupid. Programming the teacher was a mistake; hinting seemed a better strategy. The guides therefore, sought to bring the teachers into the curriculum-making activity. They suggested, but did not direct. They raised questions for discussion, but did not give answers that seemed to be presented as if by fiat. They presented options for activities, but did not specify the efficacy of any one activity over another. They were not even called teachers' guides but "Talks with Teachers." They recognized that the teacher was a human being capable of making decisions, a person who must be thought of as human if he were to think of his students as human. Bruno Bettelheim and Samuel Beckett have long since documented the failure of a mentality that treats other human beings as objects; such a mentality comes to think of itself as an object.[9] . . . *a body that is bold to come / Across clearings* . . .

Such was the curriculum development process that I went through. But it was not quite like that. Those were the pieces that we used, but that was not quite how we played the game . . . *playing the game* . . . the metaphor derived for curriculum building by the

Aesthetic Education Project.[10] It is a good metaphor, in part because it raises more questions than it solves. Is it a board game like Monopoly in which one goes around and around on a treadmill? Is it a game like chess? Like football? Like Uncle Wiggly in which one finds a way to come home? At times I am not even sure how many players there are. Certainly I am unsure as to how to define a winner. If the game metaphor is so ambiguous, why is it attractive? Games characteristically call forth the imagination and have the ordering principles that people enjoy. Games imply strategies for coping with obstacles. Games imply feelings of pleasure for those who participate. Games build upon the twin spirits of cooperation and competition.

The curriculum-building game has all of these characteristics, plus the characteristic of being simultaneously work and play. The curriculum development game perhaps describes as well as any metaphor the process by which one builds curricula; for me it describes the lore that I can pass on to others. That lore suggests that no one can build a curriculum in quite the way that my colleagues and I did and that I build different curricula differently. I build the curriculum for a graduate seminar by having to choose a year in advance a topic that I think my students and I might want to work on; six months later I am asked to submit a book list even though I know some of the books I shall probably want to use have not been published. A month before classes begin, I have an outline; when I meet the class, all starts quite differently from the path indicated by any of those preliminary steps. That is hardly the way I build a curriculum for the secondary schools. Yet by thinking of the very diversity of my own experience and by comparing my experience with that of others, perhaps I can set forth some rules of the game.

I do have a sense of the number of pieces (Figure 6-3). Many of these pieces I have already described. Certain others have not figured as strongly in our curriculum. Legal constraints appeared in the form of copyright laws that prevented certain works from being included and in the necessity for one year of American literature. Administrative structure has appeared more important in the marketing of the curriculum: Who is the decision maker in a school? Is it, rightfully, the teachers? Is it the building principal or some more remote body? How does our curriculum fit with other parts of the curriculum? I have found that if students have two kinds of courses—one that is structured and traditional in the sense of emphasizing memory and

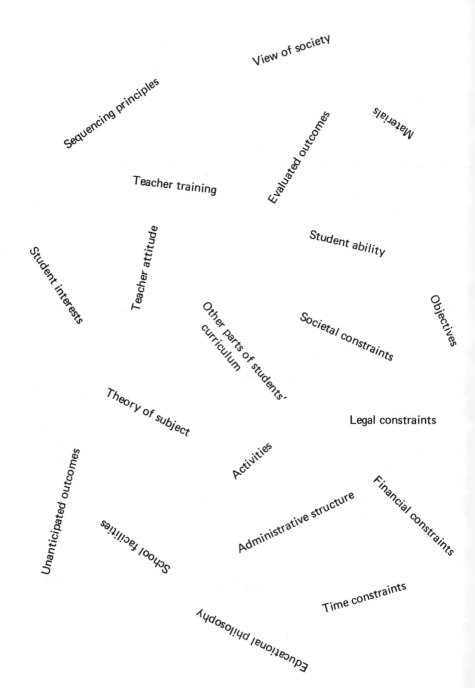

Figure 6-3. Pieces in the curriculum

analysis and one that is more open in that it encourages divergent thinking and synthesis and evaluation—the students will see the former as more important. When a choice is made as to which is to be the object of study and attention, the more open course is put aside. Why is this? Should it be? Can it be otherwise? I do not know. But I have a keen sense that the subjects, the different aspects of the curricula, compete in a student's mind. I am not sure that this is a desirable situation nor how to deal with it, save in terms of total curriculum planning. *Brilliantly, concentratedly / Coming about its own business*

In the course of working out the curriculum, we played the game in a number of different ways, or we played a number of games simultaneously. At first the game focused on theory of the subject, sequencing principles, and materials. Then came a time to consider activities. That consideration forced us to spend time on the teachers' guides and therefore on teacher training and knowledge. Consideration of that matter made us realize that we needed to write a book for teachers that would set forth the philosophy of the series.[11] We had to win their support. In setting forth the philosophy of the series it was necessary to solidify and describe the educational philosophy under which we had been working. As we were pursuing this process, the legal and societal constraints of refusal to reprint selections we wanted and incipient censorship emerged.

Had we forgotten the objectives and outcomes? No. Several of us had been concerned with this matter, and several had written on the topic of behavioral objectives.[12] Formulating the objectives and outcomes ran concurrently with the selection and arrangement of materials. The decision on how to evaluate was also being made during the course of devising the curriculum; those working on the curriculum reviewed and criticized the evaluation plan, and the items in it and finally accepted the plan and the items with varying degrees of enthusiasm.

All of the parts finally coalesced. All of the pieces in the game fell into a pattern, which might best resemble what I have sketched in Figure 6-4. This is an attempt to put the random parts in Figure 6-3 into some sort of meaningful order, to provide some sense of the dynamics of the construction of the curriculum. It is a game board, but how to play the game and how to move on it remains something of an enigma. *Till with a sudden sharp hot stink of fox . . .*

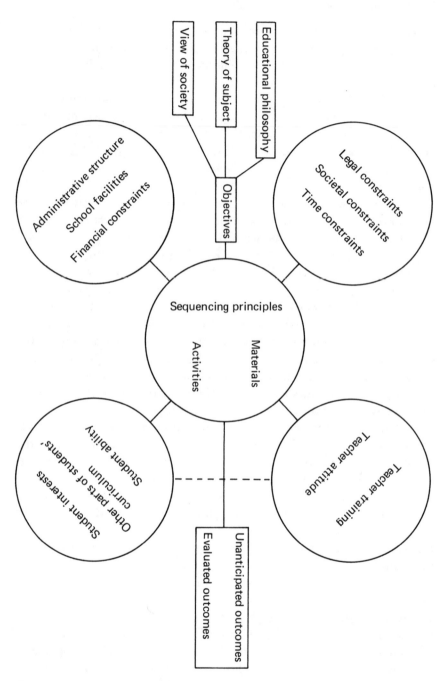

Figure 6-4. Structure of the curriculum

The game board gives one the pieces. Where one starts is another matter. Some curriculum builders start with a sense of what the classroom should look like—whether it should be orderly or chaotic—and build a curriculum from there. Many have begun with a view of how society should be. A good number have started with evaluation and have built a dog to fit the tail, which has certainly been true in the case of Advanced Placement curricula and British A-level curricula. Some have begun with behavioral objectives and others with a learning theory—behaviorist or cognitive. Some have started with a set of materials, which we almost did. Others began with a theory about the subject. We had a plan, I am sure, but we did not articulate it early in the game. I suppose, however, that theory about the subject was closest to where we began. I think that one must start at the point that seems most apposite to one's temperament, but it really may not matter where one starts.

Since it may not matter where one starts, that might be Rule 1 of the game: A PLAYER MAY START WITH ANY PIECE. It does matter, however, that all the pieces be picked up. I have a sense that in thinking about and building our curriculum we did not consider early enough the relation of it to other parts of the students' curriculum. I am not sure that we considered the financial constraints of the school in packaging our materials. I am sure that we attended to the unanticipated outcomes of other curricula, but how could we anticipate the unanticipated outcomes of our own? One was the potential transmutation into a laissez-faire curriculum, a bastardization of open education. We envisioned a sequence from lesser to greater independence of students from the teacher, and we tried to plan for that sequence in the teachers' materials. We chose to ignore some of the social constraints, particularly some of the taboos. Others we decided not to ignore. In general, however, we did follow Rule 2: ALL THE PIECES MUST BE PLAYED.

Figures 6-3 and 6-4 illustrate Rule 3: THE PIECES MUST FINALLY BE PERCEIVED TO BE IN SOME RELATIONSHIP TO EACH OTHER. In Figure 6-4 certain of the pieces are grouped into circles of society, of the school, of the student, and of the teacher. All bear relationship to the central circle which is the curriculum, the things and actions of students arranged in some sequence. Principles, theories, objectives, and outcomes exist independently of the circles, but are related to them in that they take the circles into account. One could delineate other connecting lines. The fact that this was not done does not mean that they are unrelated, but that the intersection comes not at the level of theory but at the level of practice. Theory pays little attention to constraints. Though that might well be my bias, I have created my dynamic and have followed Rule 3. . . . *It enters the dark hole of the head . . .*

Rule 3 leads to Rule 4: THERE ARE SEVERAL WAYS OF WINNING THE GAME. One way is to be able to play out the pieces as I have indicated in this chapter. The books and materials exist. Salesmen are at work, and we have done our part. The pieces can be perceived to exist and thus to exist in relationship to each other. Another way is to have the finished model approximate a structure like that laid down by Ralph Tyler. Such a way of winning is important, for it means that the player has created a curriculum that fits a model of rationality. Its formal properties meet a criterion of tried logicality and pragmatism. Another way of winning would depend entirely on the outcomes of the learner, that is, "No matter how you play the game, it's whether you win that counts." This way of winning looks only at the achievement of the tested objectives. The other outcomes are immaterial. Such has been the kind of evaluation that looks at the manifest curriculum of the school but not at the latent curriculum. One may well wonder whether the curriculum projects that attended solely to the intellectual training of a technocracy might not have had as partial by-products (would Mark Rudd have existed were it not for Admiral Rickover and PSSC?) the student unrest of the late 1960s. Other forms of victory may also arise. Some, for example, might declare themselves victors by virtue of the attractiveness of the materials (creative packaging). Others might pride themselves on intellectual modernity or incorporation of the latest educational panacea (television, computers, or the like). There are many definitions of winning, and in a society as diverse as ours and with so many conflicting views, the *real* winner *sub specie aeternitatis* may not be possible to discern. . . . *The window is starless still; the clock ticks.*

What new strategies might I suggest for playing the curriculum game? I have set forth some of the rules as I have learned them. There may well be others that I have not yet learned or become aware of. I have learned, however, that the models of curriculum, and certainly Tyler's seminal model, are a fine way of looking at a curriculum. Figures 6-3 and 6-4 seek to show how one builds a curriculum so that it approximates that model. Just as the analysis of a finished essay does not tell one how to write the essay, and just as a set of blueprints does not fully tell one where to begin building a house, so a model of the components of a curriculum does not tell the curriculum builder how to proceed. The pieces, the game board, and a few rules are there. The curriculum maker must then deal with his own thought fox. *The page is printed.*

Notes

1. Ralph Tyler, *Basic Principles of Curriculum and Instruction* (Chicago: University of Chicago Press, 1949).

2. See Alan C. Purves, *Responding, Ginn Interrelated Sequences in Literature* (Lexington, Mass.: Ginn & Co., 1973), Vols. I-XVIII; A. C. Purves, *How Porcupines Make Love* (Lexington, Mass.: Xerox College Publishing, 1972).

3. This premise comes from the future watchers who observe that people in our society are continuously forced to make choices, but the choices that are offered them are typical. They are bombarded with information about cars and have to choose between makes and models, but the choice of whether to have a car or not is already made. So it is with television programming. The three networks present the viewers with seemingly momentous but actually trivial choices. Real choice is seldom offered and to few. General education needs to address itself to that fact of our existence.

4. Among other works dealing with the reader and communication are Frank Smith, *Understanding Reading* (New York: Holt, Rinehart and Winston, 1971); and C. Cherry, *On Human Communication* (Cambridge, Mass.: M.I.T. Press, 1966).

5. We assumed that it is the function of general education to prepare the citizenry to act as citizens, to socialize them, and at the same time to teach them to be informed rather than merely indoctrinated. This last point is, I realize, an unresolved problem. There are values in indoctrination into a certain set of social norms: norms of citizenship, respect for property, respect for individual differences. In the United States we have prided ourselves on being more open and critical than conformist, to believe that a "free, inquiring mind" is a desirable end of education. In time of ecological, political, and social crises, I can see an argument against the strongly individualist position, but I would adhere to it out of belief in its long-run virtue.

6. See Alan C. Purves, "Of Behaviors, Objectives, and English," *English Journal* (September 1970): 793-797.

7. For further discussion of this model, see Alan C. Purves, "How to Love Big Brother, Live in Walden Two, and Enjoy Consciousness Three," *Goal Making for English Teaching*, ed. Henry B. Maloney (Urbana, Ill.: National Council of Teachers of English, 1973).

8. See Alan C. Purves, "Structure and Sequence in Literature Study: A Second Look," *Journal of Aesthetic Education* 3 (April 1969): 103-117.

9. See Bruno Bettelheim, *The Informed Heart* (Glencoe, Ill.: Free Press, 1960); Samuel Beckett, *Waiting for Godot* (New York: Grove Press, 1955).

10. Manuel Barkan, Laura Chapman, and Evan Kern, *Guidelines: Curriculum Development for Aesthetic Education* (St. Ann, Mo.: Central Midwest Regional Education Laboratory, 1970).

11. Purves, *How Porcupines Make Love.*

12. See *On Writing Behavioral Objectives for English,* ed. John Maxwell and Anthony Tovatt (Urbana, Ill.: National Council of Teachers of English, 1970).

7 Four Perspectives on Curriculum Development

Howard D. Mehlinger

Introduction

The overarching purpose of curriculum development is to improve instruction. Through a process of identifying a curriculum problem and developing a generalizable solution to the problem, curriculum developers attempt to supply teachers with new instructional products and procedures that are demonstrably superior to those previously available.

In addition to creating and testing improved instructional products and practices, some curriculum developers have attended to the cultivation of curriculum development as a field of professional activity within education. They prepare students who wish to become curriculum developers, and they publish essays, articles, and books about both practical and theoretical problems in curriculum development. From their efforts have come a number of paradigms, models, strategies, and prescriptions relating to the process of curriculum development. The purpose of this chapter is to consider some of the paradigms, models, strategies, and prescriptions that appear to influence curriculum developers and to make judgments about their utility on the basis of actual experience within the Social Studies Development Center at Indiana University.

The chapter is organized around four topics: the role of the curriculum developer, stages of curriculum development, lesson development, and universities as sites for curriculum development. In the first section I identify the multiple roles that must be satisfied for successful curriculum development to occur and indicate how these roles may be filled differently depending upon the size of the project staff and the personalities of the individuals involved. The second section examines stages in the curriculum development process from the conceptualization of a new instructional program to the time when the program is available for general use. The third section explores lesson development within an overall program, with special attention given to the utility of behavioral objectives for guiding development. The final section raises questions about the conditions that are necessary to support high quality curriculum development and considers whether typical universities can meet these conditions. In each of the four sections I provide one paradigm, model, strategy, or set of prescriptions that have attracted attention in the field. These are then weighed against the experience acquired through the various projects of the Social Studies Development Center.

The Role of the Curriculum Developer

The term curriculum developer is used in various ways. When the journal *Educational Leadership* describes curriculum development, it usually means something different from its use in the journal *Educational Technology*. The traditional meaning of the term curriculum developer is almost interchangeable with curriculum planner. It refers to a person who theorizes about the goals and values to be served by instruction and who decides upon appropriate sequences of courses. More recently the term curriculum developer has been used synonymously with instructional materials developer (a person who produces various kinds of instructional media for classroom use). Interviews with curriculum developers reveal that their work also requires that they engage in research, evaluation, and diffusion.

Because the overarching purpose of curriculum development is to improve instruction, the product of curriculum development invariably requires a change in current classroom practice. If the change is minor, the curriculum development task may be easy. Projects of curriculum development are, however, usually funded to undertake difficult, complex problems that present massive obstacles to change. In such cases successful development requires that a number of roles be played satisfactorily.

One way to gain perspective on multiple developer roles is by referring to a schema developed by David Clark and Egon Guba. In 1965 they presented a paper that set forth a schema identifying processes they believed to be "related to and necessary for change in education."[1] (See Table 7-1.) The authors identified four components in the process of educational change: research, development, diffusion, and adoption. Their schema identified a major objective for each component, criteria to judge the performance of each element, and the relationship of each component to educational change.

Clark and Guba did not intend that their model be used to account for curriculum development only. Rather, they used the term "development" to refer to any product or practice designed to solve an operating problem in education and that could be replicated and used successfully by those who were not members of the original development staff. While the authors' intentions were to refer to change processes broadly, their schema can illuminate some of the special responsibilities that accompany curriculum development.

The Clark-Guba schema is frequently cited as one example of a "linear model" of educational change, in contrast to the "cybernetic," "linkage," or "problem-solving" models that have appeared subsequently, partly in response to their schema. A linear model is one in which a process is seen as beginning at one point in the model and proceeding directly to another point. Thus, some critics of the Clark-Guba schema have interpreted the model as indicating that ideas for educational improvements begin with research and are then engineered and packaged by developers for diffusion to passive adopters. The critics charge that this view of educational change is both naive and immoral. In defense of the authors it should be noted that they were never supporters of the notion that ideas in education move in only one direction. Indeed, they were quick to point out, for example, that development frequently stimulates research, that development often must proceed without a research base, and that potential adopters often trigger ideas for development. The major purpose that led to the schema—and its central contribution—was to identify components of a process, each having unique objectives and

Table 7-1. Classification schema of processes related to and necessary for change in education

	Development			Diffusion			Adoption	
	Research	Invention	Design	Dissemination	Demonstration	Trial	Installation	Institutionalization
Objective	To advance knowledge	To formulate a new solution to an operating problem or to a class of operating problems, i.e., to innovate	To order and to systematize the components of the invented solution; to construct an innovation package for institutional use, i.e., to engineer	To create widespread awareness of the invention among practitioners, i.e., to inform	To afford an opportunity to examine and assess operating qualities of the invention, i.e., to build conviction	To build familiarity with the invention and provide a basis for assessing the quality, value, fit, and utility of the invention in a particular institution, i.e., to test	To fit the characteristics of the invention to the characteristics of the adopting institution, i.e., to operationalize	To assimilate the invention as an integral and accepted component of the system, i.e., to establish
Criteria	Validity (internal and external)	Face validity (appropriateness) Estimated viability Impact (relative contribution)	Institutional feasibility Generalizability Performance	Intelligibility Fidelity Pervasiveness Impact (extent to which it affects key targets)	Credibility Convenience Evidential assessment	Adaptability Feasibility Action	Effectiveness Efficiency	Continuity Valuation Support
Relation to change	Provides basis for invention	Produces the invention	Engineers and packages the invention	Informs about the invention	Builds conviction about the invention	Tries out the invention in the context of a particular situation	Operationalizes the invention for use in a specific institution	Establishes the invention as a part of an ongoing program; converts it to a "noninnovation"

Source: From Essay Six, "An Examination of Potential Change Roles in Education," by David L. Clark and Egon G. Guba, in *Rational Planning in Curriculum and Instruction.* Published by National Education Association. Copyright ©1967 National Education Association of the United States. Used by permission of the publisher.

special evaluative criteria, and each offering discrete contributions to educational change.

The importance of the schema for curriculum development is that it draws attention to a variety of functional processes that require the attention of a development team if its instructional innovation is to succeed. While developers hope to find existing research on which to base their work, often new research must be undertaken to support the development of instructional materials. The "development" component of the schema is self-evident; the design, creation, and testing of an instructional innovation lie at the heart of the curriculum development process. While others can help with the diffusion process, curriculum developers cannot assume that the efforts of publishing companies, professional associations, the ERIC system, and informal networks will be sufficient. Even adoption falls under the purview of developers. They must attend to the problems of adoption and find ways to help potential adopters overcome the political, economic, and intellectual hurdles that lie in the path of state, district, or school adoptions of new instructional products.

An example drawn from an ongoing project in the Social Studies Development Center, Indiana University, may illustrate how developers are required to play multiple roles. The Center has a contract with the National Science Foundation through the American Political Science Association to produce a high school political science course. The title of the course is "Comparing Political Experiences." Aided by a conceptual framework, students are led to compare four types of political systems—elite, bureaucratic, coalitional, and participant—across various levels of political activity. These systems are identified and analyzed in schools, communities, nations, and transnational organizations. Not only are students taught certain concepts and generalizations about political systems, but they are also instructed in certain types of intellectual skills that aid their understanding and in certain participation skills that enhance their capacity to be effective political actors. A special feature of the course is the use of the school itself as a laboratory for testing propositions about politics and for practicing political participation skills.

Though much more could be written about the program to aid the reader's understanding, this superficial treatment should provide sufficient background to demonstrate how one of the multiple, developer roles, that of researcher, is exhibited in this project.

First of all, the conceptualization of the course is original. Although courses in comparative government and politics have existed for years, given the rationale and the goals of the project, it was not possible to depend upon existing formulations of comparative politics. The program framework itself may prove, therefore, to be a contribution to political science. One of the factors that led to the need for an original conceptualization was a desire to cross levels of political analysis and to represent everyday political life rather than institutional aspects of politics. A second factor was the intention to make use of schools as laboratories for the study and practice of politics.

The commitment to tap school experience for instructional purposes has stimulated the demand for new knowledge. Despite much rhetoric about "schools as political systems," no one has adequately studied schools, using political science perspectives, to learn if schools satisfy the minimum conditions of political systems. Can schools, like other political systems, be categorized as elite, bureaucratic, coalitional, and participant? This cannot be known with certainty without research that parallels the development of instructional materials. Because a description and an analysis of school life through a perspective of comparative politics is part of the content as well as the conceptualization of the course, moreover, it is necessary to obtain reliable information about the typical political experiences of students in schools. While abundant data exist on the operation of political systems at most levels, almost no information exists on the school political system. In order to include data on school politics within the course, the developers must conduct their own research.

New problems are encountered when the developers apply existing knowledge about learning to instruction in this course. A novel program conceptualization has prompted novel propositions about learning that require testing. For example, the developers hope to increase student capacity for political leadership through a combination of classroom instruction and laboratory experience in schools. Can this be done? What are the most effective ways to achieve this objective? These are questions that can be answered only through careful pilot testing and evaluation of the instructional products.

Problems of Multiple Developer Roles in
Small as Compared to Large Projects

Successful curriculum development depends upon the successful performance of multiple roles. For this reason curriculum development is typically described as a team process. Members of an ideal team include instructional designers, media technologists, specialists on human behavior, experts on the subject matter to be taught, evaluation specialists, and individuals responsible for diffusion. Large teams tend to limit the number of roles played by any single team member, leading each individual to specialize in one or a limited number of development functions. On a small team, in contrast, a developer may be asked to play many or all of the development roles at one time or another.

None of the curriculum development projects of the Indiana University Social Studies Development Center has had sufficient funds to employ a large, full-time, professional staff. Its development teams have, therefore, ranged in size from small (six people) to very small (two people). Despite the lack of opportunity to participate as a member of a large, curriculum development team, my experience as a member of teams of varying size has stimulated some observations about the chemistry of curriculum development and the kinds of personalities that may be attracted to various kinds of teams.

The opportunity to employ full-time specialists for particular aspects of curriculum development tends to ensure more professional performance of each member of the development team. For example, the quality of evaluation is likely to be better if the project can employ a full-time evaluator than if the evaluation function must be satisfied by instructional designers who occasionally use evaluation specialists to consult on the evaluation plan. On the other hand, the staff's overall commitment to the project may be higher when each individual must assume at least partial responsibility for many roles. The evaluator may be unconcerned, for example, if the production of materials begins to lag behind schedule or if the diffusion process is handled poorly because these functions are not his or her responsibility. The response of such an individual may be typical of assembly line workers in an automobile plant. If developers commit their own egos to each aspect of the project and their own reputations are on the line at each stage, however, they may become more deeply committed than if their responsibilities are more narrowly circum-scribed.

If the above is true, it may be that the type of personality needed for curriculum development will vary according to the size of the project and the degree of specialization it permits or requires. A person who is unhappy unless he can be involved in all phases of the development process should probably avoid large projects. The latter projects need to employ people who derive satisfaction from per-forming their specialized roles well; large projects also must seek ways to enhance norms of teamwork and a commitment to a joint enterprise, norms that are less necessary in a small project where the responsibility for the ultimate success or failure of the project as a whole can be clearly assigned to a very few people.

Stages of Curriculum Development

Curriculum development is a process through which an idea for improved instruction acquires concrete form, is tested in representa-tive settings, is revised and retested until judged successful, and is ultimately made available for use in classrooms throughout the na-tion. Thus, successful curriculum development not only requires that multiple developer roles be performed adequately; it also depends upon a set of procedures. Just as the quality of research is judged not only by the outcomes but also by the methods and procedures used by the researcher, so too developers are judged in part by their adherence to accepted procedures in the development process.

Table 7-2 identifies those steps in the development cycle that are practiced by the Far West Laboratory for Educational Research and Development. The most salient feature of the development process, as shown in that table, is the cycle of program preparation, testing, new preparation based upon test results, new testing, new revisions, and renewed testing described in the third through the ninth stages. Indeed, the principal characteristic that distinguishes the process of high quality curriculum development from high quality, but typical, publishing company practice is the dependence upon careful field testing of instructional products and the identification and elimina-tion of deficiencies prior to the publication and dissemination of the product. While textbook publishers increasingly accept the utility of testing instructional products prior to the manufacturing and

Table 7-2. Major steps in the development cycle

Steps	Functions
1. Research and data gathering	Includes review of literature, classroom observations, and preparation of report on the state of the art.
2. Planning	Includes definition of skills, statement of objectives, determination of course sequence, and small-scale feasibility testing.
3. Developing preliminary form of product	Includes preparation of instructional and model lessons, handbooks, and evaluation devices.
4. Preliminary field test	Conducted by Laboratory personnel in one, two, or three schools, using between six and twelve teachers. Includes collection and analysis of interview, observational, and questionnaire data.
5. Main product revision	Revision of product as suggested by preliminary field test results.
6. Main field test	Conducted by Laboratory personnel in between five and fifteen schools using between thirty and one hundred teachers. Includes collection of quantitative data on teachers' pre- and postcourse performances, usually in the form of classroom videotapes. Results are compared with course objectives.
7. Operational product revision	Revision of product as suggested by the main field-test results.
8. Operational field test	Conducted by regular school personnel in between ten and thirty schools, using between forty and two hundred teachers. Includes collection and analysis of interview, observation, and questionnaire data.
9. Final product revision	Review of product as suggested by operational field-test results.
10. Dissemination and distribution	Reports at professional meetings, in journals, etc. Includes work with publisher who assumes commercial distribution, and monitoring of distribution to provide quality control.

Source: Walter Borg, "Research-Based Development—A Strategy for Educational Change in the '70's," paper presented at a meeting of the Social Science Education Consortium, Denver, Colorado, June 13, 1970, reprinted with permission of Macmillan Publishing Co., Inc., from W. R. Borg, M. K. Kelley, P. Langer, and M. Gall, *The Minicourse: A Microteaching Approach to Teacher Education,* developed by Far West Laboratory for Educational Research and Development, copyright © 1971, Far West Laboratory for Educational Research and Development.

marketing of them, up until now the high costs of maintaining an authentic development cycle have discouraged publishers from incorporating full-scale development procedures into their own operations.

While the steps identified in Table 7-2 would satisfy most curriculum developers, it is possible to modify the table so as to emphasize some important features of the development process that might otherwise escape notice. Figure 7-1 represents steps in the development cycle as practiced by the Social Studies Development Center at Indiana University. It does not conflict in any important way with the Far West Laboratory list, but it has the advantage of showing how evaluation and diffusion permeate a project from beginning to end.

Though it is not possible to treat in detail each of the steps indicated in Figure 7-1, three of the steps deserve special attention because they are frequently misunderstood or undervalued. These steps are: design and conceptualization, diffusion, and evaluation.

Design and Conceptualization Stage

Articles about curriculum development tend to focus primarily on the procedures used to write and test instructional materials. Substantially less has been written about the design and conceptualization stage. And yet curriculum development is mostly the art of making good judgments, and decisions made in the first stage of a project can bless or curse the project throughout its duration.

The first stage of a curriculum development project should be approached with the same patience and attention that would ordinarily be accorded the start of a multiyear, team-directed research project. Indeed, the two types of enterprises require similar procedures in the beginning. The research team must have a clear statement of the problem in order to focus its research; the development team needs a thorough understanding of the curriculum problem it hopes to solve. It is necessary for the research team to have a theoretical framework or a logical structure to guide its inquiry; a rationale in which statements concerning goals are linked logically to one another accomplishes a similar purpose for the development team. A research team must decide on the context for its study; a development team has to choose which settings are most appropriate for project interventions. The research team formulates hypotheses to be

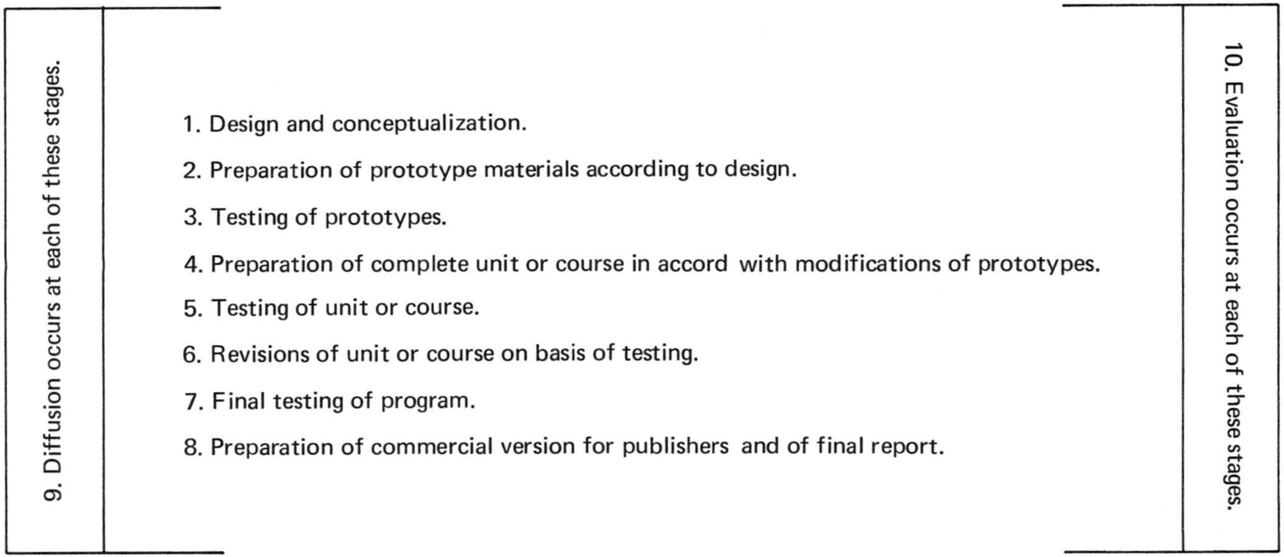

10. Evaluation occurs at each of these stages.

1. Design and conceptualization.

2. Preparation of prototype materials according to design.

3. Testing of prototypes.

4. Preparation of complete unit or course in accord with modifications of prototypes.

5. Testing of unit or course.

6. Revisions of unit or course on basis of testing.

7. Final testing of program.

8. Preparation of commercial version for publishers and of final report.

9. Diffusion occurs at each of these stages.

Figure 7-1. Major steps in the development cycle used by the Social Studies Development Center

tested by the study; the development team hypothesizes about the type of instructional product or practice that will resolve the curriculum problem, thus leading to desirable results, and tests the product in order to measure its effects.

There are other ways in which factors relating to curriculum development are similar to those accompanying educational research. Like researchers, curriculum developers are sensitive to peer approval. While the public posture is that developers attempt primarily to solve real problems in schools, in practice developers commit themselves to tasks that are professionally rewarding. Thus, what is defined as a "curriculum problem" is almost certain to be one that the developer finds interesting and one that has a reasonable chance to attract professional notice. Given the multiyear commitments that curriculum development projects require, developers must derive excitement and professional reward from a project if it is to secure their best efforts and prove successful.

Some writers discuss the conceptualization stage of the development process as if it were primarily a data-gathering exercise. According to this view developers conduct a "needs assessment," which includes appraising what the "target learners" know, sampling teachers' opinions, examining existing products, and consulting with experts in the subject field. After the data are collected, developers decide what should be done. It is a neat picture, but it is incomplete.

All of the activities listed above can be useful, but they are certain to leave developers dissatisfied. Knowledge of what a particular group of students thinks about a topic or of what the intellectual capabilities of a particular age group is can be helpful, but developers can seldom bear the expense of drawing a wide sample of youngsters, approaching the range they hope will ultimately use their work. Thus, the conclusions they reach are tenuous at best. When they sample the opinion of teachers, they are likely to learn that teachers "want" what they already have or what is available through commercial publishers. Although idiosyncratic desires may appear, developers can no more afford to trust them as representative of all teachers than they can their own judgments. If a large number of teachers want a particular product, it is almost certain that it already exists or that one or more publishers have a solution under way. While it is useful to examine competing products, these primarily inform developers about what *not* to do, as they should not devote energy and resources to replicating what exists. Subject-matter specialists can provoke developers' thinking, perhaps stimulating them to an interesting conceptualization, but most subject-matter authorities are insufficiently familiar with the schools to be very helpful. If a number of authorities agree on what should be done, moreover, it is likely to have been done before.

A major dilemma for developers is that they are not creating products to be used at the time they are conceptualizing the program; they must gaze into any available crystal ball and imagine what the schools will want five to seven years hence, when their project has terminated. The best way to be obsolete is to prepare a product the schools want *now*. Developers cannot be distracted by charges that the schools are not ready for their ideas. The question is, "Will they be ready or can they be prepared for them in six years?" Developers must speculate about the future characteristics of students, teachers, class scheduling, available technology, school budgets, educational ideologies, and the state of the discipline they represent.

Both funding agencies and developers are often troubled by the amount of time required to puzzle through the conceptualization stage. It is easy to become impatient and to want the preparation of materials to begin before basic commitments and conceptualizations are under control, but it is unwise to attempt to use shortcuts. On the one hand, developers must discipline themselves in order that they do not waste time during this beginning phase; on the other hand, they require the luxury to try out a wide range of ideas without being forced to make premature commitments.

Diffusion

Diffusion begins the day the project is funded and continues long after the development grant has expired. Not only is diffusion necessary for the success of the project, but the development team is obligated to share information about its work. Unlike textbook publishers who may try to withhold information about their new products for fear their competitors will steal their best ideas, by accepting a grant that buys their time to work on projects, developers must assume that their ideas, if not their products, are in the public domain. Usually curriculum development projects are supported by public agencies and private foundations for the purpose of affecting change in education; from the funder's point of view, it is better that ideas concerning the project are "stolen" and used than not used at all.

The purposes of diffusion vary across the life of a project. At the outset the development team should be eager to spread its ideas in order to gain feedback for revisions of the rationale and the statements on goals. The project staff is also trying to stimulate professional discussion about its ideas. It can do this by distributing its paper on conceptualization, by brochures, and by publishing newsletters and articles about the project. During the stages of testing the prototype and the full course, the developers are eager to gain feedback on their materials; they are also seeking to create a future market for their product. They can distribute widely examples of the instructional materials, demonstrate materials at conferences and meetings, and provide reports on the results of classroom testing. When the product has been published, the developer should help the publisher market the product validly and facilitate school adoptions. Developers should approve the marketing program, including advertisements about the project, and should assist the publisher by making presentations to state and school textbook adoption committees.

One product of the Social Studies Development Center is a high school civics course entitled *American Political Behavior* (APB). This program, published by Ginn and Company, was developed with support from the U. S. Office of Education. Although the grant for development was relatively small, making it impossible to employ people full-time to perform the role of diffusion, the project staff engaged actively in diffusion activities throughout the five-year life of the project. The developers published articles in professional journals, made more than one hundred presentations to professional audiences, produced "occasional papers" on various features of the project, and distributed thousands of examples of instructional materials from the course. In 1969-1970 the staff conducted six dissemination conferences in various regions of the nation for school officials who were eager to learn about a new approach to the study of politics and government.[2] In the spring of 1972 when the published materials appeared, the Center supported a former APB teacher to travel across the country to demonstrate the instructional materials to classroom teachers. During this period, and subsequently, the developers reserved large blocks of time for speaking about the project to various meetings of teachers and school officials. It is not accidental that the program experienced the best first year's sales of any social studies product in the history of Ginn and Company.

Evaluation

As in the case of diffusion, evaluation is a process that occurs throughout the life of a project and even beyond it. It begins when the development team seeks out critical readers to judge the rationale of the project, the statement of goals and assumptions about the competence of learners. An evaluator is clearly important in helping to select pilot schools, in designing instruments to test the efficacy of the instructional materials, in monitoring the field tests, and in interpreting the data for developers and ultimately for future adopters. And evaluation is needed as the materials are marketed in order to plan for future revisions.

Much is made of the distinction between "formative" and "summative" evaluation. According to Scriven, formative evaluation refers to those practices that produce data enabling developers to improve their products through revisions following classroom trials.[3] The primary consumer of formative evaluation data is the developer himself. Summative evaluation refers to an overall final evaluation of the product, the primary purpose of which is to produce information deemed useful to the ultimate consumer.

The principal problem with this formulation is that a fully useful and authentic summative evaluation is rarely provided. What typically passes for a summative evaluation is a control group-test group performance evaluation over the final, experimental version of the course. This version inevitably differs substantially from the one that will subsequently be published and marketed. By the time the published version of the program appears, the project has exhausted its funds and has ceased its operations; the publisher usually has little enthusiasm for conducting a summative evaluation of the published version and for disseminating the results. Consequently, consumers have access to evaluation results on the best, experimental version of the course but not on the version they can purchase. It would be helpful if, in the future, developers were to concentrate all their energies on the formative evaluation of their work prior to publication of the program. Then they should make certain that provision for a summative evaluation of the published program is made a part of the publisher's agreement.

Lesson Development

This chapter has discussed thus far the multiple roles developers play and the stages in the curriculum development process, with particular attention to conceptualization, diffusion, and evaluation. It has avoided the most time-consuming and critical part of the process: the production of instructional materials. And yet the best rationale, the most competent evaluation, and the most skillful diffusion are wasted if the individual units of instruction lack merit.

A number of developers have written about the production and testing phase of curriculum development in order to offer suggestions that may reduce the risk of failure and increase efficiency. What is wanted is some system of procedures that can streamline what is primarily a creative act.

Figure 7-2 is an example of one model developed to guide instructional development.[4] This model, created by Gene Faris and Richard Stowe, was prepared for use in an institute comprised of Indiana University professors. The purpose of the institute was to teach professors from a number of academic disciplines about instructional design. While the model was created to help professors improve their own courses and was not intended as a guide for curriculum developers generally, the principles contained in the model are common to the field of curriculum development.

The diagram is based on the development of a one-semester course, consisting of five units. The sixth through the fifteenth steps suggest a sequence for developing instructional materials within the third unit. The model is linear with possibilities for feedback loops, when revision seems necessary.

Although the entire diagram deserves discussion, the eighth and ninth steps are especially important. The eighth step asks the developer to state what a student can do prior to beginning instruction (entry behavior) and to state what a student will be able to do following instruction (terminal behavior). The ninth step requires that the developer indicate how he will measure the "terminal objectives" in order to ensure that learning occurs. In short, Faris and Stowe asked the professors to state their instructional objectives in behavioral terms and to write the tests they would use to measure their objectives prior to writing or selecting instructional materials.

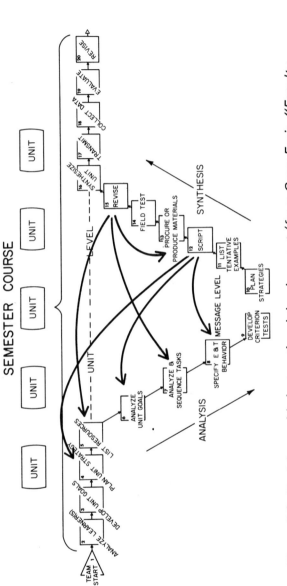

Figure 7-2. Model to guide instructional development (from Gene Faris, "Faculty Development—The Key to Instructional Development," Viewpoints, Bulletin of the School of Education, Indiana University 46 [March 1970] : 133)

Within the field of curriculum development, it is likely that more has been written about behavioral objectives—their use, analysis, classification, sequencing, and misuse—than any other single topic. It is not necessary to review this literature here, as it is familiar to those who follow curriculum development. It is appropriate, however, to indicate the extent to which the sequence described in Figure 7-2 has proved practical within the Social Studies Development Center.

Curriculum development is neither a linear nor a mechanical task. When developers begin work on a series of lessons, they have some goals in mind. If they lacked goals or purposes, they would wander aimlessly. Developers recognize, moreover, that eventually they must descend from the more abstract goals that guide a course or unit to the more specific and limited objectives that should be satisfied within a particular lesson. Nevertheless, it does not seem common for developers to specify each of their instructional objectives in detail, sequencing them from one lesson to the other and preparing measures of the objectives before they undertake the task of writing materials for students. There is, indeed, much more serendipity in the process than the sequential model suggests. A developer may begin with an idea for a new kind of game or simulation, leading him to search for a place to put it into the course; or he may have an idea for an application exercise before he has developed the lesson that will instruct students in what they will be asked to apply later.

It is probable that the developers who profit most by a careful specification of behavioral objectives and criterion measures prior to beginning lesson treatments are those who specialize in programmed instruction. For others, especially those who have the responsibility to develop semester-long or year-long courses to be directed by teachers, the need to vary instructional style, to prompt the student's interest, and to strengthen the teacher's sense of security and achievement seems very important. For such developers, the creative, instructional idea is more important initially than specifying lesson objectives. This seems frequently to encourage a reciprocal process in which developers move back and forth from a "great idea" for a lesson, to specifying the objectives that justify its place in the course sequence, to modifying the lesson once the objectives are stated, to a restatement of the objectives, to the preparation of a test over the objectives. By beginning with an idea for a lesson rather than with a statement of objectives, developers frequently find new objectives that might have been overlooked if they had tried to express them in advance of beginning work on the materials for students.

This is not an argument that goals and objectives are unimportant for curriculum development or that development occurs in only one way. It is, rather, intended to make clear that the creation of instructional materials is more dynamic and spontaneous than Figure 7-2 indicates, even with its feedback loops. When a project's materials are finally published, the instructional objectives, the treatment, and the criterion measures may appear as an integrated piece supporting competency-based instruction, but it is unlikely that they were developed as systematically as the teacher's guide might imply.

Universities as Sites for Curriculum Development

A major task for funding agencies that want to support projects in curriculum development is making judgments about whom to support and about the kind of institutional base that is necessary for high quality development. During the past two decades much money has been wasted because unwise investments were made in agencies or in people who lacked the necessary capabilities.

Four different types of agencies have received grants for curriculum development: school districts, regional laboratories, colleges and universities, and industry. All four have sponsored successful projects; each has experienced failure. No foundation can be certain that investing its funds in one kind of agency as opposed to another will ensure success.

Richard Schutz has argued that development in education can be done more effectively by industry than by higher education.[5] He claims this to be true because universities are characterized by "individual autonomy, conceptual elegance, and fragmented specialization." This has permitted universities to become ideal sites for educational research but poor places for curriculum development.

In my opinion, Schutz is mistaken in his belief regarding the capacities for universities to sponsor curriculum development. It is true that some university-based curriculum development projects have failed in the past, that sponsoring curriculum development is a relatively new experience for most universities, and that many universities may prove unable or unwilling to establish the conditions necessary to support successful curriculum development. But similar qualifications could be made about industry.

In other professional fields, most notably medicine, engineering, and agriculture, universities have long been recognized for their leadership in both research and development. This suggests that universities are capable of supporting development as well as research. The fact that educational development, particularly curriculum development, has not achieved a stature equal to development in agriculture, engineering, and medicine on university campuses probably says more about the relative maturity of curriculum development as a professional field than about the capacity of universities to provide stimulating and productive settings.

It is likely that some minimum conditions are required to support successful curriculum development within any institution. At present it seems more useful to discover what these minimum conditions are than to speculate about which agency can or cannot support development optimally.

It is unfortunate that no agreed upon set of conditions currently exists. Henry Brickell, an experienced observer and evaluator of curriculum development, has, however, offered "14 Points" that he believes merit scrutiny. While the validity of his conditions remains to be tested, he hypothesizes that, when they are absent, it is unlikely that high quality development will occur. His points are as follows:

1. A group of highly intelligent people with differentiated roles. Note that a group is required—not simply an individual.
2. Fundamental knowledge of human behavior—that is, the working members of the group must have available a working knowledge of how human beings behave.
3. Fundamental knowledge of the subject content to be taught.
4. Media expertness.
5. A limited problem.
6. Available time.
7. A special place in which to work.
8. An expected product.
9. Proper equipment and materials.
10. Knowledge of parallel efforts.
11. Freedom to design almost any promising approach—freedom to break the boundaries of past practice.
12. Try-out situations.
13. The likelihood that the innovation will be used.
14. The prospect of personal recognition if the innovation is successful.[6]

Limits on space do not permit treating each of these points individually. It is possible, nevertheless, to draw upon the experience of one university-based curriculum development center—the Indiana University Social Studies Development Center—for observations about a few of Brickell's conditions. The commentary will indicate also some of the advantages and disadvantages university sites offer curriculum developers.

A Development Team

Successful curriculum development requires a group of people working together toward a mutual goal. Many factors make a group of people necessary. First, no single individual possesses all the skills and knowledge needed for high quality curriculum development. The team requires people with special knowledge of the subject matter, with knowledge of how children learn, with evaluation skills, with technical skills in media development, and with instructional experience at the grade level and in the subject matter to be treated. When these competencies are not satisfied by members of the team, they can be met in part through consultants. It is better, nevertheless, that team members possess these competencies and use consultants only to supplement their strengths. A typical cause for the failure of university-based curriculum development has been overdependence upon one or two individuals who were presumed to know all that was required or who expected to draw upon consultants for the information and skills they lacked.

Need to Tap University Resources Broadly

It is important that the curriculum development team be able to draw upon the university as a whole for its support and not be tied too closely to any one school or division. For example, a development project that is viewed only as an activity of the school of education may have problems in securing the cooperation of those who are not members of the faculty of education. One way to avoid this problem is to provide a separate location for the curriculum development project rather than base it within a single school or department. This puts the project on neutral ground, making it somewhat easier for people from any school or division to work there. It also removes staff members from their regular offices, thereby tending to divorce them from the normal academic pressures that compete for their time and attention. Finally, it helps stimulate the development of new norms that fit the group, that support their work, and that sustain them in the face of occasionally hostile academic norms and traditional departmental or divisional prejudices.

Professional Recognition

Successful development requires that the staff members consider themselves developers first and university professors second. If the developers give primary attention to their classes, to their doctoral students, and to their committee assignments, development will suffer. Despite the enormous pressures on academic personnel to assign development activities to a role secondary to their academic work, techniques exist to alter the balance of values. One has been mentioned earlier: remove the personnel from their department offices and base them in separate quarters that make possible the growth of new, psychologically satisfying norms. A second is to provide opportunities for the development staff to maintain professional visibility within the project. An evaluation specialist may find, for example, that he has a greater opportunity to advance professionally via a curriculum development project than by continuing in a typical academic position. This requires opportunities to publish the results of project work, to deliver papers at professional meetings, and to attend conferences. Third, it is important that the administration of the university be willing to accord the products of curriculum development the same status as the products of basic research. While many of a developer's colleagues will be slow to appreciate curriculum development, university administrators are often willing to recognize high quality productive work in whatever form it takes and to reward it.

If the conditions for group work described above can be achieved, then universities appear to be ideal sites for curriculum development. No other setting can match the range of human and intellectual resources that are efficiently and economically available on a typical campus. Regional laboratories, schools, and industry cannot duplicate the library resources of a university; university-based curriculum development centers can attract personnel who would not accept positions in other kinds of institutions; university-based developers have informal access to consultants who would demand consultant fees and travel expenses for providing similar advice to other agencies. Finally, university-based developers may be under somewhat less pressure to yield to immediate market demands than industry-based curriculum developers. While universities present some problems for supporting high quality curriculum development, it seems likely that on some campuses at least the conditions for curriculum development will be met as well as in any other setting.

Conclusion

Curriculum development has struggled for nearly two decades to establish itself as a legitimate and important field for professional activity in education—not identical to teaching, although contributing to instruction; not research, although based on research and contributing to knowledge; not service, although helping schools to do their job better. Curriculum development is a relatively new field in education. It has attracted people who are eager to help schools change and who wish to contribute more than pious hopes to the process. And it continues to search for procedures and standards that will discourage charlatans and dilettantes and provide satisfying professional lives to the talented and committed. As the public demand for accountability of teachers grows, one may anticipate an increasing demand among teachers that their instructional materials also be held accountable. Curriculum development exists to foster and to satisfy this demand.

Notes

1. In 1965 the schema appeared in an unpublished paper, David L. Clark and Egon G. Guba, "An Examination of Potential Change Roles in Education," presented to the Seminar on Innovation in Planning School Curricula, October 1965, 8; the schema was subsequently published as Essay 6 in *Rational Planning in Curriculum and Instruction,* ed. Ole Sand (Washington, D. C.: National Education Association, Center for the Study of Instruction, 1967), 116.

2. These conferences were supported by the U.S. Office of Education, but by a different branch from the one that supported the curriculum development project. The teacher-training branch gave the institute proposal the highest rating possible on the basis of the quality of the ideas, but at first refrained from funding the proposal because "it did not seem proper for the Office of Education to support an institute whose purpose was to disseminate a single program." The proposal was funded ultimately when it was pointed out that the program to be disseminated was one that another branch of the USOE was supporting and that, if the project was not worth disseminating, it should be abolished. This

attitude by the USOE can be contrasted to the attitude of the National Science Foundation, which is one of concentrating its dissemination support on projects the NSF has supported.

3. Michael Scriven, "The Methodology of Evaluation," in *Perspectives of Curriculum Evaluation*, AERA Monograph Series on Curriculum Evaluation (Chicago: Rand McNally, 1967), 39-83.

4. Instructional development is distinguished here from curriculum development or instructional materials development. In the latter two cases the purpose is to design replicable instructional materials, including entire courses, that can be used by others. Instructional development, however, is used to refer to the process by which one improves his or her own course of study, which might include the development of new materials as well as the more effective utilization of materials prepared by others.

5. Richard E. Schutz, "The Conduct of Development in Education," unpublished paper from the Southwest Regional Laboratory of Educational Research and Development, Los Alamitos, California, 7.

6. Henry M. Brickell, "Needed Research on Development," unpublished paper presented to the Ohio State University College of Education, March 8, 1973, 8-9.

8 Curriculum Development in Stanford's Kettering Project: Recollections and Ruminations

Elliot W. Eisner

This chapter describes from the vantage point of a four-year perspective the curriculum development work undertaken under my direction in the area of elementary school art education. In order to understand the nature of this work and its place in the history of the field of art education, it is necessary to know something about the character of teaching art at the time the project was under way. The first section of the chapter describes some of the salient characteristics of the field at the time. The second section describes the specific purposes of the project and the way in which the work was organized. The third section addresses itself to the theories and beliefs that gave direction to the curriculum development work as well as pointing out the limitations of theoretical ideas in the practical context of curriculum development. Finally, the chapter discusses the potential virtues of alternative approaches to the curriculum development process.

The Background and Aims of the Kettering Project

In September 1968, with the support of the Charles F. Kettering Foundation, I initiated a two-year project aimed at developing cur-

147

ricula and instructional materials that would improve the quality of art education in American elementary schools.[1] Although in 1968 the curriculum development movement was over ten years old, the formal and systematic development of curriculum in the field of elementary art education had hardly begun. Though in mathematics, the sciences, the social studies, and English, large-scale national projects had been launched, in art education no national project had as yet been funded.

The need for curriculum development programs in art was, I believed, apparent to anyone familiar with the general quality of art education at the elementary school level in the United States. Most school districts employed few or no art teachers at the elementary school level, and the large urban districts that had trained art teachers used them as itinerants who had limited contact with both children and teachers. Thus, most of the teaching of art that was provided in elementary schools was handled by teachers who themselves possessed little skill or understanding in this area. The majority of students encountered their first trained art teacher at the junior or senior high school levels. The best data available[2] indicate that at the senior high school level only 17 percent of the students took as much as one year of art. Furthermore, only about half of all high schools in the country offered art as a part of their curriculum.[3]

This then was the educational context against which the purposes of the Kettering Project, as it was called, were formed. I was interested in starting at the beginning of the students' school experience and in developing resources—both written and visual—that elementary school teachers not trained in art could use to improve the quality of art education they provided their students.

The statistical and demographic features I described concerning the availability of trained art teachers, the incidence of art programs in senior high schools, and the percentage of students who elected to study art represent only a portion of the picture that needs to be painted concerning the character of art education in the United States in 1968—and to a lesser degree today. The philosophic orientation of teachers, especially at the elementary school level, concerning the teaching of art is equally, perhaps even more important.

This orientation on the part of elementary school teachers has over the years grown out of a child-centered laissez-faire attitude concerning the purpose of art education and how a teacher should

behave with respect to the teaching of art. For many teachers childrens' art—their paintings, drawings, constructions, and sculpture—is
seen as an expression of the child's personality and level of physical
and intellectual development. While this assumption is undoubtedly
true, too often teachers, because of this and other beliefs, errone-
ously conclude that they should not try to influence children in art
but rather they should provide the materials and stimulation and
allow the student simply to explore them as best he can. Art, it is
believed, is not so much taught as it is caught. The programmed
developmental stages through which the child passes are believed to
define and determine what he is capable of doing in art: teachers
should not "interfere" with the natural development of the child in
this area.

This child-centered, naively developmental view of childhood is
accompanied by some very real practical problems that the teacher
encounters. Perhaps the most important of these is the fact that since
the teacher is likely to possess little in the way of artistic skill, either
in the realm of technique or in that area dealing with the perception
and appreciation of visual form, she finds it exceedingly difficult—
even if she wanted to—to provide the kind of educational guidance
that would foster the artistic development of her students. The philosophic rationale that the teacher holds, that of encouraging children
to explore without intervention, advice, or teaching, is one way of
rationalizing her lack of competency as a teacher of art.

I have provided this description of the educational context for the
teaching of art at the elementary school level in order that the reader
have a better understanding of goals toward which the project was
directed. Those goals were then, and are to a lesser degree today,
iconoclastic. They rested upon assumptions, values, and evidence
that were antithetical to many of the practices and beliefs about art
teaching that were prevalent at the time.

In preparing the proposal for the Charles F. Kettering Foundation,
it was necessary to make explicit a number of ideas that were to
provide guidance in curriculum development efforts. First, it was
made clear that the curriculum being proposed was one that included
what I have called in previous writing "the productive," "the critical," and "the historical" aspects of art.[4] The productive realm
focused upon helping children acquire the skills necessary for converting a material into a medium for artistic expression. The critical

realm emphasized the development of the student's ability to see what he looked at, to cultivate his ability to encounter visual forms from an aesthetic frame of reference and through such a frame to acquire aesthetic experience. The historical realm attempted to help the student understand that art is created in the context of a culture, that the culture influences the form and content of art, and that art in turn influences the culture.

Two of these three realms—the critical and the historical—have not been integral parts of the art curriculum at the elementary level. Most elementary school art programs have emphasized the productive realm. Teachers have not been seriously concerned with the development of artistic vision or with the child's comprehension of either contemporary art or the art of the past.[5]

A second feature of the proposed curriculum was that it was to have a sequential character. The desirability of sequence was due to the recognition that few elementary art programs provided continuity within them. Itinerant art teachers work with a class only occasionally and often initiate class projects that can be completed in "one sitting." Regular classroom teachers tend to believe that the wider the variety of projects and materials they allow children to work with the better; hence they too often offer children not so much an art program as a collection of unrelated art "activities" that are so brief in duration that children seldom have the time necessary for developing the skills that make artistic expression possible.

A third feature of the curriculum proposed to the foundation was that it should contain a wide variety of visual materials that are especially designed to develop the skills identified in the written curriculum guide. It was quite apparent that in the physical sciences, for example, curriculum developers had provided devices that visually illustrate Newton's third law. Why could not similar devices be prepared for teaching the visual arts? It seemed ironic that in a field concerned with vision, so few specially designed visual materials were available. One of the goals of the project was to prepare such materials and to relate them directly to tasks and objectives that appeared in the written curriculum guides.

A fourth feature of the proposal was its attention to the development of evaluation devices or procedures for each of the lessons and units that were to be created. I took the view, which was not widely shared at that time in the field, that it was possible to determine in a reliable and accurate way the extent to which artistic learning had occurred. Evidence of such learning is manifested not only in the quality of products children create but in the insight, sensitivity, and relevance of their remarks about works of art and other aspects of the environment. I believed it was possible, in addition, to create exercises or tests that would in specific ways elicit such skill if it had been developed in the first place.

The Kettering Project was, in sum, an effort to develop a sequentially ordered curriculum in art that contained both a written syllabus and a wide array of visual support materials that elementary school teachers could use to increase the quality of the art programs they provided their students.

How Work on the Project Was Organized

Because the grant for the project covered a two-year period, a number of tasks had to be undertaken and completed during that period of time. These included the refinement of the ideas presented in the proposal, creation of a structure for writing the syllabus, acquisition of staff for the project, production and field-testing of lessons, construction of the visual materials to accompany the lessons, evaluation and revision of both written and visual materials on the basis of field-testing, location of schools wishing to participate in the project, construction of evaluation instruments, and preparation of a final report to the foundation. Had I as director of the project fully appreciated the complexity and magnitude of the curriculum development task, I would have requested funds to cover a four-, rather than a two-year period. But, unfortunately, I did not do so and thus was forced to work within the two-year frame.

My first task after being notified that support would be forthcoming was to select eight doctoral students, five in the field of art education and three in general curriculum at Stanford University who were to work on the project during the two-year period. These students were joined by a student in product design who was to provide some of the artistic expertise for the construction of visual materials. The doctoral students and I formed the primary core responsible for the major decisions during the life of the project. This group of nine people met regularly each week to consider, for example, the way in which the curriculum would be structured, to write lessons, and to review what each had created. I tried during the two-year period to fulfill two responsibilities: to provide the leadership necessary for the project to succeed; and to make the project one that would contribute to the education of my students. This meant that decisions that I might have made more efficiently on an arbitrary basis were made less efficiently with respect to action, but more effectively in relation to the contributions that group deliberation made to the education of the students who worked with me. Furthermore, I wanted the students to feel that this was *our* project, not simply *my* project; hence collective decision making was something that I encouraged. Only when perseveration became acutely frustrating or grossly unproductive did I attempt to resolve arbitrarily an issue being discussed.

Once the core group was formed I shared with each member the proposal that was submitted to the foundation, and I described in detail the rationale for the project and some of the goals I hoped an effective curriculum would achieve. These sessions were used to orient members of the group to the kind of work that was ahead of us and to reemphasize and clarify through discussion the leading ideas constituting my thinking about the teaching of art at the elementary school level. It was clear that the kind of understanding I wanted the core group to acquire could not be compressed and secured within three or four staff meetings. Such understanding needed time to grow and would, it was hoped, occur during the course of the curriculum development work. Yet I wanted to establish a foundation that was firm enough to let the members understand the function of the project and thus feel intellectually secure in what they were trying to accomplish.

The work for the project was divided in two phases. The first phase was devoted to conceptualization of the format or structure to be used for writing lessons and designing instructional materials; writing lessons and having them critiqued by the group; designing instructional materials to accompany the written materials; securing teachers and classrooms for initial field-testing; revising the materials, both written and visual, as a result of initial field-testing.

The core group decided to invite elementary school teachers to join the group as consultants and to use their classrooms as the places in which the initial testing of the materials would take place. Four teachers, each of whom worked in a different elementary school near

Stanford University, were subsequently employed as consultants to the project. Their role was to read the material that had been prepared and to let us know what aspects of the work were clear, obscure, useful, relevant, or significant. The teachers were, in a very real sense, our contact with educational reality, and, although we did not expect or want them to function as experts on art, they were informed about and sensitive to children and to life in their classrooms and were in a position to tell us whether what we were developing had any chance of succeeding in an elementary school classroom.

Thus, the staff of the Kettering Project for the first year of its existence consisted of a project director, five doctoral students in art education, three doctoral students in general curriculum, one master's student in product design, and four elementary school teachers. Meetings consisting of the project director and the students occurred two to four times per week, while meetings that included the teachers occurred once every month to six weeks. Virtually all meetings were held in a small house located about half a block from the Stanford School of Education. All of the doctoral students were on about half-time support during their work on the project, which meant that they were usually enrolled in two graduate courses per quarter.

One of the first tasks to be undertaken after the initial orientation session was the development of a structure or format that could be used to organize our lesson writing and that could be easily read by elementary school teachers. Although the rationale for the project and the three realms of artistic learning had been formulated, the specific format within which our curriculum writing would occur had not been developed. I now believe, although I did not appreciate it at the time, that decisions about the character and form of this format are crucial for the process of curriculum development. This format reveals implicitly the assumptions and values embedded in a project and provides the constraints within which curriculum writers must work. It is clear that when eight to ten people come together to prepare a syllabus for others to use, some common format must be developed that all members of the group can use if the syllabus is to have continuity and cohesiveness. We devoted the first month of the project to the development of the categories that would constitute the format for our work. These categories were:

1. Concept;
2. Principle;
3. Objective;
4. Rationale;
5. Introductory Motivating Activity;
6. Learning Activity 1, 2, 3;
7. Evaluation Procedures;
8. Materials Needed.

"Concept" referred to an idea, such as color, or line, that was the focus for a unit. A unit consisted of seven to ten lessons. "Principle" referred to a general proposition about the concept that the curriculum was designed to help children understand in some way. Thus, "Color can express feeling" is a principle in which the concept color is embedded. "Objective" referred to instructional objectives that, it was hoped, the children would attain. "Rationale" provided the teachers with reasons that justified the importance of the concept, principle, and objective we had formulated. The "Introductory Motivating Activity" was a procedure we suggested to help the teacher prepare the students for the lesson. "Learning Activity 1, 2, 3" refers to the fact that each lesson contained one to three learning activities, each of which we believed was instrumental to the achievement of the objective for that lesson. The availability of three learning activities was intended to provide teachers with choices regarding the learning activity that seemed most suitable for their particular classes. "Evaluation Procedures" described how the effectiveness of the lesson or unit could be evaluated, while "Materials Needed" listed the materials we provided and those the teacher needed to provide to use that particular lesson.

As I have already indicated, each unit consisted of seven to ten lessons. This meant that, once a teacher chose a unit, it was hoped she would stay with it to its culmination. We did not encourage teachers to shift from lesson to lesson in different units since we believed this would vitiate any continuity that we were able to build into our materials. The organization of lessons into a unit is schematically illustrated in Figure 8-1.

Using the curriculum format described above, we selected seven units for the development of lessons. In the productive realm units focused upon drawing, graphics, and painting. In the critical realm units dealt with line, color, and composition. In the historical realm

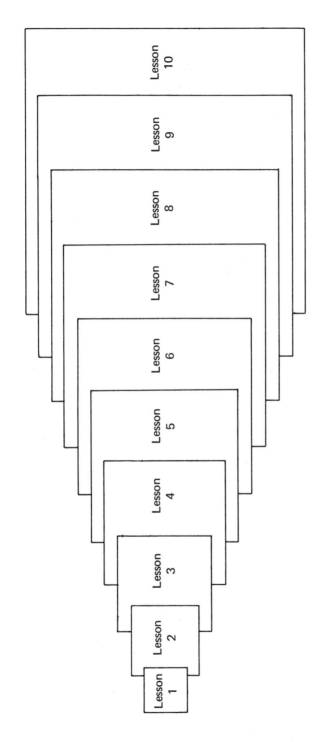

Figure 8-1. The organization of lessons into a unit

they concentrated upon the general features of art history. Using these units, the core group of the project staff produced sixty-seven lessons and about seven hundred pieces of specifically designed instructional materials that accompanied the lessons in the units. These materials, both written and visual, are sufficient for over two years of art instruction assuming that a teacher allocates about two hours per week to the study or creation of art.

How the Group Worked

To produce the lessons within each of the units the core group was organized into teams of two members each. These teams were responsible for writing ten lessons in each of the units and for conceptualizing the type of visual support materials that they believed would increase the effectiveness of the lessons. Our working procedures provided for each team to write a draft version of the lesson and to have it reviewed by either the project director or by the total group. After this initial review, the material was revised and reviewed by the teachers who served as consultants. Following their recommendations the lesson was used in the classroom of the teacher-consultant, and subsequently further revisions were made.

It is important to note here that the process of group planning and review of curriculum materials is complicated and time consuming. Even seemingly minor decisions, such as whether to use slides of works of art or cardboard reproductions for a particular lesson could elicit a full hour or more of discussion. Though these discussions appeared to some to be inefficient and frustrating, I am convinced they are a necessary part of curriculum planning. I will not explain here why I believe this to be true, but later I will go into the matter in some detail.

As was already indicated, the teams that wrote curriculum were also responsible for conceptualizing the instructional support materials to accompany their written work. In most cases members of the team also constructed these materials and made seven copies of each so that eight complete sets of materials were available for testing in classrooms. When the materials were especially complex or could not be efficiently fabricated by a team member, the student who served as our product designer undertook the responsibility for production. As I have noted earlier, the project produced about seven hundred pieces of visual instructional materials, each having a code number corresponding to a number found within a lesson in a particular unit.

The first phase of the project, which extended from October 1, 1968, to August 1, 1969, culminated in the production of two large syllabi containing the units for each of the three realms of artistic learning that the project was interested in fostering. Also produced were eight pairs of "Kettering Boxes" which contained sets of instructional support materials. These materials, both written and visual, had been revised at least two times, and most of the lessons had been tried out in the classroom by teacher-consultants or by members of the team that developed the materials.

The second phase, which occurred during the second year of the project, was one in which the demonstration of the materials expanded from four teachers to twenty teachers working in five schools in two school districts near Stanford University. During this stage of the project units that were not completed during the first phase were concluded, and observations of the use of the curriculum and instructional resource materials continued.

Because it was my aspiration as project director to develop materials that did not require extensive in-service education, only one formal in-service session was held for the twenty elementary school teachers who participated in the project during the second year. Whatever additional in-service education that occurred was provided informally by the core staff as they observed teachers and students when they were using the materials in class.

In addition to expanding the field tests of the curriculum materials that were developed, the second phase became the period in which evaluation procedures and instruments needed to be developed. With most of the curriculum development work completed by March 1968, the attention of the staff shifted to the conceptualization of aspects of artistic learning that were to be evaluated in ways that were not provided for in the evaluation procedures suggested at the end of each lesson. This effort required for its successful completion as much time and support as went into the development of the curriculum itself. The project staff did not have the amount of time nor I the kind of resources that would have been optimal. Nevertheless, the types of competencies the staff sought to assess and the procedures that were conceptualized were, in my opinion, promising and ambitious. These materials included appraisal of the visual products that children in the classes produced, interviews with teachers, and analyses of the written comments they made in the curriculum syllabus that they were using. Evaluation procedures also employed specially prepared tests of comprehension. The staff of the project made every effort within the time constraints to secure a wide variety of evaluative information that would be useful in determining the effects of the project on the students as well as those aspects of the curriculum that needed further revision. The data from these procedures and instruments were collected in May and June of 1969 and analyzed during July and August.

As the last formal task of the project a final report was prepared for the foundation. This report was divided into eight sections, and each member of the core staff was asked to prepare a chapter or portion of the report. As project director, I wrote both the introductory and concluding chapters and reviewed all of the material prepared by the staff. In addition to the final report, which described the project in detail and which presented a critical analysis of its strengths and weaknesses, a collection of sample lessons was also prepared. This collection was intended to provide those interested in the project with material necessary for understanding the format of the lessons and the level of detail with which they were written. Thus, two final written products were prepared during the summer and fall of 1969: a final report and a collection of sample lessons from each of the units that had been written.

One might ask after a substantial fiscal investment,[6] not to mention the investment in time and energy, how the results of the project were disseminated to the field of art education, aside from the information provided in the final report and sample lessons. To disseminate information about the project to the field a wide variety of channels became available, most of which were neither consciously sought nor anticipated. These channels emerged, in part because of a growing interest in the work we had done and in part because the ideas in the project were a "natural" part of ideas I worked with professionally in the field. I prepared, for example, two articles for two of the major journals published in the field of art education.[7] One of these was published when the project was initiated and described its goals and rationale; the other was published after the project had been completed and provided a description of what we had learned. Other channels for dissemination included invitations to speak about the project at conferences and conventions. The *New York Times* and the *Christian Science Monitor* had articles about the project. One of the largest school districts in the United States asked me to make a video tape dealing with the project for in-service training of teachers. The state of Hawaii invited some of the core staff and me to work with elementary school teachers to develop materials similar to those used in the Kettering Project that would be appropriate for schools in Hawaii. When I was in England and Israel I described the project to various groups of educators in those countries. In addition, people in art education from various parts of this country had visited schools where the materials were being used. The opening chapter in *Programs of Promise*[8] is devoted to a description of the Kettering Project, and my own book. *Educating Artistic Vision*,[9] describes the project in some detail. I am, in addition, using the materials and ideas of the project in my own teaching and training of teachers. Finally, the California State Curriculum Framework for the Visual Arts[10] recommends an approach to curriculum development that, in significant measure, grew out of the curriculum development work done on the Kettering Project.

As I have indicated, these channels for dissemination were not systematically contrived at any point during the life of the project. I knew, of course, that a final report would be written, but I did not plan the events or opportunities that flowed after the work had been completed. It is important to point out that in disseminating information about the project there was no attempt to offer the curriculum as either a completed or a flawless program. In the first place, I realized at the outset that it would be impossible within a two-year period to produce a finished program that would be either educationally optimal or commercially marketable. In the second place, whenever lectures were delivered or articles published, we made every effort to point out the difficulties and limitations of the work as well as its benefits. We did not attempt to market the materials, either literally or psychologically, to the professional public. Our main concern, in addition to developing the best materials we could produce, was to acquire a more adequate understanding of the problems involved in curriculum development work and to share such understanding with those in the field.

Theories Used to Develop Curriculum Materials

I have described thus far the goals of the Kettering Project and the kinds of tasks that were undertaken in its first and second phases. This information was provided so that the reader could understand the relationship of the project to the ideas that were employed in its development.

When one talks about theories underlying or guiding work in curriculum development, there are at least two aspects of the term "theory" that need clarification. If by "theory" is meant a systematic set of interrelated statements that explain, through their power to predict specific consequences flowing from certain conditions, then theory in education generally and in curriculum particularly can be used in only the loosest sense. If ideas that are used to guide action and if general beliefs about what children ought to learn are considered theoretical, then this is much more like the status of theoretical ideas in curriculum work than the type of theory referred to earlier.

A second clarification deals with the referent of theory—that to which theoretical ideas refer. In work in curriculum development, theory can refer to ideas about the nature of the subject matter being taught, about how children learn, or about how a particular enterprise might pursue its work. For example, aesthetic theory deals with explanations concerning the defining characteristics of art, behaviorism presents ideas that purport to explain the conditions necessary for learning, and organizational theory is supposed to explain why an organization functions the way it does and by implication what sorts of changes might make it more productive.

In the development of the lessons and the visual materials one psychological idea guided much of what we produced. That idea deals with the process of visual differentiation. We worked with the idea that seeing is not identical with looking; the former is an achievement verb while the latter is a task verb.[11] Seeing is an accomplishment, something that is learned, and it is not an automatic consequence of maturation. Hence in the development of materials and tasks we were intent on providing visual images that students could compare and contrast so that in the process they would become more visually differentiated. That is, they would gradually become able to see visual qualities in visual form that previously went unseen. To do this required that we produce tasks and materials whose differences from a visual point of view were at first obvious. The differences between visual images students were asked to look at and compare gradually became increasingly subtle. Many of the materials we developed, such as transparent overlay boards that were used to alter the quality of reproductions of works of art, were intended to foster visual differentiation.

The point here is that beliefs about both what is desirable from an educational point of view (developing greater visual differentiation) and beliefs about the ways in which such learning can be fostered were important in providing direction to our practical work.

Another idea that played an important role in our work concerned the importance of time and practice in the acquisition of the skills necessary for artistic expression. First, in my writing in the field of art education I have differentiated between expression and what might be called self-disclosure.[12] The former requires that an individual have sufficient control over a material to be able to use it as a medium for expression. Expression requires the application of intelligence for the purpose of converting a material into a medium.[13]

To be able to achieve expressive ends with materials requires, from an educational point of view, that the student have sufficient time and opportunity to acquire, practice, and refine the necessary skills. In the language of curriculum discourse both continuity and sequence should be provided for in the materials developed. These ideas about the meaning of expression and the conditions necessary for its achievement function, in practical terms, as the intellectual justification for the development of units as compared with a grab bag or an ad hoc approach to the development of learning activities.

The significance of these theoretical beliefs in our work in curriculum development can perhaps be better appreciated if we mention some psychological ideas that we did not employ. The concept of reinforcement (a central idea in behaviorism) was nowhere purposefully employed in the preparation of written materials. We did not want teachers to use, for example, secondary reinforcers to sustain interest or to motivate children. The idea of giving Brownie points for work completed would have been abhorrent to the group, and at no time was it considered.

Another idea that was not employed was that of using immediate, as compared to delayed, feedback to guide or reinforce the student's learning. This psychological idea simply was not a part of the intellectual body of beliefs that gave direction to our efforts and consequently was not considered when we prepared our written materials for teachers.

In discussing the ideas that were central and those that were absent from the project, I do not wish to imply that ideas about visual differentiation and those dealing with continuity and sequence provided prescriptions that must be followed. While some ideas were of greater significance than others, it is more accurate to say that these ideas were embedded in a constellation of more general ideas about art, education, and artistic learning that had permeated my writing for about a decade. These ideas formed what Walker[14] has called a platform: they constituted a body of beliefs that were shared by members of the project staff and that provided an almost inarticulated covenant that gave direction to our work.

It is both interesting and significant that the beliefs that become a shared aspect of group endeavors often seem to be internalized by members in a covert way, much as social habits are learned during childhood. The language that becomes salient in a group, the way in which values are communicated, the general intellectual style of leading group members seem to create a climate—or a culture—to which members adapt. In our case there was no manifesto that presented the values and beliefs the group came to share. In the first place, an important characteristic of deeply held beliefs and values is their ineffable quality, and yet this does not mean they are not communicable. I believe, in fact, that the total configuration of decisions within a group expresses, and at the same time reinforces, such beliefs and values.

Though curriculum development on the scale on which we worked is inevitably a group enterprise, there is virtually nothing in the literature on curriculum that discusses curriculum development from the standpoint of group processes. When one thinks of the types of theory guiding curriculum work, the most prominent ideas that come to mind are those concerning how people learn and the nature of the subject to be learned. For example, *Science, A Process Approach,* is structured largely by ideas about the nature of cognitive operations and the conditions that will refine them, while *Man: A Course of Study* is based on certain significant ideas that are believed to be important for children to learn and understand. When it comes to ideas that can be used to structure curriculum development groups in order to maximize ideational fluency, social compatibility, or morale, little is available in the written material published in the field of curriculum. Yet, for groups that organize their work as ours did, the importance of group process is enormous. We found that while psychological ideas, for example, could provide some general guidance, they were too general to be of much use in making specific decisions concerning a particular lesson or instructional support material. While members of the core group used such ideas as a general intellectual backdrop, we had to employ sustained deliberation to arrive at a decision with which we could feel comfortable. There are several good reasons why these deliberations required so much time. First, we were trying to anticipate the possible effects of taking one course of action rather than another. Since theoretical ideas are by definition general, and since we were dealing with a specific instance, we could not confidently extrapolate from the theory to the consequence of the action we were considering. We felt compelled, therefore, to explore a wide range of possible consequences flowing from a particular action in order to avoid miseducational side effects. Blind alleys as well as direct routes need to be identified, and group deliberation is one way of doing this.

Second, through group deliberation a variety of perspectives is presented. This variety makes it possible to see the problem from different angles; thus, when one makes a decision it is much more likely to have been arrived at after having compared it to a host of alternatives. It is paradoxical that "inefficiency" in group deliberation can be more efficient than efficiency.

Third, it is often the case as revealed in group deliberation that more than one educational value attends to a variety of decisions being considered. In a sense the decision finally reached is partly a matter of which group member has been most persuasive in the decision-making process. For example, there are assets and liabilities attached to the use of, say, cardboard reproductions of works of art as compared to colored slides. The former are easily movable, and there is no need to turn down the lights. However, the quality of such reproductions is inferior, and some might not have the very qualities that one hopes children will learn to experience. Slides, while often of high visual quality, require a darkened room, a screen, and a projector. In addition, teachers might not want to take the time to set up the equipment if only a few slides are to be shown.

What happens in group deliberation is that the pros and cons, from an educational, practical, psychological, and social point of view, are discussed. The decision the group finally makes will depend not only on the "objective" evidence but on the persuasiveness of a member who feels deeply and argues cogently about either slides or reproductions.

Because the actors in this drama are human, all of the human emotions come into play. Group members gradually learn how to couch their criticism in forms that are not so abrasive. There are times when someone's ego must be the salient consideration. In short, the viability of the group qua group is not a trivial consideration when curriculum development is undertaken as a group effort.

In an interesting way the process of group deliberation in curriculum development has certain similarities to the kind of deliberation that goes on when juries are deciding the disposition of a case. In both situations, the evidence is weighed, which is a telling metaphor. What are being considered and compared are not qualities or anticipations that can be put on a common yardstick and measured; they are, rather, more of comparing incomparables. For any problem there are usually several credible solutions, which is also true of curriculum problems. Thus the problem for the curriculum group is to "weigh" the various putative virtues and the costs of each and finally to arrive at a decision that is then subjected to empirical testing. This process includes not simply acquiring the facts, which are probably more difficult to secure in curriculum planning than in jurisprudence; it also includes assigning values to these facts. In both situations the absence of recipelike solutions is notable.

The various rationales and concepts found in the literature of curriculum and the empirical generalizations produced in the behavioral sciences should not be considered blueprints for curriculum construction but rather mnemonic devices that enable a curriculum construction group in their more passive and reflective moments to remember what might be an important consideration. The concepts of objectives, continuity, sequence, integration, formative and summative evaluation, and the categories describing the changing cognitive structure of the child provide only the most general criteria against which decisions about the curriculum can be appraised. And none by itself is adequate to resolve the range of diverse and at times competing educational values that can be justly claimed for different courses of action. There is not now, and there very well might never be, an architectonic theory of curriculum capable of resolving and integrating the conflicts in interpretation, fact, and value emerging from different theories within the several social sciences. Theoretical consistency in curriculum development, even if it could be achieved, might in fact be an educational Pyrrhic victory.

If one uses three common factors in the literature on curriculum— the student, the society, and the subject matter—as criteria with which to identify what considerations were most prominent in our own curriculum development, it appears in retrospect that subject matter was easily the most prominent consideration of the three. The student, though important, was simply too remote during the course of curriculum development to play a really central role in our work. In addition, we believed—or took comfort in the thought—that the classroom teacher would make whatever adaptations of our material that were necessary to suit the particular child or class or situation in which the curriculum would be used.

And the society simply never appeared in our deliberations, perhaps because our value commitment toward the visual arts already implicitly embraced the belief that the development of childrens' artistic abilities would be important for the improvement of society. Whatever the reason, once the group was launched into the process of curriculum development its focus on the needs of society did not seem productive for meeting our immediate needs: creating learning activities and instructional support materials that would teach nontrivial artistic content to elementary school children.

Possible Alternative Approaches to Curriculum Development

It is far easier for me to identify those aspects of the curriculum we created that need modification and improvement than to identify those aspects of the curriculum development strategies we employed that need improvement. Though we attempted to identify the strengths and weaknesses of the curriculum throughout the process of curriculum development and through "achievement testing," we did not try to identify the difficulties that might have resided within our style of curriculum development work. I do not believe that a style of work can be legitimately appraised outside the context, values, and purposes of the project for which it is an instrumentality. I believe that significant interaction occurs between the kind of platform one embraces for a curriculum and the working arrangements one formulates. The tool and the product are interdependent. What I sought was a program that would nurture the artistic development of children. I do not believe such a program could be created within a set of working arrangements that were, for example, mechanical or authoritarian in nature. The context within which we worked was, furthermore, educational in character. I had an educational as well as an administrative responsibility for the people who worked in the core group. This educational responsibility necessitated, in my view, particular types of working relationships that might not be critical in, say, a regional educational laboratory.

I would not, in retrospect, have made radical changes in the basic way in which we operated, given the conditions I laid down in the proposal I prepared for the Kettering Foundation. Those conditions stipulated that there would be developed at Stanford University a set of curriculum materials, both written and visual, that could be used by elementary school teachers to increase the quality of art education in their classrooms. There are, however, approaches to curriculum development that differ significantly from the model that we employed. One of these, which I used in the development of the materials in Hawaii, is to bring groups of elementary school teachers together for workshops in which examples of the lessons and visual instructional materials that have already been employed are presented and discussed. Teachers then use these materials as prototypes for curriculum development, and they act as curriculum writers and as artists who produce instructional support material to accompany the written materials they prepare. Like the working arrangements used at Stanford, teachers can be grouped in teams of two or three, perhaps from the same elementary school. The major conceptual work—the format, its categories, and the development of exemplary lessons—will already have been completed. This aspect of the task of curriculum development is both difficult and time consuming, but I have found when working with teachers that they are able to produce much promising material quite quickly. The supervision of such teams must, of course, be close, and people competent in art need to be available for consultation, especially with respect to the separation of ideas and skills that are trivial from those that are significant.

One of the potential strengths of such an approach to curriculum development is that it removes the responsibility from a single group of people for creating a complete "packaged curriculum." It uses instead the core team to conceptualize the basic curriculum structure to be used and to develop prototypal materials. The structure and materials created are then used as resources for teachers to employ in developing their own materials. The core team functions, in addition, as consultants to the teachers.

This procedure for curriculum development also has the potential advantage of increasing the teacher's understanding of the project by putting him in the position of having to think through the project clearly enough to be able to prepare materials that not only he can use, but that others can use as well. This last condition for devising curriculum is important. Teachers must write their materials and develop their visual support devices so that other people can use the materials without direct consultation with the person who created them. Such a criterion provides a new frame of reference for teachers to use in curriculum writing.

This procedure for curriculum development has, I believe, an important contribution to make to the in-service education of teachers. It has the virtue of being practical and concrete; at the same time it requires teachers to consider concepts such as continuity and sequence as well as other matters that so often appear to be little more than educational slogans. In identifying this method of curriculum development as an alternative to the way our group worked, I am not suggesting that it is without liabilities. Our problems in education are not to be characterized as having ideal solutions; their solutions are always imperfect and need to be weighed with respect to competing strengths and weaknesses. For example, although broadening the responsibility for curriculum writing is likely to yield products whose quality is uneven, at the same time it is likely to increase motivation and comprehension of the project's objectives. What kind of trade off is most beneficial from an educational point of view? As far as I know there is no metric that can be confidently applied to resolve such a problem: it is a matter of making a judgment rather than applying a standard. In making such a judgment the image one holds of teachers and of schools comes sharply into play.

If schooling is seen as a quasi-industrial venture and teachers as a work force to be directed by management, the likelihood of being sympathetic toward a program that is teacher-proof—one in which the teacher functions as a conduit for a totally prepackaged program —is higher than if one conceives of teachers as professionals who, with students and other teachers, jointly plan the educational program. I am not in *this* essay advocating one image over another. I am trying to point out that strategies for curriculum development are inevitably appraised by the images all of us have of idealized educational practice. This is not a liability to curriculum development that strives to be educational but a necessary condition for its existence.

Notes

1. The final report of the project is entitled *Teaching Art to the Young: A Curriculum Development Project in Art Education* (Palo Alto, Calif.: School of Education, Stanford University, 1969).

2. *Music and Art in the Public Schools* (Washington, D.C.: National Education Association, 1963).

3. *Ibid.*

4. Elliot Eisner, "Curriculum Ideas in a Time of Crisis," *Art Education* 18 (No. 7, 1965); *id.*, "The Development of Information and Attitude toward Art at the Secondary and College Level," *Studies in Art Education* 8 (No. 1, 1966).

5. Manual Barkan, "Transition in Art Education: Changing Conceptions of Curriculum Content and Teaching," *Art Education* 15 (No. 7, 1962).

6. The amount allocated to the project by the Kettering Foundation for the two-year period was approximately $70,000.

7. Elliot Eisner, "Curriculum Making for the Wee Folk: Stanford University's Kettering Project," *Studies in Art Education* 9 (No. 3, 1968); *id.*, "Stanford's Kettering Project: An Appraisal of Two Years Work," *Art Education* 23 (No. 8, 1970).

8. *Id.*, "Stanford's Kettering Project: A Radical Alternative in Art Education," in *Programs of Promise*, ed. Al Hurwitz (New York: Harcourt Brace Jovanovich, 1972).

9. Elliot Eisner, *Educating Artistic Vision* (New York: Macmillan, 1972).

10. *California State Framework for the Visual Arts* (Sacramento: State Department of Education, State of California, 1971).

11. For this distinction I am indebted to the work of Gilbert Ryle, *The Concept of Mind* (London: Barnes and Noble, 1949).

12. This distinction grows out of John Dewey's writing, especially *Art as Experience* (New York: Minton, Balch and Company, 1934), Chapter 13.

13. *Ibid.*

14. See Decker Walker, "Strategies of Deliberation in Three Curriculum Development Projects," unpublished doctoral dissertation, School of Education, Stanford University, 1971.

9 Strategy for Curriculum Development: SRA Mathematics Learning System

M. Vere DeVault
Leo Anglin

The literature of curriculum development includes many papers about projects funded by government agencies and foundations.[1] It is unfortunate that almost no attention has been given to the ways in which commercial publishers develop their programs, even though most of the instructional materials in schools come from such sources.

This chapter describes the strategy used by Science Research Associates, Inc. (SRA), in the development of a basal text series in mathematics for kindergarten through the eighth grade. This strategy is not typical, however, of previous SRA developmental efforts or of educational publishing in general. Probably a larger share of the developmental budget was devoted to field-testing and verification of this series than ever before in commercial publishing. To assure maximum benefits from this investment, a systems strategy was employed throughout, from the initial needs assessment through continuing implementation.

In this report we shall document the systematic nature of the SRA strategy; consider the major problems addressed in planning and implementing that strategy; and review our experience and suggest points at which the strategy might be improved.

Description of Curriculum Development Strategy

The basic components of the strategy followed by SRA in the development of the Mathematics Learning System (MLS) are needs assessment; initial development, developmental tryout, feedback, and redevelopment; field verification study; and implementation.

Needs Assessment

Product development at SRA may begin in several ways. Some products result from efforts by an outside author who submits the ideas, outlines, or manuscript for a product for which he believes there is a need in the schools. More often, SRA staff members detect a need for a product and begin to determine what that product should be. In the case presented here, two editors in the Mathematics Department initiated the needs assessment for a new mathematics program.

Assumptions and Priorities

The most important element of the strategy was that of making assumptions and setting priorities.[2] This element demanded much time and attention initially, as well as throughout the five years during which the program was developed.

A question that was considered early was whether instructional materials in the style of present commercial texts were appropriate for the 1970s. If so, then the task was one of improving on existing materials rather than building instructional materials to respond to a new set of needs. The initial needs assessment indicated that demands for new kinds of materials were coming from a number of sources, and the idea of simply building better materials in the mode of present texts was rejected.

Curriculum planners were, for example, placing increased emphasis on behavioral objectives,[3] and yet many questions were being raised about the manner in which objectives were being used in materials development and in instructional activities.[4] The mathematics community, which had provided major impetus for the reforms of the 1950s and 1960s, began expressing second thoughts and seeking ways of maintaining improvements in content while teaching mathematics in styles more appropriate to children.

The needs assessment also looked at changes in school organization and building designs, and at the increased concern for variety in learning and teaching styles, in order to determine their impact on program development.[5] The requirements of the community and of society were examined, as were demands for relevance and the need to avoid racism and sexism in instructional materials. Efforts of government and industry to adopt the metric system represented a different kind of societal influence to be considered.

Setting Goals

Based on the initial needs assessment, major goals were established to give direction to the development of the new mathematics program. These goals included:

1. The program should be a learning system.

2. The structure of the MLS should be flexible, to allow its use in a variety of teaching-learning situations.

3. The mathematics content should be correct but less formal than that of the new math programs of the 1960s.

4. The materials should be designed to permit use with a variety of other instructional materials.

5. Races, sexes, and ethnic groups should receive equitable treatment.

6. The materials should be fun to use and should provide successful mathematical experiences for the child.

These goals were continuously reviewed and refined throughout the development and implementation of MLS. At the time of their original statement they helped determine the personnel resources that would be needed for program development.

Determining Personnel Resources

Competent personnel were needed for five kinds of tasks: manuscript preparation (authors, consultants, developmental staff); production (typists, artists, designers, photographers, printers, controllers); data collection and analysis (measurement specialists, statisticians); administration (managers, forecasters, financial analysts); distribution (home office and field marketing, advertising and promotion). Although these personnel categories were itemized separately, their interrelatedness was seen as essential to the development and implementation of the program.

The authors were carefully selected on the basis of the needs assessment. Each had many years of experience in a variety of responsibilities in mathematics education. Each was knowledgeable in areas outside of but related to mathematics education. One of the mathematicians selected for the team, in addition to his involvement with innovations in mathematics education, was also a recognized research scholar. Another author, a mathematics educator, had extensive experience in curriculum planning projects, instructional systems, and teacher education. A third author was active as a mathematician, was a writer of instructional materials, and was the director of in-service institutes. The fourth author had been a master teacher for many years, had performed on educational television, and had worked with thousands of teachers throughout the country on instructional problems in all areas of the curriculum. Through the interaction of this varied group, progress toward the goals identified by the assessment of needs was begun.

A fundamental problem in innovation is the lack of integration between development and implementation.[6] Recent projects of the federal government and of foundations have found great difficulties in establishing communication along the research-development-implementation continuum. Researchers have seldom been interested in development; in turn, developers have rarely joined in implementation. To avoid this problem, members of the SRA marketing division were part of the developmental staff from the beginning of the project. Much of the information reviewed during the needs assessment was obtained from the SRA field sales force. The goals and priorities for MLS reflect field force knowledge and projections about school organization, individualized instruction, attitudes toward the new math, efforts to utilize behavioral objectives, and demands for cost effectiveness in the schools.

In addition to this use of the field for collecting data, sales personnel were used in more specific ways. One of the authors was already highly regarded in schools and among the field force for her competence as a consultant and teacher in elementary classrooms. As an author, her contributions were a direct reflection of the perceptions gained in the field. The field was further represented by the assignment of a former member of the marketing group as a senior editor of the program. His long association with the sales staff contributed to confidence in the marketing aspect of the developmental effort.

Developing Proposals, Submitting Proposals, and Decision

After goals had been set and personnel identified to work with the new program, a proposal was prepared for review at several administrative levels. The production, forecasting, marketing, and financial staff met with the developmental team to consider approval of the program. After studying reports concerning the market, developmental strategy, total investment, cash flow, and net profit for MLS, SRA top management authorized its development.

Writing Objectives

Once the goals of the program had been established and authorization had been obtained, the first draft of year-end objectives for kindergarten through the eighth grade was prepared. Throughout the developmental cycle they were continuously reviewed and revised.

Managing Development of the Program

The complex interrelations between groups concerned with the program required sophisticated management techniques. Each change or addition to program materials or formats required careful consideration, so that its impact on previously made decisions could be determined. It should be noted that development and the developmental tryout were under way before the needs assessment was completed and that implementation was also in progress at an early stage when the sales staff were brought into the planning discussion.

Development and Tryout

The year-end mastery objectives of the program were established as a part of the proposal for the total project. Next to be developed were enabling objectives, intermediate objectives designed to support the attainment of year-end mastery objectives, which gave direction to the writing of individual chapters. Then, first drafts of chapters were prepared and carefully reviewed by authors, staff, and consultants. As a result of these reviews, chapters were revised and, if judged ready, prepared for classroom tryouts. At times objectives were revised if they proved to be too narrow, too broad, imprecise, or otherwise unsatisfactory.

During the preparation of chapters, the identification of tryout sites was under way. Eight sites in the United States and one in Canada were chosen to represent a variety of geographic locations and types of schools and learners. A "field observer" was assigned to each site to provide in-service assistance for teachers, to serve as liaison with the developmental staff, and, most importantly, to assess the program. In each instance, the observer was identified by the administration of the local school as a person it wished to have associated with its staff; that person was, in most instances, also a national leader in mathematics education.

Before the program was initiated in a tryout school, a one-day training program was presented by members of the developmental staff, authors, and field observer. A major objective of the in-service program was to help teachers understand the philosophy of the program as evidenced by its major goals.

During the tryout year the field observer made frequent visits to each of the classrooms in which the materials were being used. In-service training sessions were held at the request of the teachers. These meetings were usually conducted by the field observer and sometimes were attended by authors or members of the developmental staff. Teachers were also encouraged to telephone the field observer or the staff in SRA's Chicago office if they had questions.

Data were collected throughout the year. Valuable assessments of the material came through page-by-page reactions written by the teachers in their guides. Those pages were collected quarterly and consolidated for the review of authors and developmental staff who were already at work on revisions for the field verification study to be undertaken during the following year. Authors and members of the developmental staff also visited the sites to observe the children's use of the materials and to discuss with teachers the merits and the problems of the program. The field observers critiqued the texts page by page and submitted quarterly reports on their classroom observations. Standardized mathematics achievement tests were given in the second through the eighth grades at the beginning and end of the year. Some comparisons between MLS and non-MLS classes were included in the data collection. The general reactions of teachers and of pupils contributed much to the final evaluation of the effectiveness of the materials. The most important information came from analyses of items on MLS chapter test results. Such analyses identified specific patterns of errors, which were extremely valuable in revising pages, adding or deleting materials, and improving instruction for the teacher.

Tryout results were compared with the assumptions and priorities established by the needs assessment. Assumptions about teachers' readiness for more informal approaches to mathematics and about children's acceptance of informal modes of presentation were strongly supported. It was necessary, however, to reconsider expectations about teachers' use of diagnostic tools. Many other assumptions were either reinforced or revised on the basis of tryout data. As results were reviewed, revisions were prepared, and production of books for the field verification study was begun.

Field Verification Study

Planning for the field verification study was under way during the developmental tryout year and started with more than eighty members of the field force. Each salesman was to select one or more schools in which the study would be undertaken. The purposes of the field verification study included:

1. Determining the effectiveness of the text for pupils and the guide materials for teachers in editions as much as possible like those to be finally published.

2. Obtaining further information about portions of the fifth and sixth levels, which the developmental tryout had shown needed major revisions.

3. Testing of substantially revised and rewritten materials for the seventh and eighth levels. These, too, had been less effective than desired with the tryout population.

4. Determining further needs for revisions and additions of the teacher's guide at all levels.

5. Providing sales staff who had experience with the program prior to implementation.

6. Designating model sites throughout the country where persons interested in the program could observe children using it and talk to teachers with experience teaching it.

Teachers attended short in-service workshops under the direction of the sales staff. A telephone hot line to the developmental staff was set up for use by any teacher or SRA salesman with a question concerning the program.

The field verification study continued throughout the year, and data were collected from a variety of sources. Authors and developmental staff continued to play an important role in observing and reacting to the success of various components of the program. Comments from the hot line provided information about the kinds of help teachers needed in the implementation of MLS. Reactions of teachers and pupils were a constant source of important data for further refinements in the program. The sales staff's suggestions and reactions were carefully considered to ensure that the materials that were successful in the field verification study would be equally successful in the marketplace. Both pre- and postachievement data were collected for approximately 1,500 learners at each level.

Field verification data were useful throughout the year. Parts of the text materials at the fifth, seventh, and eighth levels were revised a second time, and minor changes were made at all other levels. In addition, the verification data contributed to refinements and additions in the plans for supplementary materials associated with MLS. Teachers' guides were influenced extensively. And, again, the major assumptions and priorities were reviewed in the light of data analyses, and revisions were made accordingly.

During the field verification study, the final production work on pupils' texts and teachers' guides was initiated, and the developmental activities of authors and editors were directed to the instructional management system, drill materials, and correlations of MLS to other materials from SRA and other publishers.

Implementation

Implementation began almost at the start of program development, when the sales staff first became involved. Their ideas were used extensively in the assessment of needs; they were involved through representatives on the authors' team and the developmental staff; nine of them had developmental tryout schools in their territories, and about two-thirds of them were responsible for field verification schools. For two years there had been publicity in the form of written reports, meetings, and observation of schools. Efforts to make the profession aware of the program included articles in an SRA newsletter, speeches and articles by authors, national advertising, announcements at national conventions, and an invitation to teachers and administrators to visit the field verification schools.

Now that all materials are published in their first edition, the authors and developmental staff will increasingly provide in-service assistance to the sales staff and then to teachers.

A text series is commercially "successful" if it has a long life. A text series is pedagogically "successful" to the extent that it can satisfy specific educational needs. Since societies and schools change, instructional materials must also change if they are to continue to meet specific educational needs. Thus, MLS will be termed successful, pedagogically and commercially, only to the extent that it can continue to meet specific needs through several revisions. The four-year development of MLS has already included several revisions through a continuous review of the assumptions and priorities that gave initial impetus to the series. In addition, program implementation was started early and continued throughout the development of MLS. So, too, the assessment of needs, which initiated the program, must continue through the implementation of MLS. The major lesson that has been learned by the developers of this mathematics program is, in fact, that a continuous review of program assumptions and priorities and the resulting implications for program development can never end if a text series is to be successful in the dynamic societies of the 1970s.

Systemic Strategy for Curriculum Development

Systematic planning has long been a part of customary procedures in the schools. It is only recently, however, that educators have recognized the value of using the language and techniques of systems designs and analysis to help them solve problems in education.[7] Through the use of systems approaches they have come to see more clearly the nature of their efforts, have communicated more easily among themselves, and have altered practice because they better understand the interrelatedness of the diverse activities that comprise the educational effort.

Schools need systems strategies for curriculum development because of three major problems: complexity, diversity, and change. Each of these contributes to the need for systems design, and each in turn is served by effective application of systems design principles.

Complexity

Curriculum development is a complex, multidimensional activity. Materials for the mathematics curriculum represent a variety of instructional modes including texts, teachers' guides, drill materials, audiovisual aids, manipulatives, and supplementary kits. The task of designing these materials as a comprehensive, complementary set of instructional-learning aids is complex. That task is made even more complex by the need to develop materials that can be used by teachers and teams that vary considerably in competence, preference, philosophy, and style of classroom organization. And the demands are not made simpler when consideration is given to the diversity of learners the system is to serve.

The curriculum for a given subject area at a given level is in the context of the total school curriculum. The demands of philosophy and organization that give coherence to the total curriculum add to the complexity of the development and the implementation of any specific curriculum.

The complexity is further increased by the school as an institution in society. The expectations of society, the needs of society, and the differences from one locality to another add substantially to the complexities of building curriculum to serve the needs of schools across the nation.[8]

Diversity

The impact of diversity on curriculum planning can be felt in three ways. The first of these comes from the diversity of information about the curriculum to be developed. The understandings and expectations of society, the beliefs of the profession about the nature of the discipline and its role in the school, the nature of the school as an organized institution, knowledge about the nature of learners in classes, the competence and philosophies held by teachers in the schools—all of these influence decisions about curriculum. This diversity of sources of information is further complicated by the diversity within each of the sources.

A second factor contributing to diversity is the pool of human resources available for curriculum development activities. As information about curriculum needs is analyzed, it becomes increasingly clear what kinds of personnel are needed to create the curriculum.

Identifying appropriate authors, editors, and consultants is a task of great importance. There was a time when one person could write a complete program. In the 1940s a Morton or a Spitzer could almost single-handedly prepare a K-8 mathematics series in a very responsible and professional manner. But because of advances in mathematics education and the need to include more mathematics in the same time span, we must learn to do things more effectively. No individual has the genius to develop today's program alone. Hence, the array of personnel contributing to the preparation of materials for most basal series in mathematics today is quite large in comparison with those of earlier days. Editors and consultants, too, play different roles than were assumed earlier. The result is curriculum development by a team of curriculum engineers. The coordination of such a team requires expert management operating in a systems mode if the best efforts of team members are to be effective and creative.

Finally, the diversity of the target populations toward which the curriculum is directed creates major problems in curriculum development. Cultures differ from one part of the country to another; from one ethnic group to another; and from one economic group to another. A curriculum that would serve all youth must present a multicultural message. Information sources and tryouts in various cultures must be utilized continuously during development and implementation as decisions are made concerning development, refinement, and revision.

Change

Change is the one constant in our lives. Though change may come slowly in many schools, it is present in all of them. Schools are different than they were at the turn of the century; they are also better. At the beginning of the next century, schools will be substantially different than they are today. It is to be hoped that strategies for curriculum development will have changed to meet the changing demands of the schools. If they do, they will do so as a result of systems designs that respond to changing needs. Feedback at many levels is an essential aspect of the systems approach. If the plan for the utilization of feedback is adequate, there should be less need for the complete demise of a basal program and the development and installation of a new one. Rather, the revisions, the additions, and the changing utilization strategies would be determined by the nature of feedback that is continuously obtained, analyzed, and used in decision making.

Although feedback is one of the simplest ideas in the systems approach, making it functional is difficult indeed. Figure 9-1 shows a multilevel feedback system that should function in a curriculum development strategy. In the center is the functioning classroom program feedback design. Pupils' attainment of objectives is assessed, and decisions are made by the teacher or team of teachers on the basis of these assessments. If the assessment of the pupil indicates unsatisfactory achievement, decisions are made about the effectiveness of the learning activities or about prerequisites the pupil may have lacked.

At the second level the feedback system responds to the program. The evaluation of the program determines the achievement of the learners for whom it was intended, and developers review these data to determine the effectiveness of the program for various types of learners. Finally, the diagram shows that at the third level the developmental strategy is reviewed by the profession to determine its merits. This type of review is at the present time very informally accomplished; it can be hoped that, in the decade ahead, considerably more attention will be given to the careful review of various strategies for local, state, and national curriculum development projects. The request for papers of this nature by the National Institute of Education provides hope that such careful reviews will be made in the years immediately ahead.

In Retrospect

The merits of the strategy used to generate the SRA Mathematics Learning System can be considered at three levels. The manner in which the materials are received by schools and their effectiveness in enabling children to achieve the learning objectives of various school systems will provide objective data over the next several years. At a more remote level, strategies that employ systems design techniques similar to that reported in this chapter will be used and assessed by professionals responsible for the development of commercial, government-supported, or local curriculum projects. Because the data at both of these levels will be collected in the future, there will be no further discussion of them at this time.

LEVEL 3—STRATEGY FOR CURRICULUM DEVELOPMENT

LEVEL 2—CURRICULUM DEVELOPMENT

LEVEL 1—CLASSROOM PROGRAM

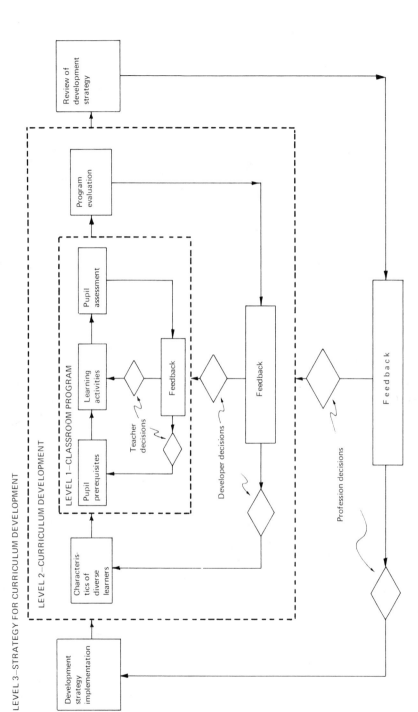

Figure 9-1. Feedback mechanism in curriculum development

At a personal level, however, it is possible to reflect on the strategy used by SRA and to consider alterations that might strengthen it as an approach to curriculum development. The authors of this chapter are in a particularly good position to make such suggestions, since one is an originator of the program, and the other served as a field observer for the developmental tryout and as a teacher for the field verification study.

There are two major areas in which improvement in the strategy should be explored. Without examining why the strategy was developed as it was, (time, money, personnel resource limitations, and so forth) we shall simply discuss these two areas.

While a comprehensive assessment of needs initiated development of MLS and is continuing as a major part of implementation, no formal model was established at the outset. With the establishment of a model to provide direction for data collection, analysis, and interpretation, more useful comparisons could be made from one time to another. Changes in society, in a discipline, and in the schools are sometimes difficult to detect over a time span of one or two years. If assessment of needs is to be a continuing aspect of program development throughout implementation, a system must be designed to reveal the subtle changes in the forces that affect curriculum decisions.

The SRA Mathematics Learning System is a comprehensive set of instructional materials including pupils' texts, teachers' guides, practice materials, audiotapes, and an instructional management system. The development and tryout phase of the strategy included elements of all of these. Elements of the management system, for example, were included in the developmental tryout teacher's guide; what was learned from that experience influenced decisions about the management materials to be used in the field verification study and in the published program. At no time, however, was there a fully functioning prototypic chapter or set of chapters installed in a classroom to illustrate a comprehensive system as it was perceived that it would be in final development. Certainly no program could be fully envisioned at the start. The team of authors and the developmental staff dedicated many months to exploring ideas that resulted in the final proposal and the decision by SRA's management to proceed with the project. The suggestion here is that even with the great amount of energy expended prior to the preparation of the proposal, the development and tryout phases would have been enhanced by having prototypic materials functioning fully within a school setting concurrently with early writing efforts.

The suggestions that the assessment of needs be more formally planned and that prototypic tryout of the comprehensive system be employed have their limitations. Each requires additional time and funds; whether such additional investments enhance the effectiveness of the strategy cannot be known at the present time. It should be pointed out also that some of the flexibility provided in the present strategy might have been lost had these suggestions been implemented.

The use of systems in educational planning and implementation must enhance rather than restrict flexibility. The success of the systems design employed in the MLS developmental strategy was a function of the delicate balance maintained between control and flexibility in each facet of the effort. The extent to which developers are able in the future to achieve that balance will determine the utility of systems in education.

Notes

1. See Elliott Duchon, James Hull, and Molly Carpenter, *Resource Guide: Evaluational Planning* (Washington, D. C.: U.S. Office of Education, 1973), 45-56, for an excellent listing of current publications, government publications, and depository libraries.

2. Kenneth Hansen, "Planning and Change," in *Designing Education for the Future, No. 4*, ed. Edgar L. Morphet and David L. Jesser (New York: Citation Press, 1968), 53-79.

3. See Ralph W. Tyler, *Basic Principles of Curriclum and Instruction* (Chicago: University of Chicago Press, 1971), 43-62, for a discussion concerning the merits of objectives.

4. See Michael W. Apple, "The Adequacy of Systems Management Procedures in Education," *Journal of Educational Research* 66 (September 1972): 10-18, for a review of the questions that were being raised concerning behavioral objectives.

5. See Laurence Haskew, "What Lies Ahead," in *Designing Education for the Future*, ed. Morphet and Jesser, 11-23, for a generic discussion of this topic.

6. Ronald G. Havelock, *Innovations in Education: Strategies and Tactics* (Ann Arbor: Center for Research on Utilization of Scientific Knowledge, Institute for Social Research, University of Michigan, 1971), 1-19.

7. For a detailed discussion of this phase of a developmental strategy, see Paul A. Twelker, Floyd D. Urbach, and James E. Buck, *The Systematic Development*

of Instruction: An Overview and Basic Guide to the Literature (Stanford, Calif.: ERIC Clearinghouse on Educational Media and Technology, Stanford University, 1972), 1-15.

8. John M. Kean and Norman R. Dodl, "A Systems Approach to Curriculum Development," in James M. Cooper, M. Vere DeVault, *et al.*, *Competency-Based Teacher Education* (Berkeley, Calif.: McCutchan Publishing Corp., 1973), Book Two, 33-37.

10 Curriculum for Career Development Education

Larry J. Bailey

Orientation and Background

Since the beginning of the modern era of career guidance in the early 1950s, the body of literature and research related to vocational behavior has multiplied exponentially. The search for unifying constructs and principles of vocational behavior has been accompanied by a surge in the area of theory building. The present status of career development theory has received extensive treatment in many recent publications.[1] As theoretical orientations and models of career development have come to be better understood, researchers and practitioners have sought to validate theory and implement career education and guidance practices derived from theory. The most comprehensive reviews of research on vocational behavior to date may be found in Perrone, Tennyson, Holland and Whitney, Crites, Herr and Cramer, and Bailey and Stadt.[2]

In March 1969 the Bureau of Adult, Vocational, and Technical Education of the U. S. Office of Education sponsored a National Conference on Exemplary Programs and Projects in Atlanta, Georgia. A primary purpose of the conference was to consider the implications of emerging career development constructs for vocational education curriculum. E. L. Herr presented a paper, "Unifying an Entire

System of Education around a Career Development Theme,"[3] that was to have a profound influence in shaping my approach to curriculum development. Herr summarized the major theories of career development and gave broad prescriptions and rationales for the role of career development in elementary and secondary school curricula. No one has put more succinctly than Herr the marriage of career development theory, the "systems approach" to educational programming, and the reorientation of vocational education. He was careful to underscore his theme: *"One of the operational goals critical to implementing the Exemplary Programs and Project Section of the Vocational Education Act relates to the need to design behavioral descriptions which would encompass the characteristics of career development, placing these at appropriate developmental levels, and wedding them to educational strategies which will facilitate them."*[4]

I became aware of Herr's paper in the late summer of 1969 at a time when I was drafting a research proposal dealing with career development curriculum for elementary schools. Three of my previous publications[5] had dealt with aspects of Herr's three main thrusts: career development principles; implications of systems development and behavioral descriptions of educational goals; and the reorientation of vocational education toward greater concern for process skills. But, in the vernacular, Herr's paper helped me to "get it all together."

Reinforced with a clearer conception of how to pursue the project, I transmitted a research proposal entitled "Facilitating Career Development at the Elementary School Level" to the Illinois Division of Vocational and Technical Education in November 1969.[6] The project, subsequently approved for funding, became known as the Career Development for Children Project (CDCP) and was directed by me throughout its duration from February 15, 1970, to August 31, 1973. The primary purpose of the project was to produce prototypical career development curriculum materials for the first through the eighth grades. Supporting aims were the development of a logical-theoretical paradigm and a comprehensive, organized curriculum framework. The theory, rationale, and curriculum model are presented in two papers by me and one by Turner, Van Rooy, and me.[7] The final project report[8] summarizes the goals and objectives, procedures, accomplishments, evaluation, and conclusions and recommendations. Various of these procedures will be discussed in the remainder of this chapter.

Procedure and Limitations

Although I have had experience and major responsibility for the conduct of four previous externally funded research and development projects,[9] the CDCP was my first attempt at curriculum development. Though this may have been a liability, it is noteworthy that Grobman, in describing the many large-scale curriculum efforts of the late 1950s and 1960s, comments that "since no *right* ways were known, each project had to build its own vehicle for operation, and, in so doing, may have enhanced the end result beyond what would have been possible in a more rigid framework."[10]

In the following pages a general curriculum model (see Figure 10-1) will be presented which has resulted from a synthesis of conventional curriculum theory and technology,[11] from application of Grobman's analysis of the "developmental curriculum project,"[12] and from my personal experience in directing the CDCP. For each of the five curricular phases a short introduction of supporting theory is provided followed by statements of relevant principles that have been borrowed from Cole.[13] Each principle is then discussed and illustrated with examples of products or procedures drawn from the CDCP.

Formulation of a Curricular Language

A "systems" approach to curriculum development begins by providing an answer to the question: what is it for? "Only if we clearly identify purpose can we specify what has to be done, by what or by whom."[14] Grobman[15] notes that all curriculum development projects have both verbalized and implicit goals. Because of readily observable disparities between what projects say are their goals and the goals implicit in their curriculum materials, the preparation of policy statements should be accorded first priority and precede more specific development of performance objectives. Bailey and Stadt call this phase of curriculum development the formulation of a "curricular language."[16] A project's curricular language should include, at a minimum, statements of basic purpose, rationale, assumptions, and value judgments. The first principles of curriculum development may thus be stated:

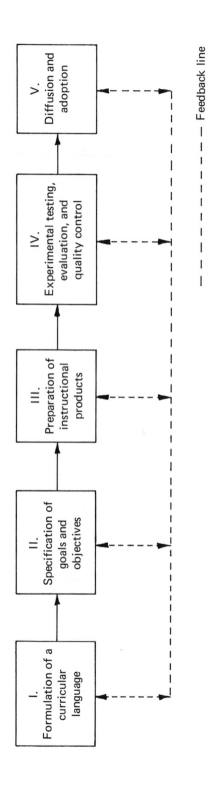

Figure 10-1. Overall structure for a general curriculum model (from L. J. Bailey and R. W. Stadt, Career Education: New Approaches to Human Development [Bloomington, Ill.: McKnight Publishing Company, 1973], 309. Reprinted by permission.)

1. The basic *purpose* of the curriculum in terms of its long-range effects on the learner should be clearly stated and based in some logical-theoretical framework.
2. A *rationale* that addresses relevant theoretical issues should be well developed.
3. The *assumptions* should be clearly identified within the context of those issues.
4. A clear statement of *values* that the curriculum espouses should be prepared and made available for inspection.

The CDCP theory, rationale, and assumptions are based primarily on Super's developmental self-concept theory of career development[17] and the related construct of "vocational maturity."[18] Career development is conceived as one aspect of general human development. It denotes the lifelong sequence and patterns of an individual's related behavior, including all experiences and activities that are relevant to work before and after entry into a formal occupation.

In its value orientation, the project seeks to provide an educational setting wherein individuals may develop broad arrays of basic skills that would endow them with a great degree of conviviality[19] and potential for career self-actualization.[20] This view is compatible with the ideal of the educated, humanized personality described by Rubins, Combs, and Cole.[21] Following are specific examples of the CDCP curricular language that have been excerpted from selected foundation documents.

Basic purpose: The Career Development for Children Project is designed to involve children, beginning in elementary school, in experiences which will facilitate the broad goal of vocational maturity . . . the intermediate goal for the project, at approximately the grade eight level, is to have students formulate a tentative occupational preference which will aid them in making decisions about their choice of a high school curriculum.[22]

Rationale: Growing unemployment among better educated segments of American society and the cry of many young people for education that has personal relevance, are causing many people to re-examine the role of education and the universal worth of a college degree. Youth, now, more than any other time in recent history are asking themselves, "What shall I do with myself?" The indications are clear; education has failed to adequately assist young people with their career planning and decision-making.[23]

Assumptions: A primary assumption of the project is that career development is one aspect of the continuing and fluid processes of growth and learning. Maturing in a vocational sense involves coping with the developmental tasks of a given life stage, in part, through a series of integrated decisions.[24]

Value judgments: There is considerable evidence in recent years that this tendency [emphasis on subject matter] is being reversed and that teachers are becoming more aware of the need to emphasize relevant and humanistic education . . . . The specific aim is increased personal freedom to make career choices based on an understanding of the tremendously varied opportunities available in contemporary society. We hope to prevent students making choices directed only by custom, geographic accident, or based on race, sex, or social class . . . . We believe a vacuum exists in the contemporary school curriculum. A belief shared with many interested citizens, educators, and legislators. This vacuum exists where a bridge should be, i.e., a bridge between the school and a productive, satisfying career.[25]

Specification of Goals and Objectives

According to Krathwohl,[26] curriculum construction involves the process of moving through descending abstractions from very general and global statements of desired program behaviors to intermediate-level statements that indicate the blocks from which the program will be constructed. Several levels of description are necessary to judicious planning of educational processes. It is very important that a curriculum have a network of logically related objectives. This leads to the next three principles.

5. The curriculum should have stated objectives in terms of desired learning outcomes.

6. The structure and organization of the curriculum should be based on some overall paradigm that takes into account the developmental capabilities, interests, and limitations of students at various age-grade levels.

7. The curriculum paradigm should have functional utility for generating a variety of learning activities, topics, and materials to be used in meeting stated objectives.

Cole[27] and Krathwohl[28] recommend a system for describing objectives at three levels of generality: At the first and most abstract level are the general statements most useful in the development of programs of instruction or the plans for types of courses and areas to be covered. These are goals toward which several years of education might be aimed. There should be relatively few of these objectives. Their purpose is primarily to inform and influence. They should reflect and be consistent with statements that describe the program's values and assumptions about basic theoretical issues.

The second and more concrete level helps to analyze broad goals into more specific ones that are useful as the building blocks for instructional units. The second type of objectives should be greater in number and specificity. They should define areas of competence, perhaps as clusters of process skills that are quite specific concerning performance but generalizable in terms of situations.

Third is a level needed to create instructional materials. This type of objectives should be large in number, and highly specific regarding performance, and even more specific concerning situations. They should be viewed as a sample of a given number of possible objectives within a universe of acts or performances that might reasonably be inferred to foster the intermediate and global objectives.

This manner of ordering objectives is compatible with contemporary theory and practice. Because many leading authorities[29] have repeatedly emphasized the importance of having clear statements of the overt behavior of learners, no additional documentation is required.

Figure 10-2 illustrates a curriculum paradigm that agrees with the principles and criteria discussed above. Six domains of career development behaviors (Cole would call these "process skill categories"[30]) have been synthesized from a review of career development theory and research. For each category of behavior a program goal (see Table 10-1) is stated with respect to four developmental stages. In defining program goals for several levels of education, I have found the concept of "developmental tasks" to be particularly useful. The compatibility of the developmental task concept with career development processes has been made obvious by Zaccaria[31] and Herr.[32] Examples of major tasks during childhood and adolescence, such as those described by Havighurst, Kearney, and French et al.,[33] have proven to be valuable aids to writing goal statements for career development education.

The method of stating objectives that I have determined to be the most practical and functional is outlined in Gronlund.[34] The major feature of Gronlund's method is the differentiation between what he calls "minimum-essential level" (MEL) objectives and "developmental level" (DL) objectives. MEL objectives are those which attempt to shape and modify student behavior to fit a predetermined minimum level of performance. These objectives are frequently stated as tasks to be performed rather than as goals to work toward. Mager[35] is the most prominent advocate of MEL objectives. DL objectives, on the other hand, represent a whole class of responses and are not stated as

DOMAINS OF CAREER DEVELOPMENT BEHAVIORS	A. Awareness K-3	B. Accommodation 4-6	C. Orientation 7-8	D. Exploration and Preparation 9-12
1. Concepts of self	A1	B1	C1	D1
2. Occupational, educational and economic concepts and skills	A2	B2	C2	D2
3. Sense of agency	A3	B3	C3	D3
4. Information processing skills	A4	B4	C4	D4
5. Interpersonal relationships	A5	B5	C5	D5
6. Work attitudes and values	A6	B6	C6	D6

Figure 10-2. A developmental curriculum model for career education (from Bailey and Stadt, Career Education, *350. Reprinted by permission.)*

specific tasks to be performed. Objectives in this form are stated as *general* objectives followed by a sample of more *specific* behaviors. This approach corresponds to the second and third levels of generality discussed above. Additional advantages of Gronlund's procedure are the relative ease with which the Taxonomies of Educational Objectives may be applied, the systematic way in which tables of specifications may be developed, and the ease with which achievement tests may be written. Following are representative examples, which illustrate the relationship among broad (Goal B1), intermediate (Objective 6), and specific (Objectives 6.1 to 6.5) career development objectives.[36]

Goal B1. Development of concepts related to self. In this phase, the child begins to conceptualize what he formerly only perceived.[37] "Self-concepts are self-

Table 10-1. Goal statements for career education paradigm

Stage	Goal
Awareness	A1. Awareness of self
	A2. Awareness of different types of occupational roles
	A3. Awareness of individual responsibility for own actions
	A4. Development of the rudiments of classification and decision-making skills
	A5. Learning cooperative social behavior
	A6. Development of respect for others and the work that they do
Accommodation	B1. Development of concepts related to self
	B2. Development of concepts related to the world of work
	B3. Assuming increased responsibility for planning one's time
	B4. Application of decision-making and classification skills
	B5. Development of desirable social relationships
	B6. Development of work attitudes and values
Orientation	C1. Clarification of a self-concept
	C2. Understanding of the structure and interrelatedness of the American economic, occupational, and technological systems
	C3. Assuming responsibility for career planning
	C4. Development of individual inquiry and problem-solving skills
	C5. Development of socially responsible behavior and more mature social relationships
	C6. Appreciation of work as a valued and enduring social institution
Exploration and preparation	D1. Crystallization and implementation of a self-concept
	D2. Executing plans to qualify for career objectives
	D3. Commitment to implementation of a self-concept
	D4. Application of problem-solving skills
	D5. Understanding the dynamics of group behavior in a work situation
	D6. Acquiring the discipline of work

percepts which have acquired meaning and which have been related to other self-percepts. A self-concept is the individual's picture of himself, the perceived self with accrued meanings."[38] Operationally, self-concept development at this level takes the form of helping students develop "self-understanding." Turner[39] points out that the greater an individual's understanding of the *activities* in which he is interested, his *ability* to participate in those activities, and the *value* of those activities to him, the more accurate will be his choice of a later career.

An additional operational aspect of self-understanding is the provision for periodic assessment of growth and learning, and the assimilation of new information. By becoming more fully aware of characteristics of the process of change which mark growth and development, the child can (1) begin to develop a better understanding of self at a certain point in time, i.e., a *concept of becoming*, and (2) recognize that his understanding of self is constantly changing, i.e., he is in a *process of becoming*.

Objective 6. Formulates present self-identity reflecting knowledge of own interests, abilities, and values.

    6.1 Summarizes primary areas of interest

    6.2 Compares present interests with those characteristics of earlier periods

    6.3 Provides examples of individual aptitudes and abilities

    6.4 Recognizes assets and limitations

    6.5 Provided with a list of activities, expresses the importance (value) of those activities to him.

Preparation of Instructional Products

"If curriculum is a plan for learning, and if objectives determine what learning is important, then it follows that adequate curriculum planning involves selecting and organizing both the content and learning experiences."[40] To this point, concern has been on the ends to be attained by curriculum. To be considered now is how these ends may be achieved. The next two principles of design can now be stated.

    8. The content of a curriculum should consist of a wide array of multiple activities, materials, and topics both within given smaller units of its content and across its total program.

    9. The organization and sequencing of activities, topics, and the design of materials should be based upon commonly, empirically understood or theoretically conceptualized theories of learning and development.

The prototype curriculum materials developed by CDCP are fairly broad and varied and begin to meet the eighth criterion. The curriculum paradigm is capable of fostering greater diversity. It is anticipated that the program will be strengthened in this respect as additional developmental work is completed.

The best examples of product developed to date are contained in Level I, Unit 4.[41] The purpose of Unit 4 is to help the child begin to differentiate human activity in terms of work and play. More specific objectives are for the child to identify general characteristics of work and play, to determine reasons why people work and play, and to assess the commonalities and differences between the activities of work and play.

The introductory activity for this unit is a poem-study print series entitled "Wango from Dango." This activity is designed to demonstrate differing but logical responses to the question, "What is work, and what is play?" This practice is well recognized by many curriculum developers who seek to develop the capacity for divergent thinking, problem solving, and expressive behavior.[42] Students are then challenged to formulate their own responses to what is the difference between work and play. The activity is managed in such a way that children are helped to identify the following four characteristics:

1. Work involves a goal—there is a task to be finished.
2. Most adults work for a living.
3. Most adults, but not all, get paid for their work.
4. The work a person does is one of the activities that identifies him, that makes him unique.

To demonstrate the goal-oriented characteristic of work, case studies of Eddie and Betty are read and discussed. Next, members of the class engage in role-playing to reveal that "feelings" about types of work and play are part of what makes each of us unique. A group simulation activity in which a simple toy is manufactured is used to demonstrate the necessity for cooperative relationships in completing a work task and to develop the attitude that "work can be fun." Finally, the teacher is provided with a listing of related commercial materials that reinforce the concepts presented in this unit. Obvious space restrictions and other limitations prohibit further discussion of curriculum materials and activities. This section demonstrates in part, however, how the CDCP has attempted to meet the design principle of providing multiple activities and materials for a given unit of instruction.

The CDCP justifies the organization of its curriculum concepts and activities (the ninth principle) via theory and empirical evidence extracted from the literature of learning and developmental psychology. Vinacke's interpretations of cognitive stages[43] are used to differentiate the major focus of the stages of Awareness (K-3) and Accommodation (4-6). The six goals for each stage are written so as to be compatible with the developmental tasks described by Havighurst.[44]

Bruner's notion of a spiral curriculum[45] is used in the sequencing of self-concept development objectives and activities. The concept of cumulative learning advanced by Gagné[46] is used to order the various curriculum units and activities within a given grade level.

Experimental Testing, Evaluation, and Quality Control

Virtually all projects of curriculum development make some provision for tryout and evaluation of materials. As might be expected, the comprehensiveness of experimental testing depends on many factors: available personnel and fiscal resources, the degree to which materials are compatible with conventional practice, the extent and quality of prior planning and in-house research and development, and the availability and willingness of local education agencies to participate.[47]

A typical model for the testing and revision of instructional materials is shown in Figure 10-3. Illustrated are the major steps in the development, testing, and revision of curriculum materials for two one-year junior high school programs entitled "The World of Construction" and "The World of Manufacturing," developed by the Industrial Arts Curriculum Project (IACP) at Ohio State University. This example demonstrates the complexity of events during the phases of testing, evaluation, and quality control. The importance of field-testing to the revision and further development of the product is made obvious by Buffer[48] in a description of the additions and changes made in the IACP materials as a result of data collected during field-testing. Accordingly, the next two principles are:

10. The curriculum should be evaluated during its development, trial utilization, and dissemination.

11. Evaluation should be primarily formative in nature with summative evaluation occurring periodically to determine how effective components of the programs are in meeting stated goals and objectives.

The theory and techniques for conducting formative and summative evaluations are well outlined in a number of recent sources.[49] Grobman[50] has observed considerable variance in the scope and intensity of the application of these techniques to the evaluation of developmental curriculum projects. This conclusion is not surprising because of inherent differences in such factors as organizational structure, personnel, funding pattern, life span, and aims and pur-

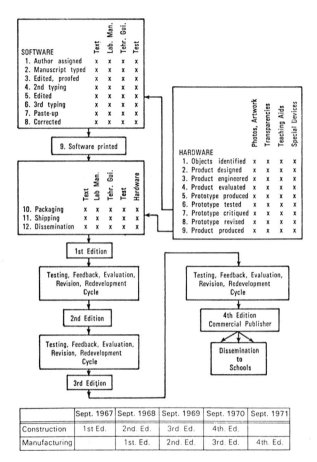

*Figure 10-3. IACP materials development system (from J. J. Buffer,
"A Junior High School Industrial Technology
Curriculum Project: A Final Evaluation of the
Industrial Arts Curriculum Project [IACP] 1965-
1971," Final Report, Project No. 70003, Grant No.
OEG-3-7-070003-1608, Ohio State University Research
Foundation, August 31, 1971, p. 35)*

poses. Because no single approach to evaluation can possibly meet the needs of all parties, and also because project directors require knowledge of available alternatives, this section surveys tested evaluation strategies that are easily replicated or adapted to new situations.

In making evaluative decisions during the formative stage of developing CDCP materials, I consistently turned to three primary reference sources for practical suggestions and solutions. The first was Grobman, *Developmental Curriculum Projects,* which is the first, comprehensive overview of the major, large-scale curriculum development efforts conducted in the late 1950s and 1960s. Chapter VI on "Evaluation" is an excellent treatment of issues and approaches related to the evaluation of curriculum projects. The second was Seferian and Cole, *Encounters in Thinking,*[51] which contains descriptive summaries of twenty curricula that are thought to have potential in process education. For each project "Selected Further Readings" provide references to relevant evaluation activities. The third was Crawford, Kratochvil, and Wright, *Evaluation of the Impact of Educational Research and Development Products,*[52] which is the final report documenting the development of selected educational products that seemed to have impact on the nation's schools. Available separately are the twenty-one *Product Development Reports* listed in Table 10-2. Following are illustrative product development and evaluation strategies employed by these projects which are generalizable and transportable to other programs. The numbers in parentheses refer to programs listed in Table 10-2.

1. Formative evaluation of the Hawaii English Program (2) was a continuous process. Eleven formative evaluation studies are summarized in Appendix A of *Product Development Report No. 2.* The initiative for many of these studies came out of questions posed by the curriculum planners or project administrators.

2. The Science Curriculum Improvement Study (4) reflects the effects of direct involvement of developmental staff in early classroom tryouts. The target audience substantially shaped the development of the product.

3. Summative evaluations were completed by external parties for three projects: "Sesame Street" (Educational Testing Service), Science: A Process Approach (Eastern Regional Institute for Education), and the Developmental Economic Education Program (Psychological Corporation). Documented reports describing these evaluations are available.

Table 10-2. Product development reports *issued separately*

Number[a]	Report
1	First Year Communication Skills Program, 62 pages (ED 072 469)
2	Hawaii English Program, 81 pages (ED 058 236)
3	Intermediate Science Curriculum Study, 47 pages (ED 058 101)
4	Science Curriculum Improvement Study, 48 pages (ED 058 102)
5	The Sullivan Reading Program, 70 pages (ED 058 020)
6	The Creative Learning Group Drug Education Program, 52 pages (ED 057 415)
7	The Frostig Program for Perceptual-Motor Development, 64 pages (ED 061 523)
8	Science: A Process Approach, 52 pages (ED 064 066)
9	Variable Modular Scheduling via Computer, 96 pages (ED 059 605)
10	"Sesame Street," 51 pages (ED 062 026)
11	Arithmetic Proficiency Training Program, 49 pages (ED 062 184)
12	The Edison Responsive Environment Learning System or The Talking Typewriter, 33 pages (ED 059 606)
13	Holt Social Studies Curriculum, 66 pages (ED 062 246)
14	Distar Instructional System, 69 pages (ED 061 632)
15	Materials and Activities for Teachers and Children—The MATCH Program, 59 pages (ED 061 774)
16	Developmental Economic Education Program (DEEP), 52 pages (ED 067 319)
17	Individually Prescribed Instruction—Mathematics (IPI-Math), 48 pages (ED 062 183)
18	The Cluster Concept Program, 69 pages (ED 064 526)
19	The Taba Social Studies Curriculum, 79 pages (ED 066 388)
20	Facilitating Inquiry in the Classroom, 38 pages (ED 064 252)
21	Program for Learning in Accordance with Needs (PLAN*), 84 pages[b]

[a]Copies of these reports may be obtained through EDRS or from the American Institutes for Research, Palo Alto, California.
[b]ED number not yet established.

4. The Frostig Perceptual-Motor Skills Program (7) revealed an effective and sustained involvement with the target audience in a setting that supported experimentation and revision of materials. Numerous small summative evaluations were also conducted and documented.

5. Science: A Process Approach (8) collected feedback data from fifteen demonstration sites that were used as a basis for program modification. A feedback form completed by teachers at the end of

each exercise is contained in Appendix B of *Product Development Report No. 8.*

6. A four-member evaluation group was included as a part of The Taba Social Studies Curriculum (19) staff to develop evaluation techniques, collect feedback data, and analyze results. Many of these techniques are generalizable to other programs.

7. In the IPI-Math (17) program the total system and many of its components were observed and continuously improved. Under this type of evaluation model the system itself provides data to demonstrate effectiveness and to suggest necessary modifications that can be instituted. With this approach there is really no final summative evaluation.

8. Science Research Associates has compiled a booklet summarizing the evaluation case studies for the Distar Instructional System (14). These arc invaluable reference sources for individuals confronted with similar problems.

Diffusion and Adoption

What happens to materials that have been developed by an externally funded curriculum project? Planning for implementation must begin during the formative stage of product development.[53] The thrust of the implementation of a new curriculum concept is dependent upon two main factors: the ability of the creator, producer, marketing agent, and implementer to understand and correlate the significant elements of a message, that is, curriculum content, the ability to communicate the message accurately, efficiently, and effectively in order to influence a positive decision. This leads to the last three principles:

12. Planning for the diffusion of curriculum materials should take place prior to the completion of prototype materials.

13. The completed curriculum materials must possess the properties of compatibility, divisibility, relative advantage, and exportability if they are to have any significant educational impact.

14. The completed curriculum should include a component for teacher education.

The approach to the diffusion of the products of developmental curriculum projects that appears to have produced the most satisfactory results to date is through regular commercial channels. The

U. S. Office of Education encourages this approach, provided that commercial involvement is accomplished on a competitive basis.

It is the policy of the U. S. Office of Education that the results of activities supported by it should be utilized in the manner which will best serve the public interest. This can be accomplished, in some situations, by distribution of materials without copyright. However, it is recognized that copyright protection may be desirable, in other situations, during development or as an incentive to promote effective dissemination of such materials. In the latter situations, arrangements for copyright of such materials normally for a limited period of time, may be authorized under appropriate conditions upon a showing satisfactory to the Office of Education that such protection will result in more effective development or dissemination of the materials or would otherwise be in the public interest.[54]

During the second year of operation of the project (1971) I began to explore actively various avenues for the diffusion of CDCP materials. The failure of many developmental curriculum projects to have a lasting educational impact was a conscious concern. Because the CDCP had chosen to develop student-based materials in a wide variety of formats, it was apparent that some type of continued support would be required beyond the period of external funding.

This awareness prompted me to convene a planning conference among representatives of the CDCP, Illinois Division of Vocational and Technical Education (DVTE), and the Southern Illinois University Foundation in August 1971 with the view toward soliciting commercial support for developing and marketing CDCP materials. This initiative ultimately resulted in the development by DVTE of a definitive handbook of administrative guidelines to be followed by state-funded projects seeking the assistance of publishers. (See Figure 10-4.) A "Request for Proposals" was subsequently prepared, a presentation was made to interested publishers, publishers' proposals were received and reviewed, and a publisher was selected. The commercial version of the CDCP Awareness Stage: Levels I, II, and III became available from McKnight Publishing Company in January 1975. It is anticipated that Accommodation Stage: Levels IV, V, and VI will be released in 1976, and Orientation Stage: Levels VII and VIII will be released in 1977.[55]

Concurrent with the development of the CDCP materials, a colleague and I wrote a proprietary text for preservice and in-service education courses.[56] The book begins with a succinct analysis and

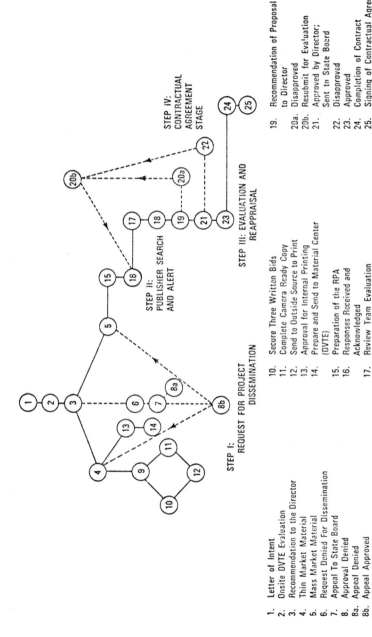

STEP I:
REQUEST FOR PROJECT
DISSEMINATION

STEP II:
PUBLISHER SEARCH
AND ALERT

STEP III: EVALUATION AND
REAPPRAISAL

STEP IV:
CONTRACTUAL
AGREEMENT
STAGE

1. Letter of Intent
2. Onsite DVTE Evaluation
3. Recommendation to the Director
4. Thin Market Material
5. Mass Market Material
6. Request Denied For Dissemination
7. Appeal To State Board
8. Approval Denied
8a. Appeal Denied
8b. Appeal Approved
9. Approved for External Printing

10. Secure Three Written Bids
11. Complete Camera Ready Copy
12. Send to Outside Source to Print
13. Approval for Internal Printing
14. Prepare and Send to Material Center (DVTE)
15. Preparation of the RPA
16. Responses Received and Acknowledged
17. Review Team Evaluation
18. Negotiate

19. Recommendation of Proposal to Director
20a. Disapproved
20b. Resubmit for Evaluation
21. Approved by Director; Sent to State Board
22. Disapproved
23. Approved
24. Completion of Contract
25. Signing of Contractual Agreement

Figure 10-4. Process for disseminating project information, Division of Vocational and Technical Education, State of Illinois (from DVTE, Administrative Guidelines for Securing Assistance in the Dissemination of Project Materials Arising from Contractual Agreements, Bulletin No. 37-972, 1972, p. 7)

synthesis of educational criticism and of recent responses to external forces. The core of the book contains brief historical and thorough theoretical treatment of three interrelated matters: career development, the foundation and evolution of career education, and models for career education and curriculum development. The book concludes with an analysis of the theory of change as applicable to education and makes recommendations to the several kinds of people who can contribute to a self-starting organization that is committed to providing experiences in career education. Suffice it to say that this text supports the fourteenth principle and should assist in the implementation of the CDCP materials.

Conclusions and Recommendations

The primary conclusion to be drawn from this discussion is that the case for using empirical findings drawn from research in product development has been considerably strengthened. Generalizations arising from the in-depth study of completed exemplary projects *can* be used to construct indicators of the potential impact of the product and to provide evidence relevant to various models of the processes of research, development, and dissemination. More specific (but not exhaustive) conclusions related to the five curriculum phases, follow.

First, the formulation of a sound conceptual base and curriculum development paradigm prior to product development has been found to be essential in communicating the intent of the project; in orienting staff, consultants, and writers; in guiding product development and decision making; in identifying areas for additional research; and in providing a basis for evaluation. Because of these roles and the (hypothesized) positive correlation between the validity of the conceptual paradigm and later impact of the product, vigorous formative evaluation should be included as a part of this phase. Cole's paper entitled "Approaches to the Logical Validation of Career Development Curricula Paradigms" describes an excellent approach to this type of evaluation.[57]

Second, the curriculum development paradigm shown in Figure 10-2, which is based on a developmental stage-developmental task approach, has demonstrated functional utility for ordering a logically related network of broad, intermediate, and specific objectives and for generating a variety of topics, activities, and materials. Further, a balanced approach between general and specific statements of objectives such as recommended by Gronlund[58] has been found to be understandable to neophyte staff, adequate for focusing product development, and manageable from the standpoint of revision and augmentation.

Third, a number of important issues related to the role of formative evaluation have been raised. Field-testing of prototype activities suggests that such practices should be carefully structured and monitored to avoid costly drains on finite personnel and fiscal resources. This is a priority decision that should be weighted against potential outcomes and not a challenge to formative evaluation per se. It is obvious that feedback from field-testing is imperative for some types of activities such as group simulation. Materials such as filmstrips, on the other hand, can often be adequately evaluated in-house by a carefully constituted panel of consultants. One teacher and a handful of students will often yield as much meaningful data as ten teachers and hundreds of students. It should be reiterated, that, to the extent that general objectives are generalizable skills, the array of possible activities, topics, and materials becomes wider and the choice of particular content less crucial.[59]

Fourth, successful management of a large-scale curriculum development project is dependent upon management by objectives and upon differentiated staffing.[60] These two concepts are mutually reinforcing. Just as the curriculum requires stated learning outcomes, so too should the program organization identify procedural goals and delineate each staff member's areas of responsibility in terms of expected results. Program objectives are best stated as "functions" to be performed, such as basic research, preparation of materials, graphics design, and so forth. Further delineation of functions in terms of a time dimension (immediate, intermediate, long-range) provides targets against which to measure progress toward ultimate goals. This approach to program management has also been found to be especially useful in working with nonstaff persons such as consultants and free-lance writers and artists. An additional advantage is continuity of effort during staff changes. Successful management is also dependent upon the economics of scale. There is, surely, an optimum range of organizational size and scope. And there is probably a curvilinear relationship between the project's complexity and accomplishments. This matter has important implications for future program planning and funding decisions and needs to be carefully evaluated.

Fifth, a curriculum development project with mass market potential requires sustained financial investment beyond the stage of formative development if it is to have any significant impact on education. This conclusion is consistently iterated by Crawford, Kratochvil, and Wright.[61] The procedure developed by the State of Illinois, shown in Figure 10-4, and accompanying administrative guidelines have been found to be an efficient procedure for securing the assistance of publishers in the dissemination of materials arising from contractual agreements. It is anticipated that this procedure will be continuously assessed and refined in the years to come.

Summary

This chapter has discussed principles and procedures of a five-stage curriculum development sequence. The model and strategies examined have proven their functional utility in developing the Career Development for Children Project. These are offered as potentials for consideration rather than as blueprints for duplication.

In concluding this paper, I should like to cite the additional cautions from Dale[62] as points to be considered during the planning and policy-making stages of curriculum development. One or more of them have been the downfall of many curriculum projects.

1. Do not design a program that varies from the basic school practices such as grade level, length of class time, or the number of days in a semester or year.

2. Do not forget to utilize existing facilities.

3. Do not begin product development before a decision-making model has been structured.

4. Do not involve an unmanageable number of field-test centers.

5. Do not develop a program without valid field-testing.

6. Do not engage in premature publicity.

7. Do not assume that materials in the public domain will be used by a large number of school systems.

8. Do not sell or disseminate test materials to persons or organizations outside the test network.

9. Do not assume that good program content or methodology is the single ingredient for successful implementation.

10. Do not let theory run away with practice.

11. Do not omit significant groups such as industry, other disciplines, teachers, minorities, parents, or businesses.

12. Do not let any single group dominate.

13. Do not retain program elements that field tests reject because "we have always done it this way," or "it's such a beautiful idea."

14. Do not be satisfied with "better than it was"; focus on relevant behavioral objectives and instructional goals.

Notes

1. S. H. Osipow, *Theories of Career Development* (New York: Appleton-Century-Crofts, 1968); M. Kroll, B. Dinklage, J. Lee, E. D. Morley, and H. Wilson, *Career Development: Growth and Crisis* (New York: John Wiley, 1970); J. S. Zaccaria, *Theories of Occupational Choice and Vocational Development* (Boston: Houghton Mifflin, 1970); R. Roth, D. B. Hershenson, and T. Hilliard, *The Psychology of Vocational Development* (Boston: Allyn and Bacon, 1970); D. G. Zytowski, *Vocational Behavior: Readings in Theory and Research* (New York: Holt, Rinehart and Winston, 1968); E. L. Herr and S. H. Cramer, *Vocational Guidance and Career Development in the Schools: Toward a Systems Approach* (Boston: Houghton Mifflin, 1972); L. J. Bailey and R. W. Stadt, *Career Education: New Approaches to Human Development* (Bloomington, Ill.: McKnight Publishing Company, 1973).

2. P. A. Perrone, "Vocational Development," *Review of Educational Research: Vocational, Technical, and Practical Arts Education* 36 (April 1966): 298-307; W. W. Tennyson, "Career Development," *ibid.,* 38 (October 1968): 346-366; J. L. Holland and D. R. Whitney, "Career Development," *Review of Educational Research: Guidance and Counseling* 30 (April 1969): 227-238; J. O. Crites, "Measurement of Vocational Maturity in Adolescence: 1. Attitude Test of the Vocational Development Inventory," *Psychological Monographs* 79 (No. 1, 1965): 36; Herr and Cramer, *Vocational Guidance and Career Development in the Schools;* Bailey and Stadt, *Career Education.*

3. E. L. Herr, "Unifying an Entire System of Education around a Career Development Theme," paper presented at the National Conference on Exemplary Programs and Projects, Atlanta, March 1969.

4. *Ibid.* 18.

5. L. J. Bailey, "Theories of Vocational Behavior," *Journal of Industrial Teacher Education* 5 (No. 3, 1968): 4-19; *id.,* "An Investigation of the Vocational Behavior of Selected Women Vocational Education Students," unpublished doctoral dissertation, University of Illinois, 1968; *id.,* "Industrial Arts and Vocational Development," *Illinois Journal of Education* 60 (No. 5, 1969): 30-35.

6. *Id.,* "Facilitating Career Development at the Elementary School Level," research proposal submitted to the Illinois Board of Vocational Education and Rehabilitation, Southern Illinois University, November 6, 1969.

7. *Id.*, "A Curriculum Model for Facilitating Career Development," Career Development for Children Project, March 1971; *id.*, "Implementing Career Education," Career Development for Children Project, October 1971; *id.*, K. G. Turner, W. H. Van Rooy, "Some Questions and Answers on Career Development: An Interview with CDCP," Career Development for Children Project, April 1972.

8. L. J. Bailey, "Career Development for Children Project: Final Report," Career Development for Children Project, August 1973.

9. R. M. Tomlinson, L. J. Bailey, L. A. Hinhede, and L. M. Langdon, "Occupational Patterns and Functions of Employed Licensed Practical Nurses," Final Report, Part I, U. S. Office of Education Contract #OE 5-85-038, January 1969; T. S. Baldwin and L. J. Bailey, "An Experimental Study of the Readability of Technical Training Materials Presented on Microfilm vs. Offset Copy," Final Report, Air Force Human Resources Laboratory Contract #F33615-68-C-1522, June 1969; *Facilitating Career Development: An Annotated Bibliography*, ed. L. J. Bailey (Springfield, Ill.: Board of Vocational Education and Rehabilitation, 1970); L. D. Holloway and L. J. Bailey, "Developing Teaching Competencies Needed by Educational Personnel in Post-Secondary Health Occupations Programs," Final Report, U. S. Office of Education Grant OEG-0-9-250340-4138 (725), August 1971.

10. H. Grobman, *Developmental Curriculum Projects: Decision Points and Processes* (Itasca, Ill.: Peacock, 1970), 6.

11. For example, E. C. Short and G. D. Marconnit, *Contemporary Thought on Public School Curriculum* (Dubuque, Iowa: William C. Brown, 1968).

12. Grobman, *Developmental Curriculum Projects*.

13. H. P. Cole, "Approaches to the Logical Validation of Career Development Curricula Paradigms," Career Development for Children Project, May 1973.

14. B. H. Banathy, *Instructional Systems* (Palo Alto, Calif.: Fearon, 1968), 13.

15. Grobman, *Developmental Curriculum Projects*.

16. Bailey and Stadt, *Career Education*, 309.

17. D. E. Super, "A Theory of Vocational Development," *American Psychologist* 8 (No. 4, 1953): 185-190; *id. et al.*, *Vocational Development: A Framework for Research* (New York: Teachers College Press, 1957); D. E. Super, *Career Development: Self-Concept Theory* (New York: College Entrance Examination Board, 1963).

18. *Id.*, "Dimensions and Measurement of Vocational Maturity," *Teachers College Record* 5 (No. 2, 1955): 151-163; *id. et al.*, *Vocational Development*; Crites, "Measurement of Vocational Maturity in Adolescence"; D. E. Super and P. L. Overstreet, *The Vocational Maturity of Ninth Grade Boys* (New York: Teachers College Press, 1960); W. D. Gribbons and P. R. Lohnes, *Emerging Careers* (New York: Teachers College Press, 1968); B. W. Westbrook and J. W. Cunningham, "The Development and Application of Vocational Maturity Measures," *Vocational Guidance Quarterly* 18 (No. 3, 1970): 171-175.

19. I. Illich, "Convivial Tools," *Saturday Review of Education* 1 (No. 4, 1973): 63-67.

20. A. H. Maslow, "A Theory of Human Motivation," *Psychological Review*

50 (No. 6, 1943): 370-396; *id., Toward a Psychology of Being* (Princeton, N. J.: D. Van Nostrand, 1962).

21. *Life Skills in School and Society. Yearbook 1969,* ed. L. J. Rubins (Washington, D. C.: Association for Supervision and Curriculum Development, 1969); *Perceiving, Behaving, Becoming. Yearbook 1962,* ed. A. W. Combs (Washington, D. C.: Association for Supervision and Curriculum Development, 1962); H. P. Cole, *Process Education: The New Direction for Elementary-Secondary Schools* (Englewood Cliffs, N. J.: Educational Technology Publications, 1972).

22. Bailey, "A Curriculum Model for Facilitating Career Development," 1.

23. *Id.,* "To the Parent," in Myron Brenton, *21,741 Choices for an Occupation,* reprinted (Carbondale, Ill.: Career Development for Children Project, 1970), 1.

24. Bailey, "Implementing Career Education," 7.

25. *Id.,* Turner, and Van Rooy, "Some Questions and Answers on Career Development," 4.

26. D. R. Krathwohl, "Stating Objectives Appropriately for Program, for Curriculum, and for Instructional Material Development," *Journal of Teacher Education* 16 (No. 2, 1965): 83-92.

27. Cole, "Approaches to the Logical Validation of Career Development Curricula Paradigms."

28. Krathwohl, "Stating Objectives Appropriately for Program, for Curriculum, and for Instructional Material Development."

29. For example, W. J. Popham, E. W. Eisner, H. J. Sullivan, and L. L. Tyler, *Instructional Objectives,* Educational Research Association Monograph Series on Curriculum Evaluation, Number 3 (Chicago: Rand McNally, 1969); B. S. Bloom, J. T. Hastings, and G. F. Madaus, *Handbook on Formative and Summative Evaluation of Student Learning* (New York: McGraw-Hill, 1971).

30. Cole, "Approaches to the Logical Validation of Career Development Curricula Paradigms."

31. J. S. Zaccaria, "Developmental Tasks: Implications for the Goals of Guidance," *Personnel and Guidance Journal* 44 (No. 5, 1965): 372-375.

32. Herr, "Unifying an Entire System of Education around a Career Development Theme."

33. R. J. Havighurst, *Human Development and Education* (New York: David McKay, 1953); *id.,* "Youth in Exploration and Man Emergent," in *Man in a World of Work,* ed. Henry Borow (Boston: Houghton Mifflin, 1964); N. C. Kearney, *Elementary School Objectives* (New York: Russell Sage Foundation, 1953); W. French *et al., Behavioral Goals of General Education in High School* (New York: Russell Sage Foundation, 1957).

34. N. E. Gronlund, *Stating Behavioral Objectives for Classroom Instruction* (New York: Macmillan, 1970).

35. R. F. Mager, *Preparing Instructional Objectives* (Palo Alto, Calif.: Fearon, 1962).

36. Bailey and Stadt, *Career Education,* 357-360.

37. M. B. Antholz, "Conceptualization of a Model Career Development Program, K-12," unpublished research paper, University of Minnesota, June 1972.

38. Super, *Career Development*, 18.

39. K. G. Turner, "A Conceptual Model of the Functional Self," Career Development for Children Project, June 1973.

40. H. Taba, *Curriculum Development: Theory and Practice* (New York: Harcourt, Brace and World, 1962), 266.

41. B. Zimmermann and L. J. Bailey, *Teachers Guide: Level I. Becoming Aware of Me and What I Do* (Carbondale, Ill.: Career Development for Children Project, 1973), 39-66.

42. For example, E. P. Torrance, *Rewarding Creative Behavior* (Englewood Cliffs, N. J.: Prentice-Hall, 1965).

43. W. E. Vinacke, "Concept Formation in Children of School Ages," in *The Psychology of the Elementary School Child*, ed. A. R. Binter and S. H. Frey (Chicago: Rand McNally, 1972), 135-145.

44. Havighurst, *Human Development and Education*.

45. J. S. Bruner, *The Process of Education* (New York: Random House, 1960); *id., Toward a Theory of Instruction* (New York: W. W. Norton, 1968).

46. R. M. Gagné, *The Conditions of Learning* (New York: Holt, Rinehart and Winston, 1970).

47. E. M. Rogers and F. F. Shoemaker, *Communication in Innovations* (New York: Free Press, 1971); R. G. Havelock *et al., Planning for Innovation through Dissemination and Utilization of Knowledge* (Ann Arbor, Mich.: Center for Research on Utilization of Scientific Knowledge, Institute for Social Research, 1971).

48. J. J. Buffer, "A Junior High School Industrial Technology Curriculum Project: A Final Evaluation of the Industrial Arts Curriculum Project (IACP), 1965-1971," Final Report, Project No. 70003, Grant No. OEG-3-7-070003-1608, Ohio State University Research Foundation, August 31, 1971.

49. R. W. Tyler *et al., Perspectives of Curriculum Evaluation* (Chicago: Rand McNally, 1967); Bloom, Hastings, and Madaus, *Handbook on Formative and Summative Evaluation of Student Learning*; PDK National Study Committee on Evaluation, *Educational Evaluation and Decision Making* (Itasca, Ill.: Peacock, 1971).

50. Grobman, *Developmental Curriculum Projects*.

51. A Seferian and H. P. Cole, *Encounters in Thinking: A Compendium of Curricula for Process Education* (Buffalo, N. Y.: Creative Education Foundation, 1970).

52. J. J. Crawford, D. W. Kratochvil, and C. E. Wright, *Evaluation of the Impact of Educational Research and Development Products: Final Report* (Palo Alto, Calif.: American Institutes for Research in the Behavioral Sciences, 1972).

53. Grobman, *Developmental Curriculum Projects*; Crawford, Kratochvil, and Wright, *Evaluation of the Impact of Educational Research and Development Products*.

54. Department of Health, Education, and Welfare, U. S. Office of Education, *Copyright Program Information* (Washington, D. C.: Government Printing Office, 1971).

55. See Bailey, "Career Development for Children Project," for more specific details of the process.

56. Bailey and Stadt, *Career Education.*

57. Cole, "Approaches to the Logical Validation of Career Development Curricula Paradigms."

58. Gronlund, *Stating Behavioral Objectives for Classroom Instruction.*

59. Cole, "Approaches to the Logical Validation of Career Development Curricula Paradigms," 53-55.

60. R. W. Stadt, R. E. Bittle, L. J. Kenneke, and D. C. Nystrom, *Managing Career Education Programs* (Englewood Cliffs, N. J.: Prentice-Hall, 1973).

61. Crawford, Kratochvil, and Wright, *Evaluation of the Impact of Educational Research and Development Products.*

62. R. E. Dale, "Implementation of Total Package," in *Career Ladders and Lattices in Home Economics and Related Areas: Possibilities for Upgrading Household Employment,* Final Report for the Contract for Technical Assistance in the Development of Career Ladders, Contract No. 11-1-0406-000 (Washington, D. C.: American Home Economics Association, October 15, 1971-June 30, 1972).

11 Questions and Requirements for the Comparative Study of Curriculum Development Procedures

Jon Schaffarzick

The preceding chapters represent the experiences and views of nine people who have directed or assumed major roles in large-scale curriculum development projects. When we asked these people to write, we hoped that the resulting essays would serve two purposes. First, we hoped that they would combine to provide other persons interested in curriculum development with a set of useful, succinct summaries of the approaches used and recommended by a diversified group of experienced, respected developers. Second, we hoped that the essays would provide a better basis for deciding whether it is worthwhile, feasible, and desirable to carry out studies designed to compare alternative development strategies. After examining the chapters and noting their consistently high quality, we feel confident that the first purpose has been accomplished. The purpose of this concluding chapter, then, is to pursue further our second objective.

Our interest in possibilities for comparative process studies stems from a concern about apparent inadequacies in the knowledge avail-

I would like to thank Lauren B. Resnick, Ralph W. Tyler, Decker Walker, Elliot W. Eisner, Robert Karplus, W. James Popham, M. Vere DeVault, Charles Thompson, Marc Tucker, and Robert Wise for thorough, insightful reviews of an earlier draft of this chapter.

able for guiding the selection or creation of the best ways of developing particular types of curricula. Funding agencies and developers are confronted with an awesome array of approaches, each of which is defended by its proponents as possessing certain virtues unshared by other approaches. Lacking reliable indications of the relative strengths and weaknesses of different approaches, developers and funders often make procedural decisions arbitrarily or solely on the basis of personal preference (sometimes better described as whim). In many cases procedural decisions are made in an ad hoc, eclectic fashion, with problems attacked individually as they arise, in the absence of an overarching, coordinated, appropriate strategy.

Does this matter? Would the availability of process research findings improve the efficiency of developmental work and the quality of the resulting curricula? Many developers and theorists seem to believe that it would. Some have criticized funding agencies for continuing to churn out products without pausing to learn from their experiences. For example, in an earlier chapter James Popham charged that the federal government has been "more interested in supporting the actual production of instructional materials than in sharpening the technology by which such materials are produced." He claims, "It is most shortsighted, nevertheless, not to expend a reasonable proportion of funds for materials production, perhaps 2 to 5 percent, in deliberately attempting to improve the technology of instructional materials development."

This is not to imply that process studies are nonexistent. A number of people have taken the time to provide thoughtful reflections and useful suggestions based upon their own experiences with development.[1] But most of these efforts are case studies of individual developmental projects. Consequently, the results do not always allow or facilitate valid, fruitful comparisons across projects and, therefore, do not provide all that we need to select among alternatives.

This apparent gap has led us to think about the possibility of designing, funding, and carrying out comparative assessments of different procedures in curriculum development. In our present positions with the National Institute of Education, we occasionally encounter situations in which comparative study might be possible. Before attempting to take advantage of such opportunities, however, we must first delineate more clearly the major alternatives to be compared, pinpoint the most crucial variable elements of developmental approaches to serve as focuses for comparative studies, determine whether comparative process research having adequate reliability is feasible, and decide whether the potential usefulness of such studies is great enough to warrant the probable expense. We must, in other words, begin to seek answers to questions such as the following:

1. What are the different ways in which individuals and projects go about developing curricula?

2. Are the procedures used in developing curricula unique in each case? Or do all developmental projects share some common, underlying characteristics that are obscured by differences in jargon and emphasis?

3. Should development procedures vary from case to case? Or are there some "best" procedures that should always be used?

4. What are the most important commonalities in alternative developmental approaches?

5. What are the most important variations in these approaches?

6. What are the causes of procedural variation?

7. Which of these causative conditions can be controlled under actual developmental circumstances?

8. Which types of process-outcome relationships are worthy of empirical investigation? Which are susceptible to such investigation?

9. Is it possible to carry out experimental or quasi-experimental studies, varying only the procedures by which programs are developed and holding constant or controlling the effects of other variables, such as program content and instructional approach? Or are particular developmental strategies so closely tied to the characteristics of the program or the developer that the use of competing approaches in developing similar programs becomes ludicrous or impossible?

The nine developers' essays included in this volume should help us in attacking these issues. What I intend to do in the remainder of this chapter is to begin extracting "lessons" that can be learned by considering the collection of essays as a whole.

One of the most valuable contributions of these chapters is an indication of which aspects of development the developers consider most important. When we asked the writers to participate in this undertaking, we intentionally provided only broad directions, avoiding the specification of topical focuses. We wanted to see which elements of development they considered most worthy of attention, as well as learning what they had to say about each such element. As we expected, this nondirectional approach has led to a fairly diversified set of statements. Each writer has organized his or her paper uniquely. Some writers give only passing attention to aspects of development that serve as cornerstones in other discussions. And, as we fully anticipated when we chose developers of contrasting persuasions, different writers can say quite different things about the same topics.

In spite of this diversity, though, there are some common threads. Some topics are addressed by everyone. And some ideas seem almost unanimously popular. These common areas would seem to suggest matters that all developers should attend to and approaches that have almost universal appeal. In this chapter I plan to treat these commonalities first, before turning my attention to the prime candidates for variation in comparative studies and to some conclusions about present needs and prospects in the study of curriculum development processes. Thus, in the first section I shall discuss nine common characteristics: the determination of the need for a curriculum; the construction of theoretical foundations; the use of goals and objectives; attention to developmental psychology and learning research; the use of group collaboration; planning for early dissemination; the preparation of staff development materials; testing and revision; and continuous development.

This list does not, of course, include all the similarities among the nine approaches. But it does include those similar aspects that the developers emphasized, and it does help us to narrow our scopes in choosing elements to vary intentionally in comparative studies.

In the second section I shall discuss the ten types of variation which, in my view, emerged as most important in the nine developers' chapters: origins and motivation; type of sponsorship; type of developer; type of target group; three major aspects of curricular content (knowledge, "embodiments," and approaches to learning); subject-matter area; type of program being developed; types and usages of objectives; staff composition; and program evaluation.

Before moving from these considerations of constant and variable elements to the concluding discussion of implications for comparative process studies, we would be wise to examine some of the realistic obstacles to the conduct of such studies. This will be done in the chapter's third section, which touches on five important problem areas: competition between program needs and study needs; interdependencies between the process and the product; the difficulty of predicting process requirements; the importance of individuals; and problems of funding agency.

Finally, in the fourth section of the chapter, I shall return to the main questions addressed by this book: should we carry out studies designed to compare alternative curriculum development procedures? If so, what forms should these studies take, and which procedural alternatives should they compare? My conclusions are, generally, that: it is unrealistic to think about experimental comparative studies in this area; we should concentrate on finding ways to take better advantage of opportunities to study curriculum development procedures naturalistically; and we should use such studies to find ways of conducting curriculum development more efficiently without sacrificing quality.

Common Procedures and Characteristics

Determination of Need

The first common procedure that emerges from all nine chapters is one that occurs as a first, or at least as a very early, step in curriculum development: the determination of whether a new curriculum is needed. This determination is generally made in one of two ways. If the developers begin with some idea for a particular type of new curriculum, they first decide whether the need for this type of curriculum is strong enough to warrant development. If the developers do not have a specific possibility in mind when they begin, they must determine what types of new curricula are most needed. In either event, needs are being assessed.

The assessment of needs varies substantially in rigor and extensity. Recently there have been frequent calls for elaborate survey and analysis techniques designed to detect new needs arising from social changes, instructional trends, advances in knowledge, changes in school organization, and changes in the learners themselves. Some developers, such as Karplus, begin with personal observations of what is lacking in education. Others combine their own perceptions with salesmen's observations of need in the schools they serve, as DeVault and Anglin did in initiating development of SRA's Mathematics Learning System. But, regardless of how needs are discovered or affirmed, few developers undertake the demanding process of constructing new instructional programs without first securing some assurance that their efforts are addressed to some want.

Theoretical Foundations

The second common feature is also an early procedure—the formulation of a curriculum's theoretical foundations. The major functions of such foundations are to explicate the purposes of curriculum development projects and to articulate the ideas that will guide development and shape the curriculum itself. Though all curriculum development projects have theoretical foundations, some are more elaborate and formally stated than others. Theoretical foundations may incorporate views about learning, about the characteristics of learners, about the subject to be taught, about society, about human relationships and group processes, or about any other topics that bear on the work to be done.

Several of the authors stressed the importance of explicating theoretical foundations and the desirability of doing so early in the developmental process. Mehlinger, for example, has declared that "curriculum development is mostly the art of making good judgments, and decisions made in the first stage of a project can bless or curse the project throughout its duration." Just as a research team needs a theoretical framework to guide its inquiry, explains Mehlinger, so does a developmental team need a "rationale" in which statements concerning goals are logically linked to one another. Tyler has stated that "an essential early step in curriculum development is to examine and analyze significant conditions that influence the construction and operation of the curriculum." These conditions include the need or problem to which the curriculum is addressed, the types of students for whom the curriculum is intended, and "contemporary educational environments" (including the home, the peer group, the larger community, and the school). According to Popham, the first step in developing a validated instructional product is "to decide, at least in general terms, what it is that the instructional materials are supposed to accomplish." Eisner has asserted that "decisions about the character and form of [a curriculum's] format are crucial for the process of curriculum development," pointing out that "this format reveals implicitly the assumptions and values embedded in a project and provides the constraints within which curriculum writers must work." DeVault and Anglin have called the making of assumptions and the setting of priorities the most important elements in their strategy. These activities demanded much time during the initial stages of their project, as well as throughout the five years during which the program was developed. And Bailey has declared that "the preparation of policy statements should be accorded first priority and precede more specific development of performance objectives." Bailey calls this first phase of curriculum development the formulation of a "curricular language." He notes, "A project's curricular language should include, at a minimum, statements of basic purpose, rationale, assumptions, and value judgments." The purposes of a "curricular language" (that is, a theoretical foundation) are, according to Bailey, to communicate the intent of the project, to orient staff, consultants, and writers, to guide product development and decision making, to identify areas for additional research, and to provide a basis for evaluation.

Most of the authors have given some indication of the topics they address in formulating their theoretical foundations. Purves has stated that "Curricula reflect the maker's understanding of the nature and goals of society, the nature of the people who are to be affected and their learning processes, the nature of the concepts, attitudes, or skills that are to be learned." In analyzing some of his own curricular foundations, Purves finds that they contain assumptions about individual differences and individual liberty, about the nature of democratic society, and about the limits of general education. Eisner has explained that theory used in curriculum development can refer to ideas about the nature of the subject matter being taught, about how children learn, or about how a particular development team might go about its work. In developing their mathematics curriculum, DeVault and Anglin asked "whether instructional materials in the style of present commercial texts were appropriate for the 1970s." They also analyzed the implications of changes in school organization and building designs, the increased concern for variety in learning and teaching styles, requirements of the community and society, demands for relevance, and the need to avoid racism and sexism in instructional materials. Bailey has added another dimension to all of these theoretical focuses by pointing out that, because developers are not creating products to be used at the time their curricula are being conceptualized, they must also speculate about the future characteristics of students, teachers, class scheduling, available technology, school budgets, educational ideologies, and the disciplines covered by their curricula.

As these examples illustrate, theoretical foundations vary in the number and types of topics they address and in the relative emphasis they place on different topics. But all of the projects discussed by the nine developers were guided by theoretical foundations of some sort.

Those who choose not to begin by explicating the ideas on which their projects are founded are forced to do so by funding requirements. In order to receive funds, prospective developers must submit proposals. And such proposals must always contain a statement of rationale. Only rarely does one receive developmental funds to spend time formulating basic ideas prior to beginning the actual work of development. There is, of course, always time to flesh out or modify initial ideas as development proceeds, but some set of broad, guiding principles usually exists first.

Goals and Objectives

The third similarity among the approaches is the statement of goals and objectives. All of the authors have utilized goals and objectives to guide their developmental efforts in one way or another. Karplus, for example, included general behavioral objectives in each teacher's guide to communicate the possible thrusts of SCIS activities and used objectives in the construction of an evaluation program for the teacher's use. The second step in Popham's "validated instructional materials strategy" is to translate the product's intended mission into specific objectives. Purves conceives of behavioral objectives in terms of a content-behavior grid, which covers the curriculum's more general objectives and provides a means for evaluating the success of the curriculum. DeVault and Anglin used their initial assessment of needs as the basis for establishing their major goals, which gave direction to the development of their new mathematics program. Once these goals had been established, they prepared a draft of year-end mastery objectives for each grade level. Then they developed "enabling objectives," which supported the year-end objectives and which gave direction to the writing of individual chapters. This approach coincides with Bailey's view that "curriculum construction involves the process of moving through descending abstractions from very general and global statements of desired program behaviors to intermediate-level statements that indicate the blocks from which the program will be constructed."

The most heavily discussed topic in recent discourse on curriculum is that of educational objectives. Theorists, researchers, developers, administrators, and teachers have debated about the proper format for goals, the pros and cons of behavioral objectives, desired degrees of the specificity of goals, the stages at which different types of statements concerning goals are most useful, and so on. The nine writers differ on each of these topics, as I shall discuss in the section on variation.

In spite of the frequent disagreements about the optimum format and use of goals, however, almost everyone agrees that curriculum development projects must be guided by goals of some sort. Tyler has described the selection and definition of curriculum objectives as a "complex but necessary task," for instance, and Bailey has stressed the importance of having "a network of logically related objectives." It is also commonly agreed that goals and objectives should be expressed early (so that developers know what they are supposed to be doing) and that goals may (and probably will) be modified as development progresses. Tyler, for example, recommends that objective selection and definition continue "both as the rest of the curriculum tasks are carried on and after the curriculum is operating." Similarly, DeVault and Anglin advise that year-end mastery objectives be continuously reviewed and revised throughout the developmental cycle.

Attention to Developmental Psychology and Learning Research

All nine chapters indicate that the developers have been influenced, in one way or another, by the work of developmental psychologists such as Piaget, Bruner, Gagné, Havighurst, Vinacke, and others who have studied the development of the traits and capabilities of learners. Karplus, for example, has stated that "current ideas of intellectual development" (particularly those of Jean Piaget) are central to the SCIS programs. In constructing this curriculum, the developmental stages of elementary school children were taken into account in three major ways:

First, the main thrust of activities had a perceptual emphasis in the very early grades, moved to a conceptual orientation with concrete referents in the intermediate grades, and then introduced some abstract referents for the upper grades . . . .

Second, the concepts introduced in the teaching program were of some help in advancing students from one developmental stage to the next, since they called attention to generalizable aspects of the children's observations . . . .

Third, the vast majority of activities could lead to student satisfaction regardless of the children's conceptual level, since each student was free to use the materials in the way he wished and could therefore adapt them to his immediate needs.

In a similar way, Bailey used developmental psychology theory and empirical evidence to justify the organization of his Career Development for Children Project. He was guided particularly by Vinacke's interpretations of cognitive stages, Havighurst's descriptions of developmental tasks, Bruner's notion of a spiral curriculum, and Gagné's concept of cumulative learning.

Tyler has referred to his syllabus (*Basic Principles of Curriculum and Instruction*), which points out "the way in which knowledge of the psychology of learning can be used to estimate the probability of attaining a given objective under the conditions found in a particular school." Resnick has provided some more specific examples of developmental psychology principles that may be utilized in guiding curriculum development: "the research makes it evident that adult concepts and skills are not 'born' full-grown, that children—and, presumably, learners of all ages—pass through successive stages of understanding and ability on the way to what we view as mature competence, and that each such stage has a kind of logic to it. 'Unskilled' performances make sense if understood in their own terms; further, they are the route to competence, a route that must be probed and clarified if instruction is to match optimally the developing capabilities of learners." Resnick has also cautioned curriculum developers about the present limitations of developmental psychology: "developmental psychology as a whole still lacks a theory or even a good set of descriptors of the environment. Thus, it is difficult to cull from developmental theory any but the most general guidelines for design of environments specifically intended to bring about changes in competence."

In spite of these limitations, however, most developers tend to examine research on learning and psychological development and to use available knowledge in these areas as at least a partial guide to the capabilities of learners at particular age levels.

Group Collaboration

Another important similarity in the projects described is that development is accomplished through the coordinated, cooperative efforts of groups.[2] None of these curricula have been created by single individuals. Most curriculum development projects are so large and complex that they require the assistance of many people and the availability of various competencies. As Eisner notes in discussing one of the smaller projects covered in this book, "curriculum development on the scale on which we worked is inevitably a group enterprise. . . ." The nature of the decisions to be made and the tasks to be accomplished require, furthermore, that the members of development groups think and work together, rather than spending most of their time functioning as autonomous members of large collections of individuals.

Group work is needed and used at all stages of development: in setting goals and objectives, in designing lesson prototypes or outlining specific activities, in writing and mediating materials for students, in organizing learning experiences, in planning and conducting trial usages, in determining the revision implications of field-test results, in revising materials and activities, and in planning and carrying out dissemination and implementation.

In discussing one of these stages—the selection of objectives—Tyler explains that group collaboration facilitates consideration of many different suggestions and judgments. Eisner extends this point by noting that in his project group collaboration heightened exploration of possible consequences flowing from particular actions, presentation of different perspectives and alternative decision options, and the articulation of varying educational, practical, psychological, and social values pertaining to issues under discussion.

It is significant to note that every author in this book has emphasized the usefulness and necessity of group collaboration.

Early Dissemination Planning

Many of the writers have mentioned the desirability of initiating "dissemination" or "field implementation" planning during early developmental stages. This may include a variety of activities, ranging from assessments of the market for emerging products to the creation of markets through the promotion of products (for example, writing articles, giving speeches, and so forth). Most developers advise that plans for dissemination begin early, run throughout a project, and involve developmental personnel as well as publishers and their salesmen. Popham, for example, recommends that developers "worry" all along about how their products will be disseminated. Bailey claims that dissemination planning "must begin during the formative stage of product development." Mehlinger has illustrated (see his Figure 7-1) how "diffusion" (dissemination) permeates "a project from beginning to end" in the development cycle used by the Social Studies Development Center at Indiana University. "Diffusion begins the day the project is funded and continues long after the development grant has expired," Mehlinger explains. Furthermore, the dissemination planning serves different purposes at different stages of development:

At the outset the development team should be eager to spread its ideas in order to gain feedback for revisions of the rationale and the statement of goals. The project staff is also trying to stimulate professional discussion about its ideas. It can do this by distributing its paper on conceptualization, by brochures, and by publishing newsletters and articles about the project. During the stages of testing the prototype and the full course, the developers are eager to gain feedback on their materials; they are also seeking to create a future market for their product. They can distribute widely examples of the instructional materials, demonstrate materials at conferences and meetings, and provide reports on the results of classroom testing. When the product has been published, the developer should help the publisher market the product validly and facilitate school adoptions. Developers should approve the marketing program, including advertisements about the project, and should assist the publisher by making presentations to state and school textbook adoption committees.

Most developers, particularly those who have produced materials that have been published, recommend early involvement of a distributor. Most often the distributor is a commercial publisher. Bailey, for instance, convened a planning conference designed to solicit commercial support for the development and marketing of his materials. Subsequent to the conference, he prepared a "Request for Proposals," made a presentation to interested publishers, received and reviewed publishers' proposals, and selected a publisher. In cases where the development itself is funded by a private firm that does its own marketing, such involvement is automatic and takes a somewhat different form. For example, SRA's sales staff became involved in DeVault and Anglin's project almost at the beginning of program development, which was when implementation planning started.

Staff Development Materials

A seventh major similarity in the approaches is the attempt to prepare those who must implement the new curricula. The publication of studies demonstrating that teachers and other implementers often do not use new curricula in the ways developers intend has increased developers' awareness of the importance of "staff development" (or "teacher education") materials. New curricula often call for the teaching of content with which teachers are not familiar or the use of instructional techniques with which teachers are not comfortable. The purposes of staff development materials are typically to assist teachers and other adults who will direct and coordinate the student's use of the curriculum to acquire a background of knowledge requisite to adequate understanding of new content and to gain an understanding of the ways in which the curriculum is meant to be implemented. Karplus has listed, for example, four goals of the teacher education activities of the SCIS: familiarity with the science phenomena in the units under study; adoption of a child-centered, inquiry-oriented classroom environment; understanding of children's intellectual development; and acquaintance with the nature of science and its logical and conceptual structure. The SCIS attempts to accomplish these goals through the use of teachers' guides and in-service workshops and preservice courses relating to inquiry-oriented science programs, especially the SCIS. Similarly, a major objective of DeVault and Anglin's one-day in-service program was to help teachers understand the philosophy of their curriculum as represented by its major goals. Bailey has tried to accomplish similar objectives by writing a "proprietary text" for use in preservice and in-service education courses.

Purves also attends to preparation of curriculum implementers, but his approaches to staff development are somewhat different than most, being strongly influenced by his distaste for "teacher-proof" curricula. Arguing that it is better to assume that teachers are collaborators rather than enemies, that teachers are "imaginative rather than cloddish," that teachers are "intelligent rather than stupid," that programming teachers is a mistake, and that hinting is a better strategy, Purves prefers to develop teachers' guides that seek "to bring the teachers into the curriculum-making activity":

They suggested, but did not direct. They raised questions for discussion, but did not give answers that seemed to be presented as if by fiat. They presented options for activities, but did not specify the efficacy of any one activity over another. They were not even called teachers' guides but "Talks with Teachers." They recognized that the teacher was a human being capable of making decisions, a person who must be thought of as human if he were to think of his students as human.

Testing and Revision

Although the authors do not agree on the best ways of testing curricula (as I shall discuss in the section on variation), they are unanimous in believing that new curricula should be tested in some fashion and that the curricula should be revised on the basis of such testing. These shared beliefs represent one of the most obvious results of the curriculum development of the 1960s, of federal funding for large-scale "team" development, and of the disenchantment with earlier approaches to development (particularly the approach by which a single author, funded by a publisher, writes text materials without the time or money to try them out before publication). Mehlinger has expressed this belief in claiming that "the principal characteristic that distinguishes the process of high quality curriculum development from high quality, but typical, publishing company practice is the dependence upon careful field-testing of instructional products and the identification and elimination of deficiencies prior to the publication and dissemination of the product." While Mehlinger's observation about the recent prevalence of field-testing is correct, his distinction between the approaches used by Regional Laboratories and those used by publishers may be breaking down. For, as we have seen in DeVault and Anglin's chapter on the development of the SRA Mathematics Learning System, at least some publisher-sponsored projects are including test-revision activities as integral components of their work.

Testing is used to obtain various types of feedback. The most common purpose of testing is to assess the performance of products in various states of completion and to pinpoint areas requiring improvement. Another function is to test empirically assumptions, such as what instructional approaches and characteristics of products will be accepted by teachers and students, what will stimulate students, what will increase learning, and so forth. The forms that feedback mechanisms take vary with purpose, stage of development, project resources, and preferences of the personnel. Some feedback activities are casual tryouts with small groups of students, while others may be "preliminary" or "prototype" tests, larger "pilot" tests, "field verification" studies under more realistic conditions of usage, and relatively well-controlled, rigorous "field tests." The typical testing pattern is to try out progressively polished versions of the product with progressively larger samples, using progressively more elaborate and expensive testing techniques. The general rationale for this progressive sophistication is that earlier versions are bound to be more rudimentary and that problems are likely to be grosser and more easily detectable during the early stages than during the later stages. Hence, there is no sense in asking large numbers of teachers and students to invest a lot of time in using more primitive versions; nor does it make sense to spend much money in testing them. Only when smaller scale usage and several rounds of revision allow confidence that the materials are worthwhile and work reasonably well do developers invest in formal "field tests."

Continuous Development

The last major common element of the nine approaches is the preference for "continuous" curriculum development. Few developers feel that their curricula are complete or in their "best" form when they are printed for distribution. There is always room for improvement. Observations of a program's use under all sorts of realistic circumstances will point out problems and suggest ways of improving the program and its usage. Furthermore, changes in various aspects of the educational scene (instructional trends, developments in other subject areas, and so forth) and advances in the subject area covered by a curriculum often create requirements for modification.

As a result of these needs, most developers argue for prolonged development-test-revision cycles and continued funding to carry out periodic updating and improvement. Karplus has pointed out, for example, that SCIS is continuing to supervise publications and equipment kits subsequent to publication, in order to "assure the necessary quality control" and to detect required modifications. DeVault and Anglin have claimed that their curriculum (the SRA Mathematics Learning System) will be pedagogically and commercially successful only if it continues to meet specific needs through several revisions. Thus, they conduct a continuous review of the assumptions and priorities that gave initial impetus to the series" and plan to continue this assessment through implementation of their program. In arguing for this approach, DeVault and Anglin have provided a strong rationale for continuous development: "The major lesson that has been learned by the developers of this mathematics program is, in fact, that a continuous review of program assumptions and priorities and the resulting implications for program development can never end if a text series is to be successful in the dynamic societies of the 1970s." This is a lesson with which all of our developers seem to agree.

Variable Procedures and Characteristics

In addition to the commonalities, the developmental approaches described by the nine authors also exhibit important variations. The significance of this diversity becomes apparent when one remembers that these are only a few of the approaches to curriculum development; many other strategies are not represented here. In this section, I shall discuss some of these variations. The ten topics treated below do not, of course, include all of the important procedural characteristics that might be varied in comparative studies of alternative curriculum development procedures. This chapter section is not, however, intended as a presentation of an "all-inclusive" set of tightly interconnected variables. Some of the variables, in fact, have little to do with one another. Instead, what I have tried to do is to list and discuss the elements that emerge, in my view, as the most significant variable aspects of the nine developers' essays, regardless of the elements' relationships.

Some of these variations (such as type of sponsorship) are primarily causes of procedural variation, while others (for example, usages of objectives) are actual procedures that may vary from project to project. Some of these differences fall within categories already listed as commonalities; we have seen, for example, that almost all developers and theorists regard statements of goals and objectives as essential guides to development. And yet these same people differ substantially in the types of goals and objectives that they advocate and actually employ. Other differences represent variations in emphasis and activity. Thus, for example, some developers endeavor to construct new curricula that differ from existing curricula primarily in the content they include, while other developers attempt to innovate simultaneously in several areas—content, instruction, organization, environment, scheduling, social relationships, and so on.

Origins and Motivation

As I pointed out in the first part of the section on commonalities, all curriculum developers try to determine, in one way or another, what types of curricula are needed. What varies is the way in which these needs are determined; the nine authors have been motivated in different ways to develop particular types of curricula.

In some of the projects described (for example, by DeVault and Anglin), the expressed and perceived needs, problems, and desires of "consumers"—administrators, teachers, parents, and students—have played major roles in deciding to develop a curriculum and in specifying the type to be developed. The initiators of such projects carefully monitor community and societal trends and requirements, reactions to other programs, and changes in school organization, teaching and learning styles and preferences, building designs, and other aspects of the educational setting. In other words, they take their cues from the consumers. They begin, in a sense, with continuous market assessments and endeavor to fill perceived gaps in ways that will satisfy the users.

Other projects (such as those of Karplus, Eisner, and Resnick) are initially motivated by the developer's (or, if different, program conceptualizer's) perceptions of what is needed. A common example of this type is the project that is started by a scholar or subject-matter specialist who feels that available programs do not provide accurate, up-to-date, or stimulating representations of a particular area. In other cases, experts of some sort think of new instructional or organizational strategies and propose to develop new programs around them. In both cases, however, the primary motivating force is the expert, not the consumer. Sometimes it is felt that the consumers are not in a position to perceive deficiencies in the programs they are using (deficiencies owing to failure to keep pace with advances in knowledge, for example). It is thought at other times that the consumers are not always able (or do not have the time) to structure or select the best ways of responding to their needs (being unable to extrapolate the likely long-term consequences of studying certain things, for example).

These variations in motivation for curriculum development suggest some questions that might be addressed in studies comparing projects that have contrasting origins. We might try, for instance, to provide more information on the reasons for the disappointing implementation records of the new curricula designed primarily by scholars. Do such failures occur because scholars have unrealistic conceptions of what children and teachers can do and want to do? Or do the problems begin when teachers perceive such curricula as impositions of ideas of "outsiders"—outsiders who have not bothered to involve them sufficiently? Contrariwise, do "consumer-initiated" curricula fare much better in implementation? If so, why? Are they actually superior to expert-initiated curricula (in terms of worth and appropriateness of content, intrinsic value of instructional approach, and so on), or do they work better simply because teachers see them as "their own" and therefore use them more enthusiastically and perseveringly? What is the optimum combination of the input of experts and consumers in deciding what types of curricula to develop? How are such diverse inputs synthesized? How are conflicts resolved?

Type of Sponsorship

Just as different types of people and groups can motivate curriculum development, so can different types sponsor development, carry out development, and serve as target audiences for the curricula being developed. The projects that have been discussed vary in all three of these areas.

Sponsorship can affect procedures and decisions throughout the course of development projects (with funding agencies recommending, approving, or even dictating courses of action), but the type of occupant in this role is usually most important in the early stages, when needs are assessed and decisions are made about the type of program to be developed. The most influential variable dimension is whether the sponsor is public or private. When the sponsor is a public institution (such as the National Institute of Education, the Office of Education, the National Science Foundation, and state departments of education), curriculum development projects may begin in two ways. In the first—in which the sponsor is most directive and prescriptive—needs are assessed and basic program characteristics are decided by the sponsoring agency itself. The sponsor usually begins in such cases with a hazy notion of need in some area (that children are not learning enough about the world of work, for example). The sponsor then attempts to clarify the need by convening conferences of appropriate experts and practitioners, examining the results and recommendations of commissioned advisory studies and reports, and listening to the advice of those who care to address the issue. At some point, which is usually determined by the cycle of events during the fiscal year, decisions are made about the type(s) of program(s) to be developed. The agency conducts a competition (via requests for proposals, grants announcements, or other funding mechanisms) and selects the group "most qualified" to produce the desired type of program. When development begins in this way, the group that takes on the actual production tasks must work within a set of rules and parameters. Sometimes the parameters are so thoroughly defined that the developer's job is essentially to "carry out orders," not to exercise creativity.

The second type of origin under public sponsorship tends to involve more initiative on the part of the developer and less direction from the funding agency. In these cases, potential developers themselves determine needs, conceive of solutions (programs designed to meet the needs), and propose their ideas to potential sponsors, usually by submitting "unsolicited proposals" or proposals in response to fairly open funding announcements. Although sponsors do exercise some authority in these cases—by approving or rejecting proposals, by requiring changes in plans prior to receipt of funds, and by reserving the right to terminate funding if progress is not "acceptable"—developers exercise much more initiative and creativity and have much more latitude than they do in the first type of public-sponsored endeavor.

When the sponsor is a private institution (usually a publisher), development resembles the first type of public-sponsored projects in the way needs are determined. Private firms are necessarily interested in producing programs that sell. Hence, in deciding what to develop, they tend to take their leads from the problems, needs, and wants expressed by potential users. Unlike some of the second type of public-sponsored projects, in which curricular characteristics some-times follow the ideas of a scientist or "expert" who claims to see problems and needs of which users are not or cannot be aware ("the public doesn't always know what's best for itself"), private endeavors invariably cater to needs that the users consider to be "real." This orientation, of course, delimits the bounds of creative possibility and generally tends to result in less drastic change.

On the other hand, privately sponsored projects more closely re-semble the less directive type of publicly sponsored projects in terms of the roles played by particular groups. When the public funding agency assumes a less directive posture, it tends to respond to ideas presented by developers. It decides whether to fund, how much to allocate, and whether to approve general program characteristics. All of these decisions are based upon possibilities advanced by the devel-opment group. This relationship approximates that which usually obtains between a private firm's board of directors or management group and the employees who will construct the program. Once the basic ideas are approved and the decision to proceed has been made, the developers—who are considered the technical experts and who have usually initiated and retooled the plans—proceed to make deci-sions concerning characteristics of the program and developmental procedures.

Type of Developer

Large-scale development of curricula that are to be used regionally or nationally can be carried out by a number of different types of institutions. The most common developers above the local level are groups in universities, private firms, and federally sponsored Regional Laboratories and Research & Development (R & D) Centers.[3] Uni-versity groups (including, sometimes, university-based R & D centers) differ from regional laboratories and private firms in their greater reliance upon students and faculty members, persons who devote only part of their time to the curriculum projects. Project staffs in labs and private firms include more employees who spend all or most of their time on the project and who specialize in particular aspects of development (for example, conceptualization, activity design, writing, mediation, dissemination, evaluation, product promotion).

Another noteworthy difference lies in the relative importance placed upon the economic utilization of available resources as opposed to the provision of learning experiences. Private firms and labs must attempt to produce curricular products as efficiently as possible. There is some training of employees, but this is usually aimed at the extension and refinement of skills rather than at the initial acquisition of skills and knowledge. In university groups, on the other hand, one of the necessary functions of development projects is to teach and train students. While this cannot serve as an excuse to ignore all considerations of efficiency, it does require a different perspective on efficiency. Eisner has described this situation in explaining the implications of having to structure his project in such a way as to contribute to the education of his students: "This meant the decisions I might have made more efficiently on an arbitrary basis were made less efficiently with respect to action, but more effectively in relation to the contributions that group deliberation made to the education of the students who worked with me." It must also be remembered, however, that university-based groups partially recoup some of this lost economic efficiency through the use of smaller staffs and substantially lower wages, primarily through employing students.

Type of Target Audience

A third curriculum-related group that varies in ways that affect developmental procedures is the target audience—the intended primary users of the completed curriculum. Most curricula are designed for use by elementary or secondary school students, but some are intended for use in professional schools or colleges. Variations in target audience have some obvious implications for the types of programs that are developed and, in turn, for procedures used in development. Curricula for older students generally require more sophisticated thought processes, include more sophisticated concepts, rely more upon reading than listening, and include larger proportions of individual rather than group activities than do curricula for younger students. These differences in program requirements combine with other differences in target audience to cause variations in developmental procedures. For example, developmental psychologists' advice is sought more by the developers of curricula for elementary schools than by the developers of graduate school curricula. Scholars participate more frequently in developing college curricula than elementary curricula. Differences in the types of curricular activities, media, and writing styles that are appropriate for particular age groups require different competencies in developmental projects. Moreover, college professors more often design their own curricula, while elementary and high school teachers usually rely more heavily on programs designed by external developers.

Aspects of Content: Knowledge, Embodiments, and Approaches to Learning

As the accounts in this volume indicate, and as examination of other development projects further demonstrates, curricula vary widely in their contents. Developers' decisions about what content to include strongly influence the types of activities that are carried out in development. In order to clarify how variations in curricular content contribute to variations in developmental activity, I think it is helpful to distinguish between three distinct (although closely interrelated) aspects of curriculum content: knowledge, embodiments, and approaches to learning.

The term "knowledge," as I use it here, refers to content in its abstract form. It includes the facts, ideas, concepts, principles, and theories that are known, regardless of how they are expressed. Knowledge is, in other words, the "stuff" to be learned. Knowledge is expressed in a variety of forms, which I term "embodiments."[4] "Embodiments" include all of man's tangible, visible, and audible vehicles for recording and communicating what he knows: books, stories, research reports, films, photographs, drawings, paintings, and so forth. These embodiments are used in a variety of ways by people who are attempting to learn or understand better the knowledge that is embodied. For example, people sometimes merely read and think about a report, while in other instances they discuss the ideas being communicated, attempt to apply generalizations in specific situations to reinforce and extend their understanding, write summaries or interpretations of what they have read or heard, or engage in other activities to assist their learning. All such activities are here referred to as "approaches to learning."

Every curriculum developer must attend to all three aspects of content—knowledge, embodiments, and approaches to learning—in one way or another. The variations lie in the ways different developers deal with each aspect and in the emphasis they place upon each. Decisions pertaining to one aspect inevitably affect what a developer does with the other two. The most influential decisions in this respect concern the choices between knowledge that is "new" to the situations in which the curriculum will be used (concepts that have never before been embodied in a curriculum for the elementary grades) and knowledge that is already taught in those situations in some other form or way. It is generally recognized that curriculum developers do not create new knowledge in the course of their work. Instead, what they *do* accomplish is to select facts, ideas, and concepts that are already acquired (which may be new to the intended learning situations, for example, the third grade) and to create new (and, it is to be hoped, more effective) ways of communicating the selected knowledge—through the creation of new embodiments, new learning approaches, or both. The importance of this function of selection should not be overlooked. As Karplus has pointed out (in a personal communication), the SCIS staff did not create any new content in science, but they did "drastically revise the conception of science as it is presented in the elementary school." In other words, he explains, they "created a new content of 'school science.'"

There are three most common patterns of the knowledge-embodiments-learning relationship. The first was more prevalent prior to the large-scale work of the 1950s and 1960s, when textbook authors would concentrate most on the creation of new content embodiments. These authors would occasionally select new knowledge to inject into the school curriculum, but most frequently they would simply incorporate the commonly taught content into new textbooks. They gave *some* attention to learning activities (such as by listing questions at the ends of chapters or by suggesting topics for class discussion), but they focused on the creation of new ways to express the content, that is, on new embodiments.

The second pattern occurs when developers select knowledge that is new to the instructional situation and that is already expressed in appropriate, usable embodiments. In these cases, the curriculum developers select embodiments (which implies the selection of certain types of knowledge) and concentrate on the creation of new ways of approaching the embodiments—ways of examining, reacting to, and learning from them. The most obvious examples of this pattern occur in curriculum development for literature and the arts. Purves selects a number of literary works (largely by considering their interest and value and the sophistication of those who will study them) and then invents ways for teachers and students to read them, think about them, talk about them, write about them. He does not have to write new novels, although many curriculum developers in elementary and secondary language arts *do* write stories for textbooks. He organizes instead the already available embodiments, looks for linkages across works (such as themes), and provides teachers and students with different ways of dealing with this raw material. Eisner carries out similar tasks in constructing art curricula. He does not paint new paintings or invent new artistic skills; he invents new ways of observing, comparing, interpreting, acquiring.

The third pattern occurs when developers decide to emphasize the introduction of knowledge that is new to the instructional situation. When this is the case, the developers usually devote much attention to the creation of both new embodiments and new learning approaches, because in most cases neither already exists in any appropriate form. Thus, crucial tasks for these innovators are to express the knowledge in a form that is appropriate for the intended curriculum users (for example, translating research findings into simplified, understandable language) and to devise potentially interesting and effective activities for teachers and students to undertake in dealing with the new embodiments. This pattern—involving attention to all three aspects of content—has been most common since the curriculum projects of the 1960s demonstrated that the knowledge presented in elementary and secondary curricula is not fixed and sacrosanct. Attention to all three aspects of content is certainly most characteristic of the projects described by the nine writers.

Subject-Matter Area

Another variable aspect of content that strongly affects developmental procedures is the subject area (or field) in which a curriculum is to be used. The present authors have developed curricula for use in science, mathematics, reading, art, social studies, English, career education, and a host of other fields. These areas (and all of the others for which curricula are developed, of course) vary in the types of concepts they include, the modes of inquiry and analysis with which they are studied, the ways in which they are viewed and treated in schools (such as the likelihood of additional resources being allocated to particular areas and the chances of new instructional styles being accepted), the structure of the knowledge they encompass, and their histories, to name but a few of the more obvious examples. These characteristics bring powerful forces to bear on the curriculum developer. They provide frameworks for what can be done, structure to much of the content, and limitations to instructional possibilities. Resnick has given a good example of subject-matter influences in her analysis of the assets and liabilities of using formalized models:

In a general sense, mathematics, especially early mathematics of the kind we have studied and analyzed, presents relatively few ambiguities. The subject matter is a closed logical system, within which informal analyses are likely to reflect actual performance reasonably faithfully and thus to guide instructional design effectively . . . . By contrast, it is very difficult to develop process descriptions for language comprehension and for advanced mathematical thinking. Many competing analyses are possible. In language, especially, the subject-matter domain is "open" and highly dependent on context, on past experience, and on details of the task as presented. It is by now quite widely agreed . . . that comprehension is not a simple linear process, that it involves use of redundancy in the structure of the language and a search for meaning—in short, it is a very complex cognitive process. For this kind of subject matter, formal process analyses and empirical tests are likely to have especially high payoff. At present, for example, there exists no generally accepted model of how a prose passage is comprehended when read, of the processes involved in taking and interpreting information from a text. In this situation much may be gained through the disciplining effort of formalized task analysis and related empirical research leading to the development of psychological models of comprehension processes.

Subject-matter characteristics can affect almost every facet of the developmental approach. For example, projects and products in some areas, such as those in which delimited sets of skills are to be transmitted, are much better served by the careful specification of precise behavioral objectives, while broad open-ended statements of goals are the only sensible vehicles in other areas (for instance, creative areas in which results cannot be thoroughly predicted). Similarly, pencil-and-paper testing for specific cognitive gains (for example, whether particular facts are learned) is sometimes useful in evaluating instruction in some subject areas, while observations of attitudinal and behavioral changes is more appropriate in others. Developers in "new" subject areas (for example, interethnic relations, contemporary social trends, some forms of career education) must engage in activities that differ from those of developers who are attempting to present more traditional subject matter in new ways. These are but a few examples; some will be elaborated in later sections.

Type of Program Being Developed

In addition to the instructional level of the target group, the various aspects of content, and the subject-matter area to be covered, other key characteristics of the curricula being developed and other facets of the developers' motives shape the actual developmental processes. This is particularly true if the conceptualizers, writers of proposals, or program designers are strong advocates of particular trends or "schools of thought." Some program architects, for example, begin by deciding that "we need programs that are more suitable for open classrooms" or "we need more programmed instruction." When this is the case, decisions about content, and even subject area, often follow decisions to build new programs.

Mehlinger has described one way in which such circumstances (including emphasis on particular elements of the program that usually results) can affect developmental processes. He suggests that some people, particularly those who are interested in developing programmed instruction, are apt to profit from a careful specification of behavioral objectives and criterion measures prior to developing lessons. Others—particularly those responsible for developing semester-long or year-long courses to be directed by teachers, and who see "the need to vary instructional style, to prompt the student's interest, and to strengthen the teacher's sense of security and achievement" as being very important—are more likely to benefit from "the creative, instructional idea" than from a detailed specification of objectives.

Types and Usages of Objectives

Although virtually all developers agree that objectives of some sort must provide guidance in curriculum projects (as I have already pointed out in discussing similarities), they differ substantially in the types of objectives they use. For example, within the present group of authors, some (Purves, Karplus, Eisner, Mehlinger) have expressed very broad educational goals, while others (Popham, Resnick, Bailey, DeVault and Anglin) have written more numerous, detailed, specific behavioral objectives.

The positions that have been advanced by Karplus and Popham illustrate some of the diversity in present theory and practice with respect to the issue of objective specificity. On the one hand, Karplus argues that in areas such as science, where "the public has no preconceived notion of what children should learn," cases where project staff consider the encouragement of various teaching styles and emphases desirable, and cases where there is little interest in rigorous evaluation (because of the belief that evaluation takes place largely through teachers' observations of children's attitudes and activities), curriculum developers should use more general objectives as guidelines, because "explicit and detailed educational performance objectives tend to preempt local decision making and are counterproductive." According to this view, detailed, specific performance objectives should be reserved for areas such as reading and swimming, where "the public has certain expectations of what children will learn," or areas such as typewriting, where there are "well-defined skills . . . that can be appraised unambiguously."

On the other hand, Popham maintains that the general goals of any development project must be translated into specifics prior to the initiation of product development. He admits that there are variations in the rigor with which this requirement may be fulfilled: some developers merely state the objectives in measurable terms; others devise criterion-referenced measures to be used in ascertaining a product's efficacy; still others explicate the limits that define the domains of the desired behavior of the learner. But in all cases, Popham asserts, the development of "validated instructional materials" should involve early explication of specific behavioral objectives; this job should never be left for teachers or other users to carry out after the product has been developed. The rationale for this position is that adequate product design, development, evaluation, and revision can be accomplished, and waste and failure can be avoided, only if the developers have precisely articulated what it is that their products are supposed to do.

As this discussion of views about the desirable degree of objective specificity has revealed, developers also differ in when and how they derive their objectives. Some refuse to begin developing instructional activities or materials until comprehensive sets of specific objectives have been completed. Others start development with only the most general intentions in mind, letting additional goals and more specific objectives evolve as development proceeds or leaving the expression of specific objectives to the users' discretion.

Developers derive curricular goals and objectives in different ways.

Some conduct extensive, painstaking analyses of the knowledge and skills to be taught or the learners to be educated. Others carry out broad assessments of social, educational, or learners' needs. Others conduct critical analyses of available programs. And still others rely heavily on personal experience, commonsense observations, and general views of society, knowledge, and learners' needs and capabilities.

Selection of the most appropriate types of objectives depends, to some extent, upon certain curricular characteristics. For example, comprehensive sets of predetermined, highly specific behavioral objectives, including specifications of criteria for minimally acceptable levels of performance, would seem to be more useful in designing programs for training relatively well-defined, precise skills (such as plumbing or computer programming) than in "fuzzier," open-ended areas that are characterized more by the unpredictable results of creativity than by thorough sets of prespecifiable skills. General, flexible goals, on the other hand, would seem to be more practicable in creative, expressive areas (such as painting and writing) than in specific skills. Mehlinger submits that careful predevelopment specification of behavioral objectives and criterion measures is probably most profitable in constructing programmed instruction, while such specificity is initially less important than "the creative, instructional idea" in developing other types of programs.

Yet, in spite of these generalities about relative usefulness, there is still much variation in practice and theory, indicating that important questions remain for empirical investigation. For example, following popular belief, one would expect "looser" goals to be more appropriate in literature, art, and, to some extent, social studies, and "tighter" goals to be more common in mathematics, reading, science, and vocational education. Karplus has destroyed this expectation, however, by developing an elementary science program without the use of highly specific, prespecified behavioral objectives.

In many, if not most, areas, it is unclear as to when and for what purposes which types of goals and objectives are most beneficial. The use and value of different types depend in some ways upon the preferences and operating styles of those who are putting them to work. But study of the strengths and weaknesses of different types of goals and usages may indicate that developers should diversify their preferences, that different types of statements concerning goals are better for different purposes, and that different types of goals are most useful at different points of any developmental effort.

Staff Composition

Because curriculum development requires many different skills, project directors must look for a variety of competencies in assembling their staffs. Limitations upon the size and diversity of staffs usually reflect the availability of resources, but also depend to some extent upon the philosophies of the project's decision makers. Two of the main decisions that must be made in structuring curriculum development staffs concern the balance between specialists and generalists and the extent to which potential users of the product (for instance, practitioners such as teachers) are to be involved in development and the roles they are to play.

Mehlinger has noted that members of projects with large staffs tend to play fewer but more specialized roles while members of projects with small staffs must participate in many or all phases of the developmental process. He sees advantages and disadvantages in each situation. Each phase of development tends to be accomplished more professionally when full-time specialists, such as instructional designers, media technologists, specialists in human behavior, and evaluators, are available and able to focus their energies on their areas of specialization. The disadvantage of using many specialists, though, is that commitment to the overall project may be less than optimal, and specialists working on different stages of development may lack understanding of and empathy for work being done in other sectors. On the other hand, in smaller projects where staff members must perform more functions and participate in more phases of development, the work done in each area might not be as professional as that done by specialists, but overall commitment to the project and coordination among parts are likely to be higher. Popham has also touched on the specialist-generalist question, noting that some leaders in the validated instructional materials movement believe that the personnel carrying on instructional development should be specialists, while others feel that personnel should be generalists engaging in all or most of the phases of instructional development. As Popham has stated, these differences of opinion "lead to substantially divergent schemes for conducting development."

With regard to the issue of the involvement of the teacher (or other user) in curriculum development, the question is not whether practitioners should become involved at all; teachers invariably participate in classroom trials of preliminary versions of a program.

Instead, the main question is whether the involvement of the practitioner should be increased and spread to other parts of the developmental process. The modal developmental pattern begins with subject specialists or scholars carrying out the conceptual work—making decisions about content, instructional approach, general design, and so forth. Professional developers next translate these general guidelines into more specific directives which they use to write, illustrate, design media, and package materials. During product development, teachers are consulted about "classroom realities," how students are likely to react, and so forth. But teachers in most curriculum development projects do not become actively involved until materials are ready for testing. And, even then, they do not actively participate in developmental activities (writing, revising, and so on) per se; instead, they merely use the new materials to instruct students, following the developers' instructions and "feeding back" their reactions. On occasion, however, some project directors, typically those with limited funds, vary this pattern, usually by hiring teachers or graduate students to finish developing materials according to guidelines and prototypes that have been prepared by subject specialists or professional developers.

Program Evaluation

Most curriculum developers evaluate their programs before, and sometimes after, dissemination. The extent and rigor of these evaluations vary widely, though, ranging from informal tryouts intended to provide some clues for revision to rigorous field tests designed to yield more elaborate "summative" information. Karplus has compared two of the common (and quite different) alternatives, which he terms the "classroom trial" strategy and the "comparative research design" strategy. The latter, as he explains, involves the use of predetermined objectives, an experimental group, and a control group. The former ignores the demands of experimental design, for the most part, concentrating instead on gaining the reactions of students and teachers to progressively refined versions of the program. Karplus claims that the comparative research design strategy has been "discredited" for the purpose of curriculum development, while the classroom trial strategy has become "widely accepted as basic to successful curriculum development." And yet some developers do continue to advocate and use elements of comparative research design in testing their programs. They claim that unless they know precisely what a program is supposed to accomplish (through predetermined objectives) they cannot adequately judge its effectiveness in achieving its intended purposes. They claim, furthermore, that, unless they can compare the results of using the developed program with the results of using something else, they cannot assess the relative superiority of competing programs and cannot determine the causes of changes in learners. They contend, more specifically, that they cannot say whether modified attitudes, skills, and knowledge are due to exposure to the program, to "outside" events, or to maturation.

Designs employing experimental and control groups are expensive. Hence, it would be of great value to compare empirically and systematically the costs and benefits of experimental-control group designs. In so doing, we must attempt to determine what it is they yield that other designs do not, when these yields are worth the cost, whether there are less expensive ways of obtaining the same results, and the stages in the curriculum development process at which experimental-control group designs are most useful. Is it best to try out preliminary versions with small uncontrolled groups and to reserve the use of more rigorous designs for formal field tests of final products? Or do small-scale experimental-control comparisons at earlier stages reveal so much more than casual tryouts and result in such better revisions that they warrant the larger investment and perhaps lead to greater returns in the end? Or are experimental-control comparisons superfluous at all stages, including final testing? Answers to questions such as these could save much time and money—in planning, developing, and testing—over many years to come.

Obstacles to Studies Comparing Development Procedures

As the preceding discussion indicates, the procedures used in developing curricula vary significantly. Almost all of the authors in this volume have raised questions about the best ways of carrying out some of their developmental tasks. They have also taken different stands on a number of issues, indicating additional questions requiring attention. Most issues revolve about relatively small sets of distinct alternatives that might be empirically compared. As many developers have declared, it would seem wise, and, in the long run, most efficient, to investigate these issues in order to provide more helpful guidance to those who must decide which procedures to use in development. Under present conditions, many decisions continue to be made arbitrarily or dogmatically.

In spite of the apparent desirability of resolving procedural issues rather than continuing to forge ahead blindly with development itself, however, there are some powerful obstacles to the required studies and to the investments they would entail. The most important of these obstacles will be summarized here, before I return, in the final section, to the central questions of this chapter: whether it is worthwhile and feasible to conduct comparative studies of curriculum development procedures, how such studies should be conducted, and which issues such studies should address. I believe that the following discussion of obstacles will provide further support for my three general conclusions: that it is unrealistic to think about experimental comparative studies of alternative curriculum development procedures; that we should concentrate on finding ways to take better advantage of opportunities to study such procedures naturalistically; and that we should use such studies to find ways of conducting curriculum development more efficiently without sacrificing quality.

Competition between Program Needs and Study Needs

A major, and almost inevitable, problem that is likely to arise in the conduct of controlled studies comparing alternative developmental procedures is the potential for conflict between the needs and wishes of those who are actually developing the curriculum and the needs and wishes of the procedural investigators. Thus, even though the investigators are likely to build in particular types of variation in the beginning (by selecting programs having philosophies, personnel, and contents that differ in certain ways, by trying to obtain assurances from the staff that their procedures will not suddenly shift, and so forth), the threats to control are numerous. Most such threats are justifiable and would be difficult to do much about.

The main problem in this respect is that the needs of curriculum development will almost always be considered more important than the needs of the procedural study. Thus, if the developers find that some of their procedures are not paying off, they will probably look for better ones. If the nature of the program changes as it evolves (which is not unusual and is to be expected in a developmental effort, after all), procedural requirements may change. Unanticipated changes in circumstances, such as funding reductions, altered relationships with schools or other external but crucially involved groups, and losses of staff, may dictate procedural modifications. And, if project personnel run across new (or hitherto unfamiliar) developmental procedures that they consider appropriate to what they are doing and superior to those they have been using, it is unlikely that they will ignore such possible changes for the sake of the process study. Their main concern is, after all, to develop the best possible curriculum, not to make life easier for the researchers. Few people would tolerate sacrifices in the quality of the program to learn more about how different developmental approaches compare.

Process-Product Interdependencies

As Eisner has explained, "interaction occurs between the kind of platform one embraces for a curriculum and the working arrangements one formulates. The tool and the product are interdependent." This demonstrates a critical problem in any attempt to compare developmental procedures. Means and ends are usually so closely and logically tied that many types of procedural variation become absurd. In order to effect many types of procedural variation, one would also have to vary crucial program characteristics (for example, subject area, content, mode of presenting content to learners). As a result, we would end up carrying out studies that concluded "Procedure A works better in developing programs such as X than Procedure B does in developing programs such as Y." What we need, of course, are studies that compare the effectiveness of alternative procedures (A and B) in developing the same type of curriculum (for example, Program X).

Difficulty of Predicting Procedural Requirements

Because most curricula are outlined in very general terms when development begins, it is usually difficult to anticipate in much detail the types of developmental procedures that will work best. Specific goals emerge, plans for learning activities evolve, and requirements for writing, illustration, and mediation become evident as development proceeds. For this reason it is usually difficult (and often foolhardy) to dictate predesigned, unalterable modes of procedure before development begins. Indeed, most developers seem to subscribe, to varying extents of course, to what Karplus has called a "pragmatic approach." By this he means that his staff on the SCIS project devised procedures for solving problems and attaining goals as the goals were set and the problems were encountered.

Such required flexibility further reduces the likelihood of a controlled comparative study. It is highly unlikely that any developers or funding agencies would willingly forgo what they consider to be superior tactics simply because such tactics do not fit the predesigned research design.

The Importance of Individuals

Another characteristic of curriculum development that dictates against well-controlled experiments, particularly against the utility of whatever findings might result from such a study, is that much of how things are done depends on who is doing them. This is not simply a matter of individual inclinations, preferences, or philosophies. If it were only that, we could simply choose the required number of project directors in such a way that we would get the desired assortment of content and procedure preferences. These leaders would then hire loyal staffs with similar leanings and would proceed to act in predictable ways. Unfortunately, the problem is more complex than that. Each individual brings to the task a different set of skills. Different individuals' skills combine in different ways on different projects, filling and leaving exposed different types of gaps. For example, some specialists in teaching also know much about mediation, and, therefore, can perform developmental tasks in both areas. On other projects two positions would have to be filled to cover the same areas, meaning that some other function would have to go untended or be covered by people in other roles.

Curriculum development projects are, in these and other ways, idiosyncratic. Each has certain combinations of people, elements, and characteristics that will not be duplicated in other projects. Hence, the generalizability of many potential findings, which would depend so much on particular circumstances, would be quite low.

Problems of Funding Agencies

The present situation in potential funding agencies, which is likely to persist for some time to come, reduces the chances of obtaining funds for a project designed primarily to study comparatively different approaches to curriculum development. After spending millions of dollars on large-scale curriculum development in the 1960s (and becoming increasingly dubious about the value of those investments) most policy makers in foundations and federal agencies feel that other things are more important and are thus reluctant to fund curriculum efforts. This reluctance is especially problematic because foundations and federal agencies are the only organizations having adequate funds to sponsor the types of studies we are discussing here. Two other possible sources—state and local education agencies—are having enough trouble maintaining their obligatory functions; sponsorship of studies comparing curriculum development procedures is beyond hope. Some people believe that publishers will be able to fill the gap. For example, DeVault has stated (in a personal communication responding to an earlier draft of this chapter) that "increasingly we will find commercial publishers do have the funds—must find the funds— to do the careful development task which during the 60's was done by foundations and federal agencies." There are signs that publishers will fund more and more development. I seriously doubt, however, that they will have sufficient resources to fund all (or perhaps even most) of the developmental work that will be required. And I am almost certain that publishers will be able to contribute little, if anything, to studying alternative development procedures.

Even if developmental projects can be funded by foundations or federal agencies, moreover, most will be sponsored by offices that specialize in particular areas, including currently popular areas of concern such as career education and bilingual education, as well as more traditional subject-matter areas such as reading, mathematics, science, and so on. This situation concerning sponsorship raises two additional obstacles to the conduct of a procedural-variation study. First, each such office is authorized to spend money only in the area(s) to which it is addressed (career education or reading, for example). Because many procedural variables are so dependent upon characteristics of content, this immediately limits the possibilities in procedural variation. Second, most such offices do not have enough money to spend on what they wish to develop, much less on projects designed to vary largely depending on how development proceeds. Furthermore, the staffs in such offices are usually there because of interests in the substance being dealt with—*not* because they are interested in studying the best ways of developing curricula.

One way of circumventing these problems would be to combine

the resources of different offices, or even of different funding agencies. The funds of offices organized around particular areas of content or approach could be supplemented with funds from a curriculum and instruction office, for example. The content offices would maintain control over the nature of the curricula being developed and would indicate mandatory and variable procedural elements. The curriculum office would study the situation across programs to determine how much variation was possible in all and to recommend developmental approaches in such a way as to achieve the desired combinations.

Conclusion: Needs and Prospects in the Study of Curriculum Development Procedures

The combination of limited resources and skepticism about the worth of national-level, large-scale curriculum development efforts almost certainly means that curricula will not continue to be developed as they were in the 1960s (unless we witness another event having impacts equivalent to the launching of Sputnik). It is unlikely that the required millions will be available to buy the time of front-rank scholars and other experts, to purchase required materials, and to allow long-term, large-scale field-test activities.

Some observers have suggested that a return to the curriculum development modes of the pre-1960s would not be a setback. For example, in a response to an earlier version of this chapter, Tyler questions whether the procedures of the 1960s really improved education and predicts that "these developments may not last very long because the teachers really determine the actual curriculum." Tyler explains that, in the past, curriculum structure (objectives, learning experiences, and organization) was "in the minds of the teachers" and "the curriculum" was developed in the special methods courses in which teachers were trained. Under this system, textbooks functioned as teachers' tools, designed to meet their needs, *but "they [the books] were not viewed as new curriculum designs."* Tyler's view is that the developmental projects of the 1960s attempted to "circumvent" this approach by producing materials that teachers would be expected to use. According to Tyler, the most important questions now are whether such "circumvention" is a desirable alternative to the older procedures and whether the "economic pinch" will require procedures that are paid for indirectly, as in preservice and in-service education.

It certainly cannot be denied that the "older procedures" are one of the important alternatives to be compared in procedural studies. And there is little doubt that funding shortages will require greater involvement of teachers in curriculum determination than we witnessed in the 1960s. We must still attempt, however, to determine the optimal types and extent of the teacher's involvement. Should they adapt "raw materials" (undirective textbook presentations of subject matter) in constructing their own curricula, should they also create the "raw materials" (by writing and illustrating their own books), or should they participate in some combination of both? My own view is that teachers will take an increasingly active role in curriculum development (through advising, evaluating, doing some of the writing, and so forth), but they will never have the time nor the expertise required to construct all of the necessary curriculum materials. Even in Tyler's view, the teachers must be given some raw materials, such as textbooks, with which to work.

Hence, whether circumstances are favorable or not, there will be a continuing need for updating and upgrading curricula (or, at least, curriculum materials to be used by teachers in developing their own curricula) and, when important new needs emerge, for developing new curricula (or curricular materials) for schools. How will this be done? One alternative is to return to the traditional approach, in which publishers hire individual authors (typically professors in schools of education or curriculum specialists in school districts) to write textbooks, usually without the benefit of diversified input or test-revision cycles. Few, including the publishers themselves, would welcome such a regression. A second alternative is to develop all curricula (including all curricular materials) at the local level. One of the problems with this possibility has already been mentioned. Teachers and most district personnel have neither the time, the energy, nor the expertise required for sustained work in developing or continuously revamping entire curricula. Furthermore, work spread across hundreds of schools and districts would lead to much unnecessary duplication. And it is virtually impossible for school districts to pull together even a semblance of the resources (scholars and other experts, as well as finances) that are possible with a pooling of funds. Hence, valid claims concerning the need for greater responsiveness to local variations notwithstanding, leaving *all* curriculum development to schools and districts does not seem promising.

A third alternative is to carry on semicentralized curriculum development projects that are economically and procedurally more efficient. It is almost inevitable, for the reasons given above, that developmental work above the district level will continue—in one form or another. If public agencies cannot or will not support curriculum development, more of this work will be assumed by the private sector. This would not necessarily be a harmful trend in and of itself, if the gains of the past few years could be sustained and built upon. A danger (although not an inevitability) would be that publishers and other private developers would opt for the quickest, least expensive ways of producing curricular materials. Without convincing proof that group collaboration, diversity of staff, careful attention to theoretical foundations and goals, consideration of the implications of research on learning and human development, extensive field-testing and revising, and other elements of the large-scale projects paid off in demonstrably superior educational programs, these private developers would be tempted to return to the one-author project. The problem is that we do not now have this convincing proof. Many people have come to believe strongly that the big projects of the 1960s generated some worthwhile procedural advances. But these beliefs are usually based upon personal experience or post hoc accounts of experiences in other projects, not upon the results of systematically designed and executed comparative studies. Arguments that the procedures of the 1960s did not represent worthwhile procedural advances (Tyler's view) reinforce the opinion that reliable comparative studies are needed.

In light of present shortages in funding—which reduce opportunities for development as well as for comparative procedural study and tempt developers to revert to earlier, less expensive, and less "rigorous" operational standards (especially in the absence of evidence bearing on the efficacy of more recent procedural preferences)—it is increasingly clear that if we are sincerely interested in more reliable indications of the relative values of alternative developmental approaches, we will have to *learn to take better advantage of opportunities to study developmental projects naturalistically; delineate more precisely the most crucial focuses for comparative study; and give more attention to questions of economic and procedural efficiency.*

Shortages in funding may obviate the conduct of more controlled experimental studies, thereby forcing us to lean heavily on more naturalistic approaches (which, as some observers have suggested, may prove to be a fortunate forced choice). And even if some experimental work becomes possible, we should continue to study naturalistically the procedures used in ongoing developmental projects, attempting to compare the effects of contrasting practices where possible. Such studies should be conducted while the developmental work is in progress (rather than relying upon the more typical retrospective analysis) and should be focused on manageable sets of important issues.

In either case—whether we employ controlled experiments or naturalistic studies of ongoing efforts—study of curriculum development processes must be preceded by thorough, logical analysis designed to yield determinations of the field's most pressing needs. The position taken here is that, *under present conditions, the most pressing needs in the study of curriculum development procedures center about the notion of economic and procedural efficiency.* Curriculum developers no longer enjoy the generous funding to which they had grown accustomed. They cannot afford procedures that require gigantic staffs, vast and extended series of coordinated activities involving thousands of people and events, and lots of money. And yet they cannot just give up, saying that without exorbitant support curriculum development cannot be done well. There are many indications that the higher costs of more sophisticated and extensive procedures are not the sole reason for the increasing expensiveness of development. In many cases, it seems, greater expenditures reflect substantial amounts of waste. Much of this waste results from developers' inability to distinguish between necessary and superfluous tasks and their ignorance of more efficient, but equally effective, ways of performing necessary tasks.

Although a period of relative austerity will certainly slow the momentum that has been achieved in curriculum development, it may also force, and allow time for, some long-needed self-study, which, in the long run, could prove to be much more beneficial than a sustained intensity of development itself. Following the line of thought presented above, it seems that two of the most important questions for such study would be: What procedures are essential to high-quality curriculum development? What are the most efficient ways of carrying out these procedures? The following discussion suggests some more specific questions of essentiality and efficiency, questions that might be addressed in studies comparing alternative curriculum development procedures. These have emerged from the analysis of variations among the projects described by the nine developers and from questions posed by the authors themselves.

Suggested Research Issues

Questions about Goals and Objectives

A first area in which more reliable empirical knowledge could help developers make more informed choices is that of goals and objectives. As we have seen, some developers begin program development with only broad goals in mind, while others insist upon the explication of numerous, detailed behavioral objectives (with levels of acceptable performance specified and criterion measures produced). Each option has potential inefficiencies. Those who start with goals that are too general may waste time as they encounter unnecessary difficulties in deciding what they want to do. Furthermore, they may end up spending as much time explicating objectives during development as others do in the beginning stages. On the other hand, the developers who adhere to hard-line behavioral objectives may get so wrapped up in specification and refinement of objectives that they unnecessarily delay development, leaving insufficient time and money for the creation of materials and activities. During the long initial periods of specification of objectives, moreover, developers sometimes become increasingly cloistered, failing to make occasional "reality checks" (for example, by discussing objectives with teachers or by trying out sample activities based on objectives). In such cases, major deficiencies in the objectives may not become apparent until development founders, necessitating the investment of more time and money in the revision or re-creation of objectives.

As we have already observed, the appropriateness of objective types and usages depends, in large part, upon the type of program being developed and upon other developmental circumstances. Developers should be guided in their choices, nevertheless, more by empirical evidence than by personal preference. Hence, we must find ways and opportunities to answer questions such as the following (while noting the effects of varying purposes and situations): Does development proceed more efficiently when initiated with general goals or when preceded by the creation of long, comprehensive lists of detailed behavioral objectives, when behavioral objectives alone are specified, or when objectives are accompanied by performance levels and criterion measures? Does the work required in carrying out the more rigorous of these alternatives pay off during development by providing such precise guidelines that the creation of learning activities and materials proceeds more efficiently? And, what is most important, which procedural options lead to the development of the most effective curricula, with which types of programs, and under what developmental circumstances?

Questions about Group Collaboration

A second way in which developers might economize without reducing effectiveness is to alter patterns of group collaboration. I am not, of course, in favor of eliminating group collaboration, an aspect of development that has been praised by all of the writers in this book. The total absence of interaction among the various participants would have one of two results: a text by a single author or overcompartmentalization of disassociated specialists that would remove valuable opportunities for educating graduate students and others who are inexperienced in development. Some combinations of a large group, a small group, and individual work may, however, be more efficient than others. At some points it may be best to involve everyone on the staff in discussions of crucial issues, while at other times discussion by a large group might be most productive and beneficial after individual attempts have been made to solve difficult problems. Studies of contrasting projects should address attention to questions such as the following: At which stages of what types of developmental sequences are which types of collaboration most efficient? What types of collaboration are best in making what types of decisions? Does failure to involve total groups in key discussions create detrimental gaps in communication between various segments of the project? Are there more efficient ways of communicating vital information and of providing staff members with a sense of involvement? Do some types of group collaboration waste time that might be more productively spent in individual work?

Questions about the Locus of Developmental Activities

Another important issue concerns the locus of developmental activities. All projects "go into the field" at some point, usually when they are ready to conduct a pilot test of preliminary versions or field-test more advanced versions. Many developers, however, have started moving toward "field-based development," a mode of operation involving work in schools and classrooms during earlier stages of the creation of the program. Arguments favoring this trend point to some new possibilities for efficiency. Do earlier field activities—such as solicitations of students' and teachers' suggestions, tryouts of the most primitive versions of the product, and the involvement of practitioners in initial stages of the program's creation—lead to the development of more realistic activities that are more acceptable to users and that require less subsequent revision? Does the feedback gained in field-based development serve some of the purposes of more typical testing, thus reducing the requirements of the more expensive later stages of pilot and field tests? When is the optimal time for projects to go into the field? Which types of activities are carried out most effectively in the field, and which are best accomplished in-house? Which types of developmental activities are practitioners (including students) most willing and most capable of carrying out?

Questions about Evaluation

The prospects of field-based development relate to three other possibilities for increased efficiency: variations in the rigor and extensity of evaluation; modifications in the timing and extensity of the assessment of needs and of studies of the market; and alternative uses of various types of personnel. We have already noted the wide variations in evaluation practices and theories. Some claim that casual tryouts with small groups of students provide sufficient indications of a product's worth; others argue for more rigorous evaluations designed to yield more reliable evidence and experimental-control group comparisons; most of the others fall somewhere between. The debates among representatives of these different camps have raised some serious questions, many of which bear on issues of efficiency. How much structure and control are required in formative evaluation and in summative evaluation? Are the results of summative evaluation useful enough to warrant their costs (particularly when such costs deplete funds available for development itself)? Can well-run, continuous, informal tryouts reduce the need for, and therefore the expenses of, more formal testing at the end point? When are large samples required? Do the benefits of large samples warrant their costs, or do they serve primarily to satisfy methodological critics? When are comparisons with alternative "treatments" and control groups necessary? Because of the brevity of most curricular experiences, do comparisons of control groups ever tell us much, or are they intended to make evaluations seem more "scientific"? What types of long-term effects are important to observe? How can longitudinal evaluations be carried out inexpensively and in such a way as to provide useful guidelines for program improvement?

Questions about Assessments of Needs and Studies of the Market

Practices in both of these areas vary tremendously. Some developers (or funders) precede program design with elaborate surveys of potential groups of users and careful determinations of demand and size of the market. Others initiate projects without consulting target audiences or conducting market studies. Much remains to be learned about the assets and liabilities of each approach. Do expensive assessments of needs—involving detailed questionnaires, interviews, and other means of determining problems to which programs might be addressed—reveal much more than casual observations, conversations with key users, or the intuitive sense of perceptive program conceptualizers? If so, how much rigor is required in these initial assessments, and which methods are most effective in revealing needs and problems? Under what circumstances does failure to conduct assessment of needs or market studies lead to misdirection, and, consequently, to wasted effort, in program development? At what points in program design and development should market studies be carried out? Which questions are best answered in market studies? For which questions can equally accurate answers be obtained through less expensive means? Which types of market studies are most cost-effective? Which are most reliable? Does overreliance upon the results of market studies lead to excessive concern over profits and, subsequently, to refusals to develop important "thin-market" programs?

Questions about the Composition and Utilization of Staff

An area that would seem to have rich potential for developmental savings in a time of funding shortages is that of staff. When funds were abundant in the 1960s, many preeminent scholars and other experts devoted all, or substantial percentages, of their time to curriculum development projects, and project directors grew accustomed to having many specialists on their staffs. As financial backing has become less robust, however, such staffs have become a luxury that few, if any, can afford. An obvious alternative is to hire scholars and experts as consultants, rather than as long-term, full-time staff members, and to bring them in only at times when their advice is absolutely essential. Concomitantly, other, less expensive, personnel—who are probably more adept at doing some tasks anyway—can be hired to carry out much of the development, testing, and revision. The most obvious candidates include teachers, administrators, student representatives of the target groups, and graduate students. These possibilities suggest several questions for comparative studies. Are the contributions of scholars and experts lower in quality when provided on an intermittent, consultant basis rather than when such participants are continuously involved as staff members? Are some types of specialized expertise required throughout developmental projects? What are the advantages and disadvantages, the costs and benefits of substituting representatives of various groups of practitioners and users for more "high-powered" (and expensive) specialists? Do results vary significantly when teachers, for example, carry out much of the actual development? In what ways do they vary? Are resulting programs more acceptable to wider audiences of teachers, administrators, and students? Do teachers come forth with different types of inputs when they are writing than when they are reacting? Does more active involvement of teachers bring about more beneficial interaction between them and scholars? If so, does such interaction tend to promote innovative insights and program characteristics? How much of what types of participation by students is most beneficial and most efficient? What is lost when students participate only in pilot or field tests and not in earlier "advisory" roles? Is there a point at which greater involvement by students does not yield returns commensurate with the costs?

A Final Word

In this concluding chapter I have synthesized, compared, and contrasted the approaches to curriculum development described by the writers of the nine preceding chapters. The purpose of this work was to initiate consideration of the two central questions addressed by the book: Is it possible and worthwhile to design, fund, and carry out studies comparing alternative procedures of curriculum development? If so, what forms should these studies take, and which procedural alternatives should they compare? After examining some of the most important procedures that are common to the writers' approaches, some of the most important variable procedures, and some of the most significant obstacles to the conduct of procedural studies, I have concluded that: it is unrealistic to think about experimental comparative studies of alternative curriculum development procedures; we should concentrate on finding ways to take better advantage of opportunities to study development procedures naturalistically; and we should use such studies to find ways of conducting curriculum development more efficiently without sacrificing quality.

Here I have touched upon only a few procedural options and possible ways of effecting greater efficiency in curriculum development without sacrificing quality. Further analysis by both theorists and developers will suggest other important focuses for comparative studies. I encourage immediate commencement of such consideration so that funding agencies and curriculum developers may continue to carry out and improve developmental projects. Failure to do so may prolong funding shortages and necessitate neglect of the procedural advances that have been made.

Notes

1. See, for example, Arnold Grobman, *The Changing Classroom: The Role of the Biological Sciences Curriculum Study* (Garden City, N. Y.: Doubleday, 1969); Robert Karplus and Herbert D. Thier, *A New Look at Elementary School Science* (Chicago: Rand McNally, 1967); William Wooten, *SMSG: The Making of a Curriculum* (New Haven, Conn.: Yale University Press, 1965); Emily Romney and Mary Jane Neudorfer, *The Elementary Science Study—A History* (Newton, Mass.: Elementary Science Study Center, Educational Development Center, 1973); Richard J. Merrill and David W. Ridgway, *The CHEM Story: A Successful Curriculum Development Project* (San Francisco: W. H. Freeman, 1969); and Gilbert C. Finlay, "The Physical Science Study Committee," *School Review* 70 (No. 1, 1962): 63-81.

2. Some curriculum theorists, such as Joseph Schwab and Decker Walker, use the term "group deliberation" in discussing the collaborative efforts of development staff members. I have chosen a broader term, "group collaboration," for two reasons. First, I wish to include in this category all of the types of collaborative effort evidenced in curriculum development work. "Deliberation" tends to connote thinking activities (for example, brainstorming) and to exclude more overt, physical activities (such as preparing materials and conducting field tests).

Second, several critics of an earlier draft of this chapter commented that the term "deliberation" carried misleading connotations associated with T-groups and the like. I wish to avoid these connotations.

3. The Regional Laboratories and R & D Centers were established by the federal government in the mid-1960s. The labs were intended to serve educators in particular geographical areas. As such, they are more service oriented, although they do engage in substantial amounts of program development. The centers are located in universities around the country. Each center is supposed to carry out research and development in a particular substantive area (such as teaching, learning, administration). Project staffs in centers tend to include primarily faculty members and students, while most project members in labs are full-time employees of the labs.

4. Several people have recommended that I find a more appropriate term to replace "embodiments," and I realize that its unfamiliarity in this context may cause some confusion. No one has suggested a replacement that more clearly communicates the concept, however, and I have personally undertaken an unsuccessful combing of the thesaurus. I shall, therefore, continue to use "embodiments" with the hope that my explanations clarify the intended meaning and with the hope that someone will eventually suggest a more generally acceptable alternative.